10th 2017

Dear Louise,

I hope you -
this as much as I enjoyed
writing it.

Mabel x.

P.S. Thanks for all the feedback
during the process

A Season to Die for

Malcolm Kidd

Malcolm Kidd

Original title
A Season to Die for

Cover design
Philip Kidd

Cover layout
Sonja Smolec

Layout
Yossi Faybish
Sonja Smolec

Published by
Aquillrelle

© Copyright Malcolm Kidd, 2017

All rights reserved. No part of this book may be reproduced, stored in a retrieval system or transmitted in any form or by any means without the prior written permission of the author and publisher. Quotes of brief passages may be reproduced in a newspaper, magazine or journal for reviews only.

Printed in the United States of America, First Printing.

ISBN 978-1-365-66137-2

Thanks:

Thanks to my long-suffering family, Jane, Lucy and Philip, my editor, and in remembrance of my parents, Philip and Mary. Thanks also to members of Ciaran Carson's Queen's Writers Group at the Seamus Heaney Centre in Queen's University, Belfast, the Linda Tavakoli Writers Group and Olive Broderick's Words For Castleward Group, for all their invaluable support, guidance and faith. Thanks also to my friends and mentors Kathleen Quinn, Martin Tyrell, Rose McGrory, Karen Ritchie, Don Fay, Robert Wilson, Paul Jeffcut, Ray Givans, Roy Gamble, Karen Legrand, Cheryl Holohan, Cousin Holohan, Shirley Bork, Maureen Hill, Diana DeCesaris Champa, Caroline Healey, Chelley McLear, John McAllister, David Morley, Chris Bethell, Michael Willoughby, Peter Cruden, Charlie Johnson, Peter Grace, Hugh Dawnay, Stephen Seager, Alex McKay, Lar Sheeran, and Alec Harper. Marcelo Berisso, Eduardo Berisso, Lalo Berisso, Buff Crisp, Tyrone Beresford The 8th Marquis of Waterford, Peter Newell, Arthur Lyons, Joan Lyons, Desmond Lyons, Michael Lyons, and The Lahore Polo Club. Johnny Kavanagh, John Carolan, Oliver Caffrey, David Corbett, Lawrence Durrell, Ernest Hemingway, Irene ffrench Eager, Susan McKeon, Louise Corry, Mary Montague, Helen Hastings, John McGuckian, Henry Shaw, Wilma Kenny, Vi Whitehead, Terry Hinckland, Yossi Faybish and all the beautiful ponies.

Table of Contents

Prologue 1

1 The Punjab, December, 1989 5

2 Dinner in Eurasia 14

3 Lahore 38

4 The International 59

5 Mona Depot 75

6 Malibu, Four Months Earlier 92

7 Florida, January, 1990 127

8 Buenos Aires 132

9 Las Heras 145

10 B.A. 158

11 Gualyguychui 172

12 Downtown 184

13 Zorro's 189

14 San Telmo 199

15 Flavia 210

16 La Boca 216

17 London 225

Polo, like Paris, is a moveable feast, and if you are lucky enough to have found love on the move then you will always have Paris.

~Malcolm Kidd 1990

Prologue

If Tom Standing's feet had not touched the ground that year, 1989, lying on his sickbed might have been a good moment to do so – but then came the letter, Sophie's letter: *Joe's gone AWOL.*

He reached for the phone, but knew it was futile. The pain from his eardrum inflamed since leaving Karachi, his head near exploding when he landed in Dublin three flights and eighteen hours later, left him deaf and a powerful sedative now rendered him incoherent. He struggled to think of how to solve the mystery of Joe Henderson's disappearance, and lost consciousness. When he awoke, while the piercing popping in his ears had eased little, the letter, still in his hand, minded him he must call Sophie.

"What's happened?"

"Tom, he's gone, my sweet Joe. He said nothing, just left one night, not even a note. I don't know what I'm going to do. Has he been in touch with you? Is he with you?"

"No, I've not heard from him since I was in California with the two of you. And I've been in Pakistan for the last few weeks. Do you want me to come over?"

"There's nothing you can do just now. My sister is staying and we've been calling people round the clock. I just hope he's safe. He obviously wants to be alone. Thanks for calling Tom, what do you think?"

"Joe's always been tortured by demons but he rarely spoke about them with me. His divorce paralysed him, you know that, and then his drinking – it really scared me. Sometimes it could go on for days, weeks."

"I told him no drink in the house, and I never saw him drunk. Look, I'll call you if we hear anything. Thanks again, Tom. Thank you for calling."

He had last seen Joe, a successful jazz pianist, in November at his home in the Malibu Colony, north of Los Angeles. Joe seemed happy, relaxed, working on an album and looking forward to its

1

launch followed by a twelve-city tour. So, what had happened after Tom returned to Dublin? He now agonized over what might have happened had he remained with him in California. Joe was a tour de force with his own agenda, and when his mercury rose, there was no knowing what he might do. From his pillow Tom noticed the mallets made for him in Lahore leaning against the wall, two with Joe's initials, and wondered if his friend would ever get to play them now. Joe's madcap ways always brought a sense of clarity to an otherwise far gone state of confusion, despite the farrago of his own life. Maybe it had been a quality of leadership he had that carried the Tojos team through four miserable chukkas on the Lawns ground at Cowdray Park in May 1987. That warm Sunday afternoon, before a bank of basking picknickers and aficionado-packed stands, Lily White, Tricky Richardson, Joe Henderson and Tom Standing took on the mighty Silver Bears. Tom, curate of his own nostalgia, never had come to terms with the events of that week, when he learnt the value of money the hard way. On Wednesday morning, with pathetic supplication, he reflected through the pools of a fool's eyes in his bathroom mirror on a momentary misjudgement when investment became madness; four days later, no recovery in sight, he took to the field with desultory detachment. Joe, fired up from a week long bender galloped past him shouting "C'mon Tom, it might never happen." Lily, recently widowed, looked as down in the mouth as her black mare. The team professional, Tricky, had torn a riding muscle and used a surcingle tied around his waist and thigh in a figure of eight to compensate. His five goal handicap would go begging until another game. When the ball went into play, Joe's encouragement would not win them the game, but it helped. When the final bell rang they realised they had been playing for more, and the tensile outset had moved from grand mal to petit mort, and some perspective had been restored. Joe could lift spirits from any level.

Thinking of Joe, only two weeks earlier, unaware of his friend's impending dilemma, and with his own stories to live, Tom Standing had caught the plane to join the Irish Polo Team in Pakistan.

Flying over England on the short hop from Dublin to Schipol, the remote landscape beneath recalled a sense of attachment he still had for the places of his childhood, seminal moments of passage through pubescence, growing up in Brighton, moving to London to study, then work. Friends, family as well as enemies appeared in his thoughts as the flight transported him. More recently, the move from England to Ireland, following the death of his father in January, had followed the turmoil of crashing markets, a burst property bubble, and many trees wind-felled across southern England. The move allowed him to regroup, tempering a loss of purpose.

Tom and his mother rented an apartment on Dublin's south side, and began searching for a house in the country. His horses yarded on the north side, Phoenix Park, where he joined the All Ireland Polo Club (AIPC). The polo could be wild, always competitive, always followed with drinking and reveling in the clubhouse. Weekend invitations took him to fine country houses, where Irish bonhomie replaced the professional pragmatism of his former English club. He indulged the welcome, while his mother would stay with family. His partner of seven years chose not to join him, leaving him to his chosen life. Of death, 'divorce' and moving country, the loss of his father was the most painful of all, and now gave him the serious responsibility of caring for his aging mother.

She had graduated in medicine from Trinity College Dublin, and after thirty-five years in general practice the devoted doctor from Ireland had paid a high price, being diagnosed with Alzheimer's disease soon after arriving in Dublin, her selfish son's duty was defined. He bid on a house in Virginia, Co. Cavan. Lien free, the house handsomely restored, he moved in with his mother and dogs. The horses arrived from Phoenix Park in September, the end of the Dublin season.

The Church of Ireland chapel in the middle of the town where the road forked right to Cavan, left to Oldcastle, had two new parishioners. Virginia, a quiet lakeside village, in part satisfied Tom's need for settlement, and the newcomers soon became well known, from whichever side of veiled windows. With help from local carers his mother, more settled, grew happier. They had time now to reflect on their bereavement and the urn sat proudly over the fire. Glad she had not left him behind, she hoped her English husband was too.

*

The travelator's speed through the transit lounge soon had him boarding the longer haul flight to Karachi, and with anticipation he now relaxed to relish the prospect of a Eurasian adventure.

1
The Punjab
December, 1989

Flashbacks to his earlier in-flight reflections on the year's events, now punctuated with casual flicking through airline magazines as he flew East might have been more restful had it not been for hushed wrestlings with his adjustable armrests. Tom Standing disembarked with limited enthusiasm for the dry-spice laden afternoon air hanging over Jinnah International. With sleep deprivation manifested in a saccadic twitching of the eyes, Tom ambled in the slip-stream of his escort, two laconic, square-shouldered terminal guards beelining through the crowds, shoes clacking on the pale marble floor. In the terminal lounge slouched Peter Struell, legs akimbo, his blonde fringe flopped over his puffed eyes. He had camped there since midday, presently tending to his jet-setter delirium with duty free spirits.

"And then there were two" he dribbled with the vocal latency of the truly snookered. "P-pull up a stool old boy".

Tom cleared his throat, parked himself on the wooden bench and looked around. The low hanging sun scattered varying geometries across the room's regular pillars while street and runway traffic echoed off the large panel windows on either end of the building. Tom leaned back and watched the ceiling bloom peach to orange until the odour of Struell's uncapped bottle gave him a stir.

"Not very politic".

"Sh-state guests old boy". Tom recalled his companion Joe Henderson once arguing for sustained inebriation on long trips.

"Think of drunkenness as a wave of bliss, old son. A rolling wave. There upon the crest you find yourself, head in the clouds, feet dangling over the frothy parapet - and the trick, the trick is keeping the momentum topped up and riding the whole thing into port".

Considering this as his sinuses adjusted to more fully appreciate the momentum gathered thus far, Tom dreaded to imagine the toll amassed for Struell by their arrival in Lahore, let alone Peshawar. Tom imagined himself indulging at some point but anticipating the merry ruckus of a complete polo team was enough distraction for now.

Drib by drab the team assembled, each as groggy as the last, having left the British Isles within a stone's throw of the witching hour. By the time Michael O'Mahony had staggered through security, gin-soaked shirt tails flapping, most of the troupe were awake and anxious to continue. A bright eyed state envoy took the team across the tarmac to a state-chartered plane.

"Please come aboard gentlemen. Your luggage is already stowed away."

"I bloody hope so!" Tom bellowed over the ignition of the first turbo-prop engine, the setting sun maintaining a low-twenties breeze. As he boarded, the second ignition sent black soot billowing by the passenger door reminding Tom of bubbly days at Goodwood and Le Mans. The generous mauve cushions of the cabin seats compensated well for the time spent on Struell's terminal bench. Vacuum-cleaner musk and the perspiration of panicked tidying lingered in the cabin air, as did several indents in the seating fabric from boxed cargo that Tom suspected had been somewhat avian.

"We will be taking off as soon as everyone is seated and comfortable. May I please remind you of..." proceeding formally through a standard airline safety demonstration, prop life-jacket and all "... Thank you very much, I hope you enjoy your flight." Dipping his head, the attendant quickly picked a roughened feather off a nearby armrest before turning to the exit.

"Hold on there captain." O'Mahony rumbled.

"Yes, sir?"

"S'there any booze on this bus or'll your commander in chief be depriving us of our victory champagne too?"

Struell displayed a wide grin, while others chortled regardless. "There's the tournament to play yet, Mike."

"I can arrange some refreshments if you like, sir?"

"Aye, captain. Good lad."

As the worn leather patchwork that was Karachi sank beneath a twilight haze, spirits soared and sloshed among the troupe. Their plane chased the days' final sunbeams up into lavender clouds, the humming engines set a backdrop to their lubricated conversations. Tom however was too bug-eyed exhausted to maintain any meaningful exchange and dozed off with a fresh drink cradled in hand and a languid eye sinking down the feather speckled aisle.

Squinting in the darkness so as not to lose their footing on the red-carpeted staircase from the plane, the team disembarked to the sounds of attendants bustling around them, unloading and driving off with the teams luggage. Tom was halfway down himself when the Lahore delegate powered up several spotlights, blasting him into sudden alertness in time to grab the cool metal handrails as his leather-clad feet lost themselves on the fine rug. Collecting, composing and promising himself to at least make their first chukka without twisting his ankle Tom searched for the tarmac, toes outstretched like a toddler feeling for the bottom of a public pool before leaping in.

The asphalt was sticky from the day's heat and clung to their shoes as the team was taken through the terminal to their roof-racked taxis which teetered unnervingly all the short distance to the red-bricked, British built Lahore Junction Railway Station – subsequently refurbished by Sultan Mohammed, the local driver noted. The first taxi was laden inside and out with bags that Tom, not presently energized or enthusiastic for cramped cab banter offered to escort, lest the driver made off with it all. As the taxi audibly skidded to a halt, Tom sensed the overhead baggage lurch forward with inertia and imagined the entire cab collapsing forward like an overloaded dung beetle. No sooner had they stopped than the driver swung open both doors, offering his hand to the pale Tom with the nervous energy of something feral. Once out, his first glimpse of the churning, swollen commuter queue induced a rush of motion sickness. With rapid precision the driver offloaded the roof-rack as uniformed attendants carried the bags through the crowd.

Tom glanced around for the other cars and for a split-second was overcome with a sinking feeling. of loneliness. Contemplating his status as a foreigner slumped against a dim, grimy street lamp, he listened to the car horns and whistles coming through a silhouetted row of palms. The clean-shaven driver also glanced around as he knelt down holding out a cupped, trembling hand. "I hope you have a very good evening, sir."

Though there had been ample time to exchange his cash at Karachi, Tom could only offer a Bank of England fiver which the driver accepted without hesitation before revving and swerving out past the bulwark of Czech hedgehogs into the turbulence of Lahore's mainstream traffic.

The mass of pensive faces was beyond him at this point. He sat solo on the cool pavement peering up and around at the red ochre minarets and clock towers of the station building, consciously breathing in evening air: ground coffee, palms, exhausts and sewage.

"Alright sport? Careful not to nod off. You'll have your 'ruddy wallet nicked out here."

He assessed himself, checking each pocket. Nothing, the remainder of two pill-based sedatives he had rationed for the initial intercontinental flight, nothing, wallet and passport. He felt teammates stepping over his stiff knees into the shuffling mass of waxed faces and dyed linen.

"In there, that's where they'll fleece you." Tom croaked.

"Here lad." O'Mahony pulled Standing to his feet.

"Not far now, our carriage awaits" Mike warbled, cruising through the drove. Tom was loose, like a board-stiff shirt after a vigorous shaking in crisp air - but a hoarse tone and glistening forehead betrayed time spent in crushing frustration. Tom scouted either side of the man's pink face, paler since stepping into the night air, for blood vessels historically prone to bursting around and about moments of questionable umpiring.

"What kept you?"

"Cabbies, cops - cowboys, the lot! 'City's full o'them. We might as well have walked but I'm not taking one step in that bloody traffic."

Digesting the second pill and clenching his duly stamped identification, Standing slipped out of Michael's wake and there after

8

nudged and pardoned a floundering course amid the uncountable, pensive faces. Human, animate and mechanical sounds thundered off corrugated roofing as a white-gloved hand shot up into view and beckoned. The attendant ploughed a manageable path along the busy platform between carriages, painted regent green with a single cream line at window level. He could barely make out the metallic clanks of his footsteps up into the train amid the engine whistles and massive collected mutters and clucks of people and livestock.

Standing stepped up into a wood-paneled interior, slid the compartment door shut with a final clack and listened to the heady thudding of his heart slow and quieten. The stillness drew attention to the private nature of this car, a fact commanding appreciation through a collective softness of speech and manner on the part of the five passengers. A softness and dignity which could not have been expected to outlast the generously stocked mobile drinks cabinet hunched beside the cushioned armchair occupied by Arthur Murray. Standing stretched and took a seat.

"Alright there Arthur."

"Black hair."

"What's that?" Tom yawned, settling in for the roughly ten hour tranist to Peshawar.

"Look at them. This is a country of black hair."

Tom followed Arthur's gaze to the river of heads just below the window frame, steadily bobbing and flowing between the carriages, adorned in shining black hair. The uniformity had a calming effect.

"Yes. It is."

This could have been the most comfortable seat Standing had ever known. Side-lamps bathed the carriage in a moody glow, complementing the warm-spice upholstery, all of which contrasted with the cool industrial air of the platform and that of the river. Tom was reminded of late evenings that had become early mornings fretting over televised stock read-outs and displays, hunting for patterns and suspect correlations. Tom felt he should find his way back to the sleepers, but was caught off guard by a striking image.

As the current continued along the platform, without any apparent lapse in density, upon the shoulders of a man – Tom assumed a man since the face remained hidden under a gleaming jet mop – sat a large goat, black but for a distinctive patch of white around one eye, into which Tom gazed, listless. The Goat seemed to gaze back at Tom through the window, silent, almost in contemplation, it's wiry main blending with that of the carrier. The animal didn't look lost or panicked as the eyes reflected only a shallow awareness of being and movement before looking away. Tom slipped away before opening an internal debate as to whether the goat had looked at him or just caught its reflection in a carriage window. He recognised a face, and snapped to. It was Struell. "Hi Peter." Peter Struell turned, grinning at his teammate.

"We wondered when you might come round. Guess the whisky caught up with you, old boy," Struell said with measured sympathy.

"Probably. What else could you do on that damned train?" It had been difficult to sleep on unsprung rolling stock, and bunks without mattresses, so they read their books and sipped whiskey through the night, stretched out on lounge chairs. Khalid, their Punjabi steward, had tended to their needs. They imagined themselves in a Kipling novel, their ruefulness tempered with stories about dacoits and thugs who'd have marauded there during his time. Although the excursion had been a joint operation involving army and police forces, it had been Rashid Mahmoud, a Pakistani railway official and polo player, who had organised the private carriages of the train which now made its way through the clear night, the carriage window framing the landscape in relief – level, lifeless, highlighted here and there in lambent reflections where moonlight found water. Michael O'Mahony had brought his fiddle to accompany any poetry reading and Struell read a chapter from T.E. Lawrence's *Seven Pillars of Wisdom*. Khalid was kept busy.

Whiskey drinking might have offended his religion, but he knew its soporific properties as he knew the discomfort of lying on a hard bench, rolling with the rhythm of old wheels on old track, and old timber furnishings, smooth with the patina of Empire, polished

10

by myriad uniforms, preserved, as the Irishmen were pickled, bound on their adventure with the esprit de corps of a Corinthian coterie. Each had paid his own way to be part of the tour of Pakistan, and their hosts had responded by providing sleeping wagons and a state room with a retinue of attendants. Rashid had left them in capable hands, giving his assurance that they would be met at Peshawar at 7.00 a.m. by the District Commissioner of Police for the Peshawar District, Rahim Allam. The party, relieved on hearing the train's fricative skirling from its whistle, and the sibilant hissing of steam from its pistons, pulled into the station on time.

Following a brief introduction to local dignitaries, the team climbed into their jeeps, three in total, all bearing regimental flags and banners for their official visit. Each vehicle had two armed guards and at least one army officer. Standing sat between the Commissioner and General Rafi Akram, a tank commander; on the front bench, Struell was flanked by a guard and the driver. The other vehicles, one in front and behind, carried Michael O'Mahony, Arthur Murray, Desmond O'Mahony and Brendan Hannigan. They moved fast on the tarmac, between craggy outcrops of a threatening stillness. "Why all the precautions?" Standing asked.

"Tribal conflict", said Allam. "They see the flags and keep their distance, so long as we keep moving."

"Better keep moving then," Standing said.

They passed just one entrance – a gap in a thick high perimeter wall, maybe twelve feet at its base, ten at the top. They could see the wide marbled forecourt that led to an imposing fort, recently constructed.

"Who lives there?" Standing asked.

"A drug baron."

"Criminals live well here."

"He pays his dues."

Some twenty miles further on, the air conditioned only by the dry rush from a draughty quarter light, the convoy drove into a yard. More armed officers, this time police, greeted them. They met the police agent for the Khyber District, Sharif Iqbal. His hospitality was warm, yet tacit, and he invited them to lunch inside the station. After a simple meal of soup and samosas, they returned to the yard to fire Kalashnikov semi-automatic rifles, their volleys striking the compound wall, its friable rendering crumbled in a cloud of dust. A blue Ford saloon with its windows smashed, riddled with bullets, had fresh blood splattered on its rear seat.

"What happened here?" Standing asked the agent.

Allam was quick to reply for him: "They did not pay their dues." Standing felt a nudge. Struell edged him away from the scene.

"Keep moving."

The path led the group of generals, visitors, police and guards to the local casbah. This was no domestic market; the only fare on offer was an extensive range of ordnance abandoned by the Russians, following their withdrawal from Afghanistan earlier in the year. The counters displayed small arms alongside mortars, and racks of heavier weapons stacked behind the traders. One produced a weighty catalogue. Standing turned the pages to see a bulging arsenal, enough to fully equip armies, navies, and air forces, on both sides – a war. Listed were gunships, cruisers, destroyers, submarines, battleships, as well as two aircraft carriers, Mi-24 helicopters, MIG fighters, long-range bombers, tanks, every kind of armoured vehicle, and twenty thousand mercenaries for hire. As they moved to another hole in the wall, a more insidious war trove became clear. What were the toffee-like substances, laid flat on the trader's surface, one grey, another dark tan, and a last one black?

The first was C-4, the second Semtex – both devastating plastic explosives being used widely by covert political groups in the Middle East, and elsewhere, explained Allam. Standing, despite the blood-stained car in the compound, could not resist touching the Semtex as he asked Allam: "And this last one – what's this?"

"You don't know?"

"No. Just like the others, I've never seen it before." Allam spoke with a guard while the visitors followed him the brief distance to the top of the Pass, to look down over 'no man's land' on the border with Afghanistan. The mountainous terrain of the Spin Ghar, which the Pass had been crafted through, traced the contours of a snake as the Silk Road evolved; the valley, lush in parts, a level plain stretched either side of its remote checkpoint. But what really caught Standing's eye were the epigraphs and regimental inscriptions chiseled into the rocks at the head of the Pass. His own father's regiment, the Royal Sussex, had entered the Punjab here in 1888. As he scanned, he took a cigarette rolled and offered by Allam's man with substance number three. He drew the smoke deep into his lungs, and the resin took control, numbing him. He attempted to focus from behind his eyes on the group of men present – the generals, commissioner, and Irish – as it all began to blur, though one thing was clear – he was not alone. Every man present was passing and enjoying the smoke, except the guards. Allam asked him did any of the weapons hold any interest. "A splendid selection, do you not think so?"

"I suppose so." He felt uneasy discussing anything with a narcotic clouding his mind.

"Would you not like to look again at some of the items? The handguns perhaps?"

Standing called to Michael and Arthur, "What time is our train this evening?" The penny had dropped. Despite the percolation of pain relief, he was anxious to change the subject. Now he knew why they were there. "Jesus God, Peter. They think we're terrorists," Standing whispered.

"You're right - Exciting, isn't it?"

They beat a retreat to the vehicles, bidding farewell to their host, descending the notorious Khyber Pass, now indelibly registered within their own duplicitous encounter, in silence. Standing slipped back into his reverie for the hour or so it took to reach the city limits. As twilight descended and temperature dropped, his mind wandered from darkness to light, considering again just how he found himself in this situation. Mostly however, the team was gagged by the same burgeoning question. "They think we're IRA? Bloody hell!"

2

Dinner in Eurasia

When they entered the centre of Peshawar the throng of the market, trading animals and much diversity of goods, the cityscape imbued with the sounds of life, a corybantic discourse of barter with banter, goats, sheep, camels, horses, all manner of fowl, rolled over by plumes of multicolored cloth, draped from the windows of mercantile rooms. Carved mosaic shutters allowed in light, but not the inquisitive. Above all this could be heard the cry of the muezzin from a towering minaret, with the help of loudspeakers, calling the city to evening prayer. They had time to pull into a hotel to freshen up, and were ushered to Victorian bathrooms of white ceramic walls, brass taps and large gilded, filigree edged mirrors – a glorious reminder of the opulence of the Raj. Starched attendants stood by, reminding Standing of the humorless Khalid, who would be preparing the carriage for their midnight return to Lahore.

"Jesus God, Peter. They think we've come to buy weapons", Standing said, sotto voce.

"Not any more" replied Struell. "Best keep shtum, old boy."

"Yes, you're right. Best to say nothing" Standing said to his friend. "Can't wait to get on that bloody train again. Hope Khalid has a good bar set up for the trip."

"Something to relish," said Struell.

"More Lawrence washed down with a good malt?" asked Standing.

"I think maybe some Wodehouse, to lighten the load."

"Good choice. I hope Arthur has some decent jokes, or possibly not so decent. Either way, he makes me laugh."

The carbolic soap was barely preferable to the lingering odours of what had been a long day, but showered and shaven, tamped dry by fresh towels in plentiful supply from their attendants, and splashed with extracts of lime and sandalwood, Peter Struell, Michael O'Mahony, Arthur Murray, Desmond O'Mahony, Brendan Hannigan, and Tom Standing stepped onto Main Street, Peshawar, in the middle of the casbah. Without disdain for their North-West Frontier hosts, the six horsemen strode forward to face whatever might lie ahead amongst the silhouettes of the bustling bazaar outlined against the crepuscular crimson of the closing evening. Tom remembered something that Alec Purcell, the President of the All Ireland Polo Club, had said to him before they entered the departure lounge at Dublin airport: "Know this, Tom. The English go abroad to fight, the Irish to make love." And in that statement Standing delegated himself a strictly Irish Ambassador. The endorsement, backed by his birthright, had qualified him as equal to the other members of the party, and he felt rather proud of this. He also recalled a similar sentiment expressed by a former City colleague, a Brazenove executive named Rupert Price who, when Standing asked on account of his tanned complexion whether he had been abroad replied: "Don't you read the newspapers?" Standing later learnt that Price had returned from the ill-fated 1979 Fastnet yacht race, when fifteen yachtsmen and three rescuers perished in a force eleven storm in the Atlantic off the Cork coast. When he next saw his colleague he apologized for his error, to which Price replied: "An Englishman only goes abroad for one reason – to fight!"

Arthur Murray, hearing the president's comment, added, "Tom, you have two passports, you know. You have your Irish passport of course, but you have a better one than that. You have a polo handicap, and that will get you into far more places." How right he would be.

The men walked deep into the heart of the market area, savouring the scents of jasmine and incense, as well as traditional naans rolled and heated, wafting along a cooling breeze to fill the air and fire their palates. The miasma of animal excrement, ever-present, failed to inure them against the more preferable aperitifs, dinner just a few steps away. Russian vodka was on sale everywhere in this Muslim market. The defiant wildness of the North West existed in abundance at the foot of the Pass where commerce embraced anything and everything marketable, from white to black, as clear as that. More down-to-earth items such as clothing, pashminas and a variety of headgear appealed to the European visitors; they were fascinated by the Afghan Pakol, worn by many including the Taliban, and the Karakul, a hat of goatskin immortalised by Nehru. The best Karakuls, they were informed by a street seller, were made from the astrakhan pelt of a newborn lamb. Standing felt compelled to buy one, without barter, if only to give the nascent creature some legacy to its brief life. Pashminas, shawls made from fine goat's wool, were stacked high on stalls. These were tan and dun coloured, and Struell and Standing went native and wore them to the restaurant. Standing had bought an embroidered pashmina of cashmere for his mother on a trip to Delhi a few years earlier and knew well how warm and comfortably they sat around the shoulders. They bought rabbit fur hats. These were Russian, and looked like the coonskin hats that North American frontiersmen had worn at the time of Davy Crockett. Aromas issued from pyramids of fruit, tangerines, dates, nuts, leatherware, tikka, dried fruit, kebab stalls, green tea shops, all covered by wide striped awnings, the bearded tribesmen beneath drinking tea and drawing smoke through the water bowls of their hookahs: Uzbeks, Shinwaris, Iraqis, Tajiks, and Afridis, their multicoloured djellabas drifting like paint strokes across a kinetic canvas. And the Irish mingled, unbothered, in the flow and counterflow of this tribal confluence.

Few women were seen here, except where returning from the Mosque, wearing the hijab, mostly black, about their heads and shoulders. Two smaller women emerged wearing the full hijab, in orange, from head to toe, with latticed visors for visibility and ventilation. Such dress defied comprehension by any of the visitors. Hannigan, the pious one among them, thought this might be the equivalent of a nun's habit. Tom thought he may have had a point as they knew he had searched high and low since their arrival for a place of Catholic worship. What terrible thing had this quiet 'prelate' done in his past, that he spent most of it since in seeking salvation? The bazaar had many storytellers, but a lack of Urdu limited the English-speaking from understanding them. The reactions from those who did understand were more easily interpreted; stories could well have been written simply from studying the faces and gestures of the animated onlookers. Following their hosts, one remaining general, Rafi Akram, who would be returning with them on the night train,

16

Police Commissioner Allam, and four of the guards from earlier, now in mufti, they entered the Khan, a celebrated Pashtun restaurant, set in the middle of a terraced row of Sehti houses. The Sehti business community of Peshawar had distinct dwellings which were also places of business, and could be recognised by their ornate carvings and narrow balconies which overlooked the street market. The Khan, formerly an indoor market for gems and semi-precious stones, had become an eating place some twenty years earlier. The large open plan hall with its exposed rafters stood as tall as its neighbours, and could accommodate up to 300 diners. The tables were long, seating up to fifty diners each, and they sat together, flanked by the general, commissioner and four guards. From a menu of Charsee Tikka, Seekhu Kebabs, Kabul Palao, along with tender barbecued lamb, they feasted. It all fell, succulent, from the bone as the fork lifted, as did the beef in the Chapli Kebab. No alcohol permitted in public made conversation polite, and formal. The commissioner revealed that he had lived in London during the 1960s while attending the London School of Economics, and in his reminiscing it seemed he was attempting to clarify much about his present responsibilities running a police force compromised by political and crime-fuelled corruption. He spoke of a rapacious wave of Russian armaments and black-market goods sweeping through the North West, though Standing did not see how this justified his position of looking the other way and taking bribes, and he would not be drawn. Following the consolidation of the Gemstones Corporation of Pakistan, nothing remained of the lustrous hues of those items, cut and rough, that had adorned the same tables on which the Khan party now dined. Standing, anxious not to agonise further, especially while they remained in Peshawar, and sensing that Allam seemed still to be under the misapprehension that all Irish were freedom fighters, he picked up on a conversation he had eavesdropped between Struell and the general.

"What is your reason for travelling to Lahore, General?" Struell asked.

"I live there," came his reply. "I believe that two of you will be staying at my house in the cantonment," he added. Standing interrupted to inform him that it was actually three of them staying in his home: Michael O'Mahony, accompanied by his son Desmond, and Arthur Murray. They too had heard the general, and a lively chat ensued, when the general spoke of his charming wife Fareeda, his entertaining father-in-law Hesky, and his three polo-playing sons, Kublai, Genghis, and Shamyl. Replete, the post-prandial mood had mellowed them as they enthused over the return journey, eager to get back to Lahore. Two jeeps parked in wait as they stepped out of the Khan. The cool evening had chilled further, dumbing down the scents of the market area to a lingering sweet remnant of that former pungent mix, the air was cleansed and refreshing to take in. At the railway station, over the urgent whistling of station masters and impatient engine drivers, the noise of freight and passenger carriages shunting into position, they said farewell to the commissioner and his remaining retinue. The whistle hailed them aboard, and Khalid was there to open the door to their state room, resplendent with flowers delivered from Lahore earlier that day; the sweet scent of Siren jasmine filled the cabin. The train blew its whistle once more, as latecomers jumped into the crammed carriages at the rear – workers mostly, for the Lahore textile and tannery industries – and their party, relaxed now for the homeward journey, began to open books, tune instruments, quench thirsts, and loosen their clothing. The adventure still had legs.

Immediately ahead of them the engine now hauled its load away from the platform, as Standing reclined in a leather armchair. Watching the city and its mountainous backdrop evanesce into the gloom of its frontier terrain, he thought about his father, and how he had been able to bring his memory to such a high point, on top of the world; he had for a moment felt closer to him than he could ever recall, not since they had gone camping thirty years earlier, before they were separated by his education; a lot can change over eight years at boarding school. Just as the bond between them had been severed back then, the moment of discovery at the head of the Pass had too been interrupted. At the very instant of a numinous link with the hereafter, he had been elevated to a very different orbit by something that had germinated beneath the earth, and his contemplations would have to keep for the time being.

18

General Rafi sat facing him, a healthy, handsome man in his fifties, and continued to speak of his sons who made up, with him, the family polo team. As Fareeda delivered him each boy, he had dreamed of the day they would all take to the field, and he would lead them from behind, in the number four position. As a tank commander and father of three querulous siblings, he had learned that it was the sweeper who would clear up any mess his inchoate offspring might leave. As they had matured into their late teens, his tenure remained as outrigger, who swept and steered his young cohorts into a cohesive, formidable side – the toast of the Lahore Polo Club, as the Irish National Polo Team would soon discover.

"How's your drink?" asked Rafi.

"Oh! Thank you."

Rafi beckoned to Khalid, who came to stand beside him, offering a whisky decanter. Rafi took the crystal vessel and began to pour. Standing thanked him. "That's fine." Rafi continued to pour the liquid until it tipped the rim of the glass. Eyebrows raised, Tom protested politely, "Whoa there. Take it easy general."

The reply from the tank commander, father of three plains warrior princes, who had lived his life as a playmaker, witnessing success and death equally, spoke with assured assertion: "Life is not a dress rehearsal, my boy!" Uplifted by the sage general, Tom stood to drink the full tumbler of Glenmorangie. Now this 'old boy' was ready to be entertained. Rafi began to recite:

> The cup of the eye is filled to the brim,
> My tears – they yearn for freedom,
> To flow, to move, to fall like the monsoon rain,
> You are required Oh! Evil soul, harbinger of pain,
> For the heart is a lamb and you are the butcher,
> Slaughter it and let the blood tear flow,
> Let men forget the rains that turn the grass green,
> Let them see the tears of blood ... the paint,
> That makes the soaking ground crimson,
> Let the sun's light think that the dew falls,
> Let it sparkle on the river of tears,

I need you beloved for the pain you give,
Return, for the cup of the eye is filled to the brim.[1]

Rafi requested that his audience indulge him when he repeated the stanza in Urdu. Khalid switched off the compartment lights, and there began a request which lifted, moved, and touched all their Punjabi and Irish souls, as together they rolled towards the divided province. Rafi poured again, incanting in his mother tongue, and Khalid, at first humming a soft chant, connecting the end rhymes with each new line, began to sing. Not so loud so as to disable the lament, their harmonious unison now inspired Irish hearts. Michael and Desmond gathered their fiddles and flutes to improvise, and so complete the session with Celtic fusion. This was truly a meeting of souls, Standing thought, nodding his head, a simple contribution to this international ensemble, less potent but in good time. This was a warrior's aubade, embracing the lustrous Asian full moon beaming onto them in their standing place. The atmosphere prevailed for the rest of the night, and they continued to chant, decant, recite, orate, sing, orchestrate, narrate their stories and their jokes. Peter responded to Rafi with a Kashmiri poem he had found in his third choice of reading, an anthology of world poetry, as the team plane had floated high above the Hindu Kush before turning South towards Karachi, their first stop on arrival in this land of ancient and exotic civilizations. Peter read with considered delivery:

The soul, like the moon,
is new, and always new again.
And I have seen the ocean
continuously creating.

Since I scoured my mind
and my body, I too, Lalla,
am new, each moment new.

---

[1] The Cup of the Eye is Filled to the Brim - Anon. c.1450, translated from Urdu c.1770.

20

My teacher told me one thing,
Live in the Soul.
When that was so,
I began to go naked,
and dance.[2]

Lalla, the seer poet and mystic, came from the Kashmir province of India. She lived in the fourteenth century, a period of religious upheaval and change. The Kashmiris had always been religiously tolerant, and welcomed the fusion of traditions, so when the region came under the influence of the rapine Islamist invaders during that century, Lalla and most of the people of the region empathised with their new occupants; they had brought with them a less doctrinal branch of Islamism, much diluted with Buddhist philosophy. Rafi knew of Lalla, and he enjoyed Peter's rendition of this soulful sonnet, backed by Desmond's somnolent whistling.

"Bravo, Peter, Bravo," Rafi praised him, wondering if he had any more verses from his book.

"I do have another," Peter told him tentatively. He was anxious not to offend when the party was going so well.

The traitor's skull, we shall drink out of it,
His teeth we shall wear as a necklace,
From his bones we shall make flutes,
Of his skin we shall make a drum
Then we shall dance.[3]

He had recently read a treatise on the harshness of punishments meted out by Muslim courts of the seventeenth century. Not any more condign, similar penalties were indulged by the high caste Hindu Marathas, so he hoped Rafi did not resent the poem. He had chosen it with its final line in mind.

---

[2] Lal Ded (14th Century).

[3] To a Traitor (Anon c. 1550).

"Let's have some dancing now," Rafi smiled and clapped his hands twice. A veiled girl entered the compartment wearing a full cloak, followed by a flautist and a tabla player. Khalid cleared an area in the centre of the floor and laid a plain rug covering, which the girl crouched down on shrouded by her cloak. The two musicians sat, cross-legged, facing their audience. They wore white djellabas and Karakuls, and were waistcoated; the drummer wore green silk trimmed with red braid, the flute player's sleeveless vest coloured a deep red with white embroidery. The tabla player began tapping a slow rhythmic beat, the girl lay coiled on the rug. As the flute found note, the young dancer lifted a hand, her fingers still touching the floor covering, then let it rest once more; her long plaited hair hung over her other hand. The beating of the drum, a gentle muted thud on the goatskin, punctuated the timing of the train as it crossed the expansion gaps. These line breaks were set by the bolt spacing through the fishplates which linked them. Steel on steel amplified through the carriage, syncopating the timbre of train with drum, break and beat, and break and beat. Flute and dancer began to stir, applying and raising their digits, his fingering the length of this conduit to his erotic soul, hers, these pathfinders for her lithe, gamine figure, her cloak shed, limb after limb, her head still bowed. This beautiful creature responded to the descant of the seated troubadours, as they did to her. The alluring quintessences of their purpose reached their climax, as the centre of all attention raised her head, heavily painted, to reveal a stunning visage, eyes closed, with sweeping eyeliner to her brows, her arms, bent at their elbow, reaching left arm to right shoulder and right to left, across her chest. Her head cover stirred and a black serpent appeared and stood, emitting it's assertive hiss. No less ferocious than any larger snake to the men from Ireland, where no snakes reside, this elongated animal, moonlight glistening on its scales, its yellow tracer lines, luminescing in similar vein, had at first shocked the travelers as they clenched fists and gripped glasses, tense, in anticipation of what might follow. The dancer, Aaban, explained to Rafi that she wished to perform an Egyptian Snake Dance, as Cleopatra had herself with a cobra. The snake on her own head, a benign Asp, was neither poisonous nor hostile, and had been trained by charmers, chosen for their illustrious skills in this ancient form of performance art. Rafi, convinced by the girl's explanation and sensing an air of apprehension from the tourists, beckoned a man at the doorway of the compartment. Any further anxieties were allayed as the dancer's minder came forward and removed the threatening reptile.

"Come, gentlemen. Are we men or mice?' beseeched Rafi.

Feeling himself a man once more, Arthur said, "Thrilling stuff, Rafi. And the snake got us all going too. I was mesmerised for one."

"An Arabian night par excellence, General," Peter said.

"Dance on, child," Rafi told the girl. Some child, thought Tom, as she turned and twisted her fine form, more quickly now, the engine picking up steam, and the music continued, with full Irish accompaniment. Aaban, or Angel, graced the carriage for a further half hour – sensually suggestive, delicately en dedans, dégagéd through her demi-pliés, rising to the balls of her feet, through ronds and pirouettes, herself now the serpent, fish and gazelle, all of them exuding from this chimeric Daphne describing the depths and highs, the rise and fall of both passion's tragedy and its comedy. The team stood, their necks craning towards the siren, their senses heightened by a tropism to the acolyte of Isis, the Sun Goddess of fertility. The harmony drove rapidly to its crescendo, and with a final ejaculated hiss, Aaban, spent, recoiled upon the rug, her two confederates silenced. Stimulated to such a state of high tension, unrequited, unreleased, how would the guests respond? How could they? A tough act to follow, they all agreed, with suggestions that Brendan "Brenda" Hannigan might rise to the occasion, everybody else's blood racing with excitement, and only one thing on all their minds. Arthur stepped up with a choral response, and began to sing "The Fields Of Athenry" and they all joined him.

But a lonely prison wall,
I heard a young girl calling
Michael they have taken you away,
For you stole trevelyn's corn
So the young might see the morn,
Now a prison ship lies waiting in the bay

Low lie, The Fields Of Athenry
Where once we watched the small free birds fly
Our love was on the wing
We had dreams and songs to sing,
Its so lonely round the Fields of Athenry

By a lonely prison wall
I heard a young man calling
'Nothing matters Mary, when you're free'
Against the famine and the crown,
I rebelled, they brought me down
Now its lonely round the Fields of Athenry

By a lonely harbour wall
She watched the last star falling
As the prison ship sailed out against the sky
Sure she'll live in hope and pray
For her love in Botney Bay
It's so lonely round the Fields Of Athenry

Still not overwhelmed by a day of reminiscence, and a night of romance, its antiquity looking back at them in the form of such a slender muse, this vision of Terpsichore, this dancer and singer of songs, a force of creation, Standing noticed the musical case in the corner of the carriage, and, when he discovered a guitar, volunteered a song. Michael and Desmond agreed to pick up the tune.

It's the long goodbye
And it happens every day,
When some passerby
Invites your eye
To come her way
Even as she smiles
A quick hello
You've let her go
You've let the moment fly

Too late
You'd turned your head
You'd know you'd said

The long goodbye

Can you recognise the pain?
On some other street
Two people meet
As in a dream
Running for a plane
Through the rain
If the heart is quicker than the eye
They could be lovers
Till they die
It's too late to try
When a missed hello
Becomes a long goodbye.

"This has a ring of Hollywood, Tom," Rafi commented.

"It's the theme to 'The Long Goodbye', a film directed by Robert Altman in the seventies. Raymond Chandler wrote the book about his detective Philip Marlowe."

"The 1970s, you say, Tom?"

"That's right, General. It's an ingenious use of motif through music. Did you ever see it?"

"I have not, but it sounds interesting." Tom was always intrigued by the diversity of arrangements of the theme; from jazz, blues, swing, piano bar, one of the film's stars singing and humming it to herself, and eventually, when the plot moved the action South of the border, a Tijuana brass band and some Spanish guitar changed its tempo yet again. Alas, sensing little mutual interest in the subject, he was content to listen to the night musicians. They all fused in play, and danced jigs, bridging the art forms of their diverse cultures. A sense of shared subjugation to British Rule galvanised a Eurasian bond they could not have imagined before leaving the 'auld country.

Rafi's hospitality was his largesse; he was indeed larger than life, a wonderful host and travel companion.

Brenda chirped in with a humorous story of an American in Ireland. The American asked directions at a five-point crossroads from a local man sitting on a wall. The local having directed him to his destination via all five paths, which the frustrated tourist could not fathom without making a complete circumnavigation of the globe, he threw his hands in the air, crying out: "Now I'm really confused," and asked the Irishman:

"Which way would you go?" to which he replied "of that I cannot be certain, now. But one thing I am sure of." The Irishman paused, holding the American in suspense at what that might be. With a finger raised before his face, a curved eyebrow over his twinkling eye, the local character informed him: "I'm not lost!"

"Not bad, Brenda", Peter said. "We might get you singing yet."

"I doubt it," Hannigan mumbled beneath his breath.

Aaban had declined the Irish invitation to join in the general dancing, sweetly bowing out. She left with her chaperone for another carriage. Arthur produced a hip flask of Remy Martin, and when Khalid overheard the name of the brandy he produced a suitable chalice befitting the spirit. Arthur approved, and finally Khalid's upper lip curled into what passed for a brief smile. At the same time, he raised an eyebrow towards Arthur, whom he clearly liked. If the single-mindedness of the train's direction had needed any reassurance, Khalid's presence affirmed that none of them were lost. Arthur had struck again, his rough charm and riveting turn of phrase may have been lost on this dutiful servant, yet Khalid recognised a kindred similarity between Arthur and his own father, Wassim, himself a loveable rogue, who had wooed women the length and breadth of the sub-continent both before, after and despite partition. He, like Khalid, had been a railworker, and traveled extensively on the India State and Pakistan Railways, romancing his way from Peshawar as far south as Madurai, and back again, many times, as a driver of steam locomotives. He had even driven one of the two engines which pushed and pulled the Victorian carriages, like the two the present company found themselves in, from Peshawar via a branch line to the head of the Khyber Pass at Landi Kotal. The twenty-six miles of British-built track traversed ravines and waterways via many bridges, and thirty-four tunnels had been engineered to facilitate the expansion of Empire. Hostile tribesmen and dacoits presented the greatest challenges to the rail travelers, and any security afforded the journey naturally lessened as the occupiers departed from the region. His father had told him of the need to carry a purse of many rupees to satisfy the plundering hillsmen, as without ready bounty a stoppage would often involve confiscation of passengers' belongings – or hostage taking, when a higher figure was demanded by ransom. The latter was paid as promptly as the weekly daytrip allowed. Only an inept robber would strike as the train descended the line; negotiations were effective only on the ascent, when the purse was full, and if not, it might be replenished on arrival in Landi Kotal. Any unfortunate hostage taken on the outward journey hoped that might ensure payment on its return. However, if taken on the descent, it guaranteed one full week in the company of these warring opportunists. Khalid's father had never been so unfortunate on any of his excursions, but had been able to tell of many he had witnessed. Wassim loved to tell stories of the Great Pass, Khalid recalled (again, Rafi interpreting), when he spoke of a dream he had while driving his engine at the head of its load, including on the occasion two freight wagons in addition to the two passenger carriages. Wassim's diurnal dream occurred as he rested briefly from stoking the fire with coal from his long, scraping shovel. He looked out over the familiar terrain, and as the engine crossed a bridge high above a ravine he saw the flow of water below. "Where did this water come from?" the engine driver queried as he leaned out, a firm grip on the holding rail. There is little rain here, he mused, and he knew the top of the Pass to be as arid as the rest of the five-hundred-mile Central Asian watershed that is the Kush. What moisture there was in the night dew must be stored in pockets within its highest range. He envisaged small pools that would quickly funnel into channels beneath the rock surface, so as not to evaporate in the heat of the day. The gentle fall of this heaven-sent liquid, "the universal solvent," added Rafi, began its long journey from a million pools, through a million million pipeways, "conduits of safe conduct." Rafi nodded to Khalid, who, continuing his father's fantasy, described how that drip of life, from its moment of divine conception, when it penetrated the mother pool, would grow, like a boy, into adolescence, playfully tumbling over rocks and rapids in the ripples of the growing stream, its pulse gaining strength, as the gravitational forces bore down into the great rivers of the Indus and Oxus. A'man river', like the Indus, would even spread its new 'roots' across the vast alluvial delta at Karachi, to procreate within the awaiting Arabian Sea. Still not at its journey's end, this only additive enriched all the life of the seas and oceans, as its cycle continued, feeding the self-sustaining system of the planet's depths. Whatever was not consumed within the water or on land, either fresh or embodied within organisms consumed on land or sea, might simply evaporate into the heavens to once more fall upon the great Kush, or some other range of mountains, many thousands of miles away.

Tom said, through Rafi: "Wassim sounds like a wonderful father, Khalid. Your childhood must have been a happy one."

Khalid, facing Tom, said: "Know your history, know yourself," in English. Tom was dumbfounded. Could Khalid speak his language, or was this a one-off expression he had learnt from his Father or some other teacher? He chose not to ask.

*

It was Rafi who related all this to their keen ears, and the perception of the voyagers being aboard a magical journey into the mystic had been further intensified. Aaban rejoined the party, and wished to sing. Rafi translated for her when she introduced her first song, a war ballad written by the highly celebrated 13th Century poet, scholar, and musician, Amir Khusro. It was written in Punjabi, which Rafi was unable to relay to the carriage. He did explain that Khusro was credited with designing the Indian Tabla, the hand drum used by one of Aaban's two backing musicians, and the Sitar, a 3 stringed lute, which the flautist had now taken up, and it leaned between his legs where he sat on the matted floor. To the tap of the

28

Tabla, and the sizzling Sitar, this young woman emoted a dirge that would have shaken the soul of any warrior. Standing had seen the highly acclaimed Sitar player Ravi Shankar in the 1960s, accompanied by Zakir Hussain on Tabla, playing to an audience at Sussex University, and he knew how hypnotic it could be. They relaxed as their rolling carpet carried them deeply higher into the tranquility of the nocturnal narrative of the Winter solstice. Aaban, wishing to continue her Egyptian theme, had asked Tamwar, the sitar player and Taki, the drummer, to sing in English. She thought this better than her own Egyptian version which few, if any, would understand. She knelt in front of her audience, the lids of her eyes shut and lips sealed, and began to hum a chant to the Pharoah Akhenaton *Hymn To the Sun*:

> *A glory,*
> *eternity in life*
> *the Undeposed,*
>
> *beauty*
> *flashing*
> *powers,*
>
> *Love,*
> *the powering,*
> *the widening,*
> *light*
> *unraveling*
> *all faces followers of*
>
> *All the colors, beams of*
> *woven thread,*
> *the skin*
>
> *alight that*
> *warms itself*
> *with life.*

The two lands,
shape themselves
that love

flows
to the
making,

Place, man, cattle, creature-kind,
& tree of every image
taking place.

Life-in-shing
shining
life,

The Mother/Father,
sees the seeing
rise upon our

hearts beat
dawn lights
earth entire

As you made. And as you
pass we settle
equal to the dead,

linen wrapping
nead nostril
plugged with

Earth that waits
return in heaven
rises overturned

the uplift
palms upturned to
Light your being is
the living
Acts the

Touch the voicing in
all land
hears man -
Womanshong en-throning
Truth

gives
heart the
food

The One, we give, to walk,
purely to your
Will, all

creatures
dance you
toward your coming every

Day, you gave your
Son, forever in your
Form he

Acts
in
beauty, saying:

I am

your Son, my heart
knows your the

strength
the seat
of powering

Eternal is the Light
you are the watchful
Maker,

solitary
every
life

Sees light that breathes
by light,
flowers

Seeding
Wilderness,
light stunned by

Light before your
Face,

(At this point Aaban, arms outstretched, fingers aflutter, arose, ascending in Arabic the descant of adoration to celebrate the sun dance of her Goddess Isis).

the dancing
creatures
feathers
up from nests a

Wavering in wing
goes around
around

& praises
living
Joy
you
Are

As her homage climaxed, Aaban, stooping her head, let drop the voile veil she had worn throughout to reveal a burnishing plate fixed to her own crown. Both moon and candle light, turning silver to burning gold, fired a scintillating candescence and set their mobile temple aglow. Standing felt his heart, beating, faster. The Angel Aaban was exalted to a level the equal of Isis, not merely her archangel. She was worthy of the status that befitted her name, at the zenith of the ninefold celestial hierarchy.

"Get a grip," he said to himself, "it's only a dance." For a moment he was reminded of the solstice he had spent in Co. Kerry that Summer. He had driven to Dingle with Nessa, a girl he had met on the Sunday evening at the end of a hectic weekend of partying, drinking, and many chukkas. From a position more vulnerable than predatory, he had gone along with Nessa's plan to travel south to the Dingle peninsula. His impression of Nessa was that she would be looking for the long-term, and he made it clear that this was not on the cards, so they would travel as friends. He was grateful she was happy to agree, and they left Dublin together on Monday morning.

The week had been filled with cliff-top walks and collecting crabs from lobster pots with Michael, the proprietor of the guest house where they stayed. Michael and his wife, Roisin, and little Michael and his sister, Brige, lived high on the approach road to the fishing village of Dingle, celebrated for its restaurants, bars, music sessions, and festivals. Nessa, Tom, and their hosts, both teachers and musicians, spent their evenings visiting the local music spots, which thronged with tourists enjoying the carnival spirit that visited the Gaeltachts in high summer. Michael played the squeezebox, and Roisin? Well, Roisin sang.

Saturday had been a sunny, cloudless day. Tom, Michael, and son, aged nine, rowed the coracle into the bay to raid lobster pots.

Tom's imagination fired, he had notions of wading ashore with a booty filled vessel in tow – contraband and treasure, acquired by rapacious means or other, for Queen and country. His buccaneer delusions were quelled when Michael assured him that the neighbouring fishermen were all his friends, and they were only too happy for him to remove the many unwanted small crabs that often clogged the lobster gates. The three boys in the boat were content to gather their tamed quarry, Michael senior because he would prepare a bisque for their supper, and the boy because he always dreamed seafaring dreams after a trip on the bay with his Dad. Tom's own thoughts turned more to a memorable Hemingway scene, when the author had tied string around the neck of a wine bottle to let it cool in the stream. Michael had thought of that, and drew a bottle from the water by the cord he had attached to a rowlock.

"Perfect," said Tom. "There's a great deal more to you, Michael O'Hanlon. Not just a squeezebox player!"

"And you've probably played more than polo in your time."

They anchored to a fishing buoy and the boy threw a line over the bow. They all lay in the sun, and its equipoise with the earth and ocean and wind was interrupted only with a little humanity, as they shared the literature they loved. They spoke of Maurice O'Sullivan's *Twenty Years A-Growing*, Hemingway's *The Old Man and The Sea*, *For Whom The Bell Tolls*, and others – Joyce, Salinger, Donleavy.

When they had finished their potation, they weighed anchor, gathered up the oars and rowed back to the shore. The men pulled the boat up the beach and tethered it to the post Michael had dug three years before. It had weathered many storms, as had its charge. Michael told Tom that only once had he needed to bring his boat to shelter beside the house; that night, the 22nd of November 1986, a high-force gale broke the back of the Kowloon Bridge, a merchant ship en route from Canada. She had earlier sought shelter in Bantry Bay, and then continued her journey to the Clyde Estuary. Her rudder was lost in deteriorating weather before she was blown onto the Stags off Baltimore, County Cork. Captain and crew were rescued by the RAF, and she sank two days later.

34

Tom and the Kerry men made their way up the cliff path. The wind was picking up; the bay remained calm. Back at the house, Roisin had made bread, while Nessa played with Brige in the garden. The men's faces were burnt from their exposure, so Roisin soothed them. She was humming a tune Tom had not heard.

"It's a ballad to celebrate the solstice," she told him. "It's tonight."

"What are the words?"

"Irish. They are about fertility, and how the sun rose and set during the many years of occupation, and how the Irish heart will always be free, and independence will glorify its fertility once more."

"And they were right, of course," said Tom.

They all sat to eat in the kitchen. Michael had bisqued the seafood in white wine using a pressure cooker, adding cream when he decanted the soup into a tureen. They ladled their own bowls and took bread from the table, Roisin's freshly-baked granary loaf, still warm. Food from the land and from the sea, a sense of delivery, that moment of connection with nature's harvest, humbled the interloper. He felt at home. He had been allowed in, and he knew no harm would come to him.

In town, they moved about to different bars, drinking in some, wherever the music took them. And still it was Roisin's humming that was dominant above all else in his thoughts. He found himself yearning for the voicing that had earlier moved him, and the proud supplication of the words she had translated for him, and which, Michael told him, she had written herself. The full bars of Dingle were not the setting for what he wanted, and he detected that Roisin sensed this also. Michael said "Let's move down the shore to Hickey's."

Nessa abstained for the evening, and drove the short journey out of town. Before she went she spoke into his ear, "maybe you'll find somebody here." *Maybe.* Hickey's was close to the waterline, set back on the edge of a pasture, accessed on foot through a field gate. On hearing the driving beat of the bodhran, fiddles and whistles, it sounded like more of the same. A feeling of disappointment filled him, though he noticed Roisin was less affected, and had begun once again to hum. Hickey's was heaving, the revelers up to the nineties, mostly local, the girls pretty, the men pretty wild. Getting drink was challenging, fighting his way through the bar. "Three pints, and a mineral water," he ordered. A tall brunette with a warm smile stood beside him, and asked was his accent Australian. He knew when he was being wound up, replying; "Could have been. My father was born there. Is that a Dublin accent you have?"

"I'm from Kerry," she informed him, as if he had not known. Feeling Guinness–fuelled and bold, he whispered closely in her ear, "I'd like to…" as a hand on his shoulder interrupted his reckless flow.

"Not from here, friend?" the warning came from an imposing fellow with a bushy beard.

"Seamus " said the brunette.

"Nearly a week now," Tom told him. "How about you?"
The glazed eyes of the bearded one suggested a week would not cut it, but the Englishman stood his ground. What else could he do but go down with pride? The two men looked into each other's eyes. His adversary's hirsute head eclipsed the girlfriend's face, restraining further distraction by the 'blow-in'. The glare seemed endless, and Tom decided to have the last word.

"You may feather me, but please let her tar me."

"And me," another girl's voice was heard.
The silence between the men suddenly exploded into a burst of laughter, and the bar room collapsed.

"You're some lad, Tommy boy! You are that. Buy this man a pint," Seamus called out. Tom was pleased to settle for a social victory, and forfeit the girl, as he stepped out the side door into the night air. As the pints mixed well with a still coolness moving over his face, he left the manic exchanges of Hickey's. He was being drawn to the source of a voice, now familiar to him, as it came ashore to greet him. He took care not to lose the trail, and trod silently in the sand. When he was around the dune, a pontoon began to emerge, and as its length became clear, it was bathed in light. The radiance of the moon and the dawning sun met on Dingle Bay, and there, at the end of the pier, a meridian mother in her tryst, Roisin sang her freedom song.

36

Now in the train, the rising light from the sun, the glorious star and giver of life, was replacing the moon as it set down behind the world, and Standing was minded once more of Dingle Bay. This thought was held in the dynamic of the madrugada and the light of the night gave way to twilight. Another time, he thought, as the night closed with daybreak, and Khalid entered with tea and toast. Both their trusty attendant and conveyance were delivering them from an indelible journey into antiquity, as they rolled into the station at Lahore.

3
Lahore

Two local hosts received them as they alighted from their carriages of privilege, but not before the throng of factory workers had hurried past them to the ticket barriers, anxious not to be late on a Monday morning. When the crowd had dispersed, the Irish polo players accompanied the two men – Tariq Akram, a local businessman, and Rashid Mahmoud, the General Manager of the Pakistan National Railway, and both members of the Lahore Polo Club (LPC). Tariq admired Peter's headgear. He was still wearing his Pakol, and his light-coloured pashmina, loose and trailing behind him, gave him the appearance of one returning from a military campaign. T.E. Lawrence came to mind as Standing admired his tall companion. But he would reserve comment as it might go to Struell's head – or worse, incur his wrath. Rashid was interested to know about the day before. Had they enjoyed the day out, and what were their impressions of the Pass, and Peshawar, the city of legend. It was not that he felt interrogated, more simply fatigue after a long, sleepless night, following a tense afternoon. He preferred to discuss the day after some rest.

The players were separated into two awaiting cars. Arthur travelled with Michael and Desmond, accompanied by Tariq, and headed to the cantonment district of the City. Peter, Tom and Brendan travelled with Rashid who sat up front with his driver. Brendan was dropped off first, at the house of Jalal Ounis, his bungalow on the edge of the city centre. Jalal's wife Shareez greeted them and invited them for tea. A charming, intelligent, young woman of European appearance, Shareez had lived in Northamptonshire as a girl, brought up by her Indian mother and English father, a physics teacher at Stowe school. His name was Campbell, and Shareez changed her name to Ounis when she fell in love and married Jalal, a former army Lieutenant, and now an officer serving in The Lahore Police Department. Jalal had learnt to ride and play polo in the army, and on retirement three years earlier when he married, the army had made arrangements for him to join the LPC, and generously continued to mount him at that club. Shareez rang Jalal to let him know of their arrival, and he walked across the lawn just a few minutes later. Things were quiet at the station, so he was able to get away and join them for morning tea. If Standing had not been so in need of his bed, he would like to have discussed the nefarious arms and narcotic exchange with Jalal; but as the warmth of the rising sun soothed him, along with the comfort of the warm lemon tea, he resigned his senses to the day.

Seeing that the three travelers were weary from their lively night with Rafi, Jalal's most formidable polo adversary and great friend, he suggested to Rashid that they should break up the gathering, and give themselves a chance to rest before evening chukkas at the club. And so they left the company of Jalal, Shareez, and their house guest, Hannigan, and drove on towards the canal road. Rashid's driver stopped the car outside the house of Imran Shin, and Peter stepped out of the car and made his way along the garden border, pulling out his door key, and entered to a warm welcome from the houseman, also known as Imran. This dutiful, jolly servant had joined his master when he was appointed Director of International Operations for Pakistan Air Lines (PAL), a post befitting the descendant of a ruling dynasty from the Gilgit region of the country; Gilgit sat in the foothills of the Hindu Kush, and polo was played there under maverick rules. Without helmets, anyone who turned up was allowed to play, making for uneven, large numbers, exceeding the prescribed four-a-side, as standardised by the Hurlingham Polo Association (HPA). The Association stipulated that all players must use the mallet while held in the right hand. Not so in Gilgit, where anything went.

"How can such a game be umpired?" Peter asked.

"That's easy," laughed Imran Shin. "They don't use umpires!"

"Are they not subject to the rules of the Pakistan Polo Association?"

"Most definitely not. Gilgit's dynasties pre-date all others on the sub-continent, and they take their guidance from none other than their own masters."

Strategically, the territory of Gilgit, a hillside enclave protected from the north by the vast Kush, had traditionally feuded with their southern neighbours for thousands of years and partition had not changed that. Struell, amused by Imran's description, was impressed mostly by the hubris of his host's forebears. He enthused at the idea of visiting the region, albeit doubtful about playing a match without rules, and he would certainly take his helmet, just in case. But alas, this was not to be. The tour had not scheduled in Gilgit, Imran informed him, though Struell felt there might be more international xenophobia underlying this omission. In spite of this, as Standing arrived at Rashid's home, he had been left with an abiding sense of how varied and intercontinental his chosen sport was, acclaimed at all levels throughout the world. He was part of something which spread to many parts, although he had yet to discover where they would take him.

Tea was brought to his room. It was 4 o'clock after all, and in postcolonial Punjab many British traditions were still observed. Or maybe it was the other way around; perhaps it was those former governors who, having been introduced to tea drinking during the time of the Raj, had then been educated by the high caste merchants and masters in the etiquette of its consumption, and more importantly, the civilised times of day to do so. The young houseboy placed the tray on an ottoman. The canal road was busy now, donkeys and cattle, driven west by herdsman carrying long sticks, keeping up with farmers driving empty carts, and uniformed children returning from school. Heading east were more carts, laden with produce for the bazaars of Lahore City, and taxis carrying office workers and other members of the business community back to their places of work and commerce.

The Englishman drank his tea and poured a second cup of the bergamot-scented blend, before showering. Chukkas would be at 6pm. He pulled on his playing whites, a tee shirt, sweater, fleece jacket, and loafers. His boots sat in a bag, which he had left in the hall beside the three mallets he bought the week before. When he joined Meera and Rashid in the drawing room, they asked him how he was feeling.

40

"Ready to play. Who will be playing this evening?"

Rashid replied, "I am umpiring. Jalal is captain, and he will be playing with Imran, Tariq Thakral, and Wakir Sikarwar." As Standing told him that he thought the six players from Ireland would probably share the chukkas, Rashid was called away to take a telephone call, and left the two of them. Meera asked Tom to explain how it was possible to share a game, and soon he realised that she knew next to nothing about the sport which occupied her husband on a weekly basis. Rashid had taken up polo before starting his Business Studies degree at Karachi University in 1959, and had not missed a season in thirty years. For his knowledge and experience of the game, both as umpire and player, he was held in high esteem within Pakistan and India, as well as further afield in the Middle East and widely in Africa. Yet Meera, who met him at a tournament, the 1985 Punjab Cup, knew so little about this game, despite its intrusiveness into her marriage. All the same, they were loving towards each other, and did appear to be quite happy.

"What I meant was that four of us will play, while two sit out, and when there is time out, for example at the end of a chukka, maybe one will substitute while somebody else sits out."

"A chukka is a period of play, isn't that right?" she asked.

" That's right. And it lasts for seven and a half minutes," Tom informed her.

"That is not very long."

"It can seem a pretty long time when you're galloping the length and breadth of such a large ground. It's hard on the ponies, constantly pulling up and changing direction," he said. "We play four chukkas per game. And each pony is restricted to two chukkas, with a break of at least one chukka's length."

Tom was delighted to impart what he knew about his chosen sport. He asked her if she had a sheet of paper and a pencil so that he could firstly illustrate the layout of a polo ground. It is three hundred yards long, and two hundred yards wide. In the centre of the ground a white "T" is drawn, to divide the two halves. There are white penalty lines drawn the width of the ground at thirty yards, and spots mark the forty- and sixty-yard distances from each back line. The goal-posts are ten feet high, and eight yards apart." Meera followed Tom's description from the lines he drew on the sheet.

"A game is divided into 4 periods, known as chukkas, and each lasts seven and a half minutes. The first bell is rung at seven minutes, and the chukka continues until either a goal is scored, a foul occurs, or the ball is hit off the field, out of play, or time runs out. The last chukka, though, ends on the seven-minute bell. A pony may be played twice during a game, with a break of at least one chukka. Many players only use their ponies once, so they need more than the minimum required, which would be two. Polo is very demanding on ponies. They are galloping most of the time, but frequently need to pull up and turn, to follow the direction of play."

"So you need two ponies?" Meera asked him.

"Minimum, for each player," he replied. "A team would need at least eight ponies. Many players use more, and keep spares in case of injuries, so a team might well bring twenty or more ponies to a game," he told her.

"Rashid has seven ponies I think, but I don't know if he uses them always. He tells me that his handicap is two, and ten years ago it was four, but he has never explained this to me. Could you tell me what it means, Tom?" He could not remember anyone ever asking him to explain polo before, and he had found the prettiest ears on the subcontinent.

"The handicap system is applied to all players, from minus two goals for novices, rising to a maximum of ten goals. There are not too many ten-goalers, as these are the very best in the world. Most of them come from Latin America. If Rashid made four goals, then he must have been a very good player. And of course a team handicap is the sum of its four players' handicaps." Handicapping is the other way round in golf of course. The lower your handicap, the better rated the player. The great Carlos Gracida is currently the best in the world. He is Mexican, and began playing when he was five years old. He has won every tournament, and plays the Argentine Open with the ultimate of all teams, La Espadania. They have four ten-goal players, which gives them a forty-goal rating."

"Your team handicap is how many?" she asked.

"We are six or seven goals depending on who is playing; we have a three, a two, and four one-goal players. Does that make things any clearer?"

"Yes," she replied, "I think so. Thank you so much. Perhaps I will understand a little more when I go to a match, which is not very often."

"At the start of a game, the teams line up in the middle of the ground, each team on either side of the "T". The umpire bowls the ball in underhand between them, and the game begins. A goal is scored when the ball crosses the line between the posts. Each time a goal is scored, the teams return to the middle, but they change ends, and the ball is rolled in again. If the ball goes out of play across the back line, wide of the posts, then the defending team hits in from the back line, with all opponents at least thirty yards from the hitter, on or beyond the thirty-yard line. If a defender hits the ball over the back line, then the attacking team is awarded a free hit from the sixty-yard line, rather like a corner kick in soccer – except that in polo the ball is placed directly in front of the goal. The defenders must be positioned thirty yards from the hitter and can only impede the attack after the ball has been struck.

"Most rules of polo concern the 'right of way', often referred to as the 'line'. This is the direction the ball was travelling in when it was last struck, and it must be respected by all players. The player with the primary right to the line will be to the left of the line, so that the ball is on his stick side. Think of the white line down the centre of the road, and you are driving on the left of it. You have priority, and no player may cross in front of you. A player can 'tackle' you by riding you off the ball, and this is done by a player riding alongside and moving his horse into yours until one of you concedes to the other. If a cross does occur, then the umpire will award a penalty against the offender. This may be a free hit from the spot, or from the centre of the field, or further up on either the sixty, forty, or thirty-yard line, depending where the infringement occurred. If a foul is committed directly in front of the goal by a defender, then a goal may be awarded automatically. The other way to tackle an opponent is to hook his stick. Players must always hold the mallet with their right hand, and must not hook each other's mallets above shoulder height, for safety reasons. And we strike the ball with the face of the mallet's head, not the end, as with croquet. A stick or mallet is between forty-eight and fifty-three inches in length, depending on the height of your horse. We still refer to them as ponies, because there used to be a height restriction; but that doesn't apply anymore. The term pony has just kind of stuck. There is more to fouls and penalties but too much detail now might be confusing, and the best way to learn, actually, is by playing. That is, if you were to take up the game. Do many women play in Pakistan, Meera?"

"Only men," she replied.

"Really? Many women play in Europe, and America, and in the Southern Hemisphere. I have played with and against many," Tom told her. Meera had no children, did not work, was well tended by an entourage of staff, and driven wherever she needed to go. Her birth family were nearly all from Karachi, and Tom wondered what she did with the time her charmed life afforded her.

"As there are six of us, two sit out at any given time, as I was saying. But in an official match we play off our declared handicap whoever is on the field. Peter is our Captain, so we always need him. He plays off three goals."

"And what makes one player better than another do you think?" Meera asked.

"Well, you need to be fit, and have well-schooled horses, and the better you can ride the better player you'll make. But above all those things, just like most sport, the key is anticipation. If you can read the play accurately, then anticipation of what will happen next will give you the edge. All players of one or two goals and higher have the required skills in their repertoire to cope with most situations, but the player who has read the game better than the rest will be waiting for the play to come to him, rather than chasing after it, playing catch-up. 'Ball chasers' are bad players. A strong player makes the play by being one step ahead at all times." Rashid came in to say that they were leaving for the game. He had spoken with the head groom, and the ponies were in the lines, at the ground.

"Anyhow, Meera, I hope this has helped, so now you'll have to come and watch more."

*

If it had taken twenty minutes normally to reach the ground from Rashid's house, the greater congestion on the canal road this time increased a sense of urgency in Rashid's driver. He thrust through the beast-drawn vehicles ahead, mounting verge and curb, swinging out to overtake others, barely missing the hooves of the oxen and donkeys, whose nonchalance suggested they were either used to it or sleepwalking. The canal stretch had Standing thrown from one side of the rear bench to the other, until he discovered the strap over the door. A policeman waved them on, recognising Rashid, the Head of the Railways network for the Punjab. Tom, despite feeling privileged, was uncomfortable with the disdainful way the other road users were brushed aside, as if the pursuit of pleasure naturally took priority above the daily journeys of those lives that depended on them, especially when he had seen so much poverty in the rural districts. With an open mind and difficulty, whilst trying to assimilate the paradox of opulence and penury that this binary culture was clearly steeped in, he could not sense that there might be a leap from pre-industrial society to any kind of European modernism. The masters of old would always dominate, he thought, as the driver emerged from his dodgem run and instantly decelerated to cruise the outer city carriageway to the polo club. All the pilot's former exigency had disappeared, tardiness no longer an issue.

"What the hell was all that about?" Tom said.

"Oh! He likes to be on time, don't you Ranjit?" said Rashid.

"Yes sir!"

Ranjit had driven for a General stationed in Kashmir, and had made regular trips across rough terrain, day or night, the length and breadth of the Punjab. On these stressful journeys – to meetings in Rawalpindi, Karachi, and as far as Peshawar, Ranjit had learnt to move with stealth across the provincial countryside, and with assertive guile through any urban destinations. At the wheel of the general's military limousine, this driver's road rage, horn blaring beneath the winged flags of his regiment and country, received deference from all in his way. Any other response, whilst he was uniformed, to an encounter with this bullying 'Toad' would have proved costly, Tom thought. Thus, Rashid and Tom were swept through the gates of the Lahore Club and delivered to the clubhouse enveloped in a plume of swirling dust which issued like a nebular cloud from this rush to the finishing line. Tom had him down as either a frustrated, unrequited polo player, or possibly a rally driver. Ranjit was almost certainly asserting his position of superiority above the grooms, and maybe even the players; after all, he could drive, and had driven generals, and all they could manage were horses at the Lahore Polo Club. Rashid and Tom were greeted by the other players, who were relaxed, laughing as a group, sharing something about Ranjit. They considered that Rashid and Ranjit made a good team, as one always kept the other waiting, thus providing the other with the opportunity to relive his military driving days, resulting in these hallmark dramatic entrances. They all wished Ranjit drove for them.

"Enough, gentlemen!" Rashid exclaimed. "To our mounts."

The Irish players collected their stick bags and made their way across the playing ground to the pony lines. Twenty ponies were tied up in a line like serried soldiers on parade, with four grooms standing beside them. Standing met Hanif with his two ponies at one end and walked up to him, greeting him with a smile and a nod. The mounts looked well turned out, brushed clean, clipped, their tack immaculate. Their bridles, all with Pelham bits, shone from the soap Hanif had spent the afternoon working into them. The reins were supple and the saddles wiped with more soap. Standing was impressed with his dedication and the pride he took in his work, and Hanif recognized this as he was punctilious in his diligent manner towards the visitor, and remembered everything that Standing had pointed out from previous meetings.

Standing liked girths to be slackened between chukkas as this was less restricting on the horse, and enabled it to relax, get its breath back. Standing himself would always tighten his own girth. If

46

the evening was hot, then he liked buckets of water and sponges to be at hand for cooling the animals. He also wanted all his horse's legs to be bandaged, not just the forelegs. He had brought tape with him in order to wrap and secure these bandages; he also insisted that the tails were wrapped with tape, and not merely tied up. Hanif knew to bring an antiseptic spray to treat minor injuries and cuts, as well as an astringent gel. The two men had a respect and mutual equestrian understanding which oiled the parts of a working machine on and off the field. And if this spirit of gestalt could be established between horse, rider and groom, then so much more might be achievable by four like-minded players in a team. Hanif had cleaned Standing's boots, which he brought to the ground with the horses. Embarrassed by this indulgence, he had never seen his boots look as polished, like mirrors, buffed and balled to a glass finish. For Hanif it was pure pleasure, and he delighted in providing good service.

Standing offered rupees into Hanif's hand the second time they met, but he refused them. Not sure whether Hanif should be seen to take them, he decided to place them into a boot, and no dispute. Rashid's horses were all from New Zealand, which bemused Standing, as he knew the Pakistani Army still had cavalry regiments, and Rashid had told him that all the horses they used were either from the region or from neighboring regions. The New Zealand horses, more expensive largely because of the transportation costs, were better trained and, with the exception of Jalal and Rafi, who used military mounts, most members of the club used Antipodean animals. The Irish were mounted on these. Standing's horse for the first chukka was called Chiquita, a curious name, he felt, for a horse from down under, playing in Asia. She was black, light-mouthed, and tended to overrun, but Standing attributed this to his lack of familiarity with this fine-limbed eight-year-old, 15 hands mare.

The play began smoothly, with meaningful calls that produced positive consequences. Their hosts, generous in every way, did not desist in this practice game, seeming to allow their guests a fair degree of slack. As the first bell rang at seven minutes, the score was one apiece. In the closing thirty seconds before the second bell,

Struell took the ball to within thirty yards of the goal and tapped it through, running out the chukka at 2–1 to the Irish.

Back in the lines, Standing congratulated his friend, under pressure from Jalal when he attempted to hook his stick. He had explained to Meera that hooking sticks, like hockey, is permitted in polo so long as the player trying to hook is placed on the same side of the opponent's horse as the opponent's stick, which must be carried in the right hand. So, the hooker must be on the same side as the opponent's stick, without crossing over the other player's pony. In addition, hooking can only be attempted below shoulder height, as it would clearly be dangerous to lock sticks at head or neck level. It makes sense, he told her, to carry the stick or mallet upright when not targeting the ball, as it is then out of harm's way. Any infringement of this rule constitutes a foul, and the umpire will award a penalty against the offending player's team. Again he hoped he had made this clear to her. Jalal had been 'unable to engage' Struell, who scored a straightforward goal.

Standing barely touched the ground as Hanif took Chiquita, offering him his second mount, a robust chestnut gelding with powerful haunches, his nose bearing a long flash, and two white socks the length of his cannon bones, standing just over 15 hands. Rashid named the mighty steed Cezar, and he regarded him as the captain of his string, much as Kipling had personified the 'Maltese Cat'. Standing knew this classic story, about a military mount who bore an army officer, the team captain, and had courageously given all but his own life as well as his rider's in order to score a winning goal, rendering them both fit only for umpire duties for the rest of their days. The 'Cat' commanded the other horses when they were tied in the lines, and they followed their leader's orders. Cezar too was dominant in the pony lines, Standing sensed, and felt in safe hands when they galloped back onto the field for the second chukka.

The teams formed two straight lines beside each other, pointing towards the umpire, Rashid. He demanded that they move apart to create space between them for him to throw the ball in. They were now playing to the opposite end of the field before the last goal had been scored, since play always reversed direction as a result of a score.

"Ready?" he called. All players looked at him, anticipating the start. "Play!" he roared, throwing the ball into the gap between them.

The number one players on each team clashed sticks, neither making contact with the ball. The next player, for the home side, nicked the ball, and it ricocheted forty feet up-field. Struell was quick to pick up the direction, and sent a backhand shot down onto it; it soared thirty feet above the horses, heading for the home goal, fifty yards or more. Standing, at number one, was soon behind it, on its line of trajectory; this gave him priority to strike it next. He took a half-shot, sending it a further thirty yards directly to goal. Two more taps and the goal was his, he thought.

Not so. Jalal, wearing the number three shirt, normal for the field captain of a team, rode up Standing's left side, and thrust the weight of his own horse against Cezar. The ride-off forced the attacker over the ball, and backing up right behind the action was Imran Shin, who then hit the ball around the tail of his pony with a backhand stroke to the side of the ground. It went too far, out of play. Rashid moved rapidly to the scene and collected the ball with his pick-up stick, calling "Line up!"

The players lined up once more, this time to the side of the ground, and Rashid threw the ball between the teams. It passed right through to emerge beyond the last players. They turned vigorously in on each other to claim the line of the ball. All the players understood that the line demarcated the right of way, which is the first rider to have the direct route to the ball on his stick side, the right-hand side. A player finding himself on the right side of the player who has claimed the line of the ball may hook sticks to prevent a clean shot, or may even strike at the ball himself, so long as he does so by swinging his mallet only on the nearside of his own pony, and at no time must he cross the implied line established by the player with the right of way. Like driving on a major road the first car has right of way, and any other road users needed to observe the highway code before engaging with or joining the highway. Tariq Akram, for the Club team, was first onto the line, and struck the ball with strength sixty yards towards the visitors' goal. Struell engaged him with a ride-off left to right. Tariq was pushed so far to the right of the line that Struell was able to play a backhand shot, lofting the ball high over the ensuing teams, shifting the direction of play from defense to attack in one move. Arthur picked up the momentum, moving the play aggressively to the home goal, as he roared; "Back me up!" Desmond was already behind him, alert to Arthur possibly missing his next hit, which would have left him to pick up the slack, at the same time as keeping a defender at bay. Arthur did miss his shot, and Desmond, unmarked, struck with his mallet; the ball went wide to the left.

Not having a goalkeeper, as in soccer, the player wearing the number four shirt is the last defender of the goal, although the play interchanges constantly, and so it fell to Imran Shin to hit the ball in from the back line. This set play required that the opponents be no closer than thirty yards up the field from the hitter, beyond the thirty-yard line. As Imran began his canter to the ball, both he and the umpire called: "Play!" His own players were placed one to his right, within the thirty-yard line, thence untouchable by any members of the opposition, and another to his left, close to the border of the ground. These two players were respectively the numbers three and two. Imran hit the ball twenty-five yards and moved onto it at a gallop, his number three Jalal coming in behind him in support. This signaled Wakir, at number three, to block Struell from engaging Imran while he had the strike.

At any time, as they all knew, polo held each and every one of them in a grip of attack which could reverse in an instant into defence, in a shifting paradigm of competition. Wakir held Struell, mount against mount, preventing the Irish player from encroaching upon Imran's charge. The Lahore number four wound his mallet up to deliver a fine blow, and the ball did not hit the ground until it had cleared the halfway line. With ball still rolling, Tariq was next to claim the line, and dealt a spirited shot as he galloped over the ball. Desmond was first to it, and yelled "Open!" as he cut the ball more than forty yards out to the right with a well-executed backhand.

Standing responded, picking up the new line. Taking the ball down the field he felt in complete control, unimpeded by any opponent. This time he was going to close the deal. He stroked the ball with half shots. Three shots maximum should do it, he thought.

He just had to keep his composure and not go for the millionaire shot, which always failed; the 'hyperbolic hit of hubris' he had heard it called, as its execution so often would lead to nemesis. Must not waste the effort, he kept repeating and repeating, stroking the ball on the second hit. With just fifteen yards to go, he heard hooves behind him, threatening the outcome. His mallet fell ahead of his pony's for the third time, and swung back passed his right boot, describing a pendulum above the ground, and with his eye firmly on the sweet spot of the ball, let the returning pendulum tap it through the goal mouth. He rode on to the runoff area with the great Cezar, turning round to be greeted by a noisy ovation from his fellow players. No time to waste: both teams returned to the centre of the ground, changing ends, Rashid waiting with ball in hand.

"Play!" he cried. Standing, the bit between his teeth now, met the throw from the front of the line-up. Struell called out.

"Back it, Tom!"

Aware that Struell was moving up the field from the back of the line-up, Standing dug deep beneath the ball to loft it downfield. The team was motoring now, and with that Arthur raced ahead for Peter's pass. Peter did get his shot in, slightly sliced to the right, finding Desmond who had escaped Jalal's gripping ride-off. Desmond knocked the ball up to Arthur, and he finished the move with a mighty blow to goal. If anybody could do it, Arthur could, Tom thought. "Well done, Arthur. Great shooting." On a roll, the Irish team raced back to the centre of the ground, eager to extend their lead, now 4–1.

The ball went in. This time Jalal connected, moving the ball away from the line-out, calling his forward echelon to prepare for attack. "Move up, move up!" he instructed Wakir and Tariq. By the time Jalal had penetrated Irish territory, his players were in position, anticipating his next move. He roared, "Take them out!" He wanted Wakir and Tariq to clear the path, open the way for him to bring the ball through, backed up by Imran, his number four. Wakir stuck with Struell like mud to boots, forcing him out to the left field, as Tariq imposed his own horse on Desmond's, and the pair were locked out to the right of the goal. Jalal, who had created the opportunity, now seized the moment, pushing ahead firmly, concentrating on the accuracy of his stick work as he approached the Irish goal, at the same time aware of the threat from Struell and Standing, who were now both unmarked.

Struell was on Jalal's stick side when he swung in to avert him from his course. Jalal immediately locked his right leg in front of Struell's, restricting his mobility, whilst applying an equal amount of force in retaliation. Struell had to concede to Jalal's dominance, hoping he had jeopardised any attempt at a shot. Jalal's hold on Struell's leg enabled him to bring pressure to bear, manipulating his own horse to the right, pushing his opponent's likewise. Jalal had a clear path now on his pony's nearside, and played a forward shot. It was plum, the ball sailed through the goal. 4–2. As they returned to the centre once more, the bell rang to end the chukka, and they rode off, back to their lines. Time for some refreshment. Standing drank from a large flagon of water, then poured it over Cezar's head. The chestnut whinnied as the liquid ran down his white nose, spraying Hanif and him with beads thrown wide from his flared nostrils.

"Well done, Cezar me boy!" Standing said, slapping his steed on the neck. Rashid was close by, and Standing called out to him. "Thank you for this guy. He has a heart of gold - gave me a great chukka!"

Struell told Tom that Michael would play the next chukka, and he told Arthur that Brendan would replace him for the third chukka also. Tom and Arthur would then play out the fourth and final period. His team leading by two goals, Standing climbed the small stand to watch. Hannigan played number one, and Michael, his age beginning to show, was still able to make good impact in a ride-off, and Standing felt confident that they could hold the lead. Beneath the stand was a small club room, and he stepped down to get a drink. A steward poured him a glass of cordial, asking him if he wanted whisky. "Better not," said Standing "I have to play again."

Back on top, the game was underway. He saw Jalal take the ball from the throw-in to the end of the field and score another goal; 4–3. Jalal was riding a robust black mare, which had a long stride; no more than six made the distance from the halfway line to the goal, one hundred and fifty yards.

Rashid called "play!" again.

Jalal made contact, but this time Hannigan hooked his stick, smashing its willow head. Play continued as Jalal rode to the side of the field where his groom was standing with a choice of replacement mallets, or 'chaugan'. Jalal threw down the broken cane and took up another of similar length. Standing had noticed an epigraph which hung on the wall downstairs in the club room.

Man is a Ball tossed into the Field of Existence,
driven hither and thither by the Chaugan –
Stick of Destiny, wielded by the hand of Providence.

The inscription bore no attribution, so he imagined it might have been a quotation from way back when conflict prevailed on the plains of Persia, perhaps at the time of Alexander the Great. The renowned conqueror was reputed to have been sent a chaugan by King Darius (c. 350 B.C.) by way of an insult, suggesting that the mallet better suited his nature to the art of warfare or diplomacy. Alexander rebuked the gesture, and it is claimed he said :"The ball is the earth, and I am the stick." Alexander succeeded to become King of Asia, and Darius was defeated.

It was with this in mind that Standing turned to a fellow spectator and asked when polo was first played in Pakistan. This small man had sharp facial features and a well-groomed moustache. He was dressed traditionally in white pajama bottoms, black shoes, a long chemise worn outside the bottoms, tweed waistcoat, and a tan pashmina about his shoulders; he held his karakul. He introduced himself as Heski Beid. "I am the father-in-law of Rafi Akram."

Heski told him that history dated the sport's origins to hundreds of years before the birth of Christ, when it was played by trainee horsemen and boys of the warrior castes in Iran and throughout Persia. It was the invading Mohammadans in the thirteenth century who had brought the game to India, whence it developed, in particular when the British cavalry regiments formalised its rules in the 1900s. These became the substance of the Hurlingham Polo Association rule book, established in 1875. The

Pakistan Polo Association was not set up until 1947, following partition from India, by which time the HPA rules were recognised internationally, if not completely adhered to.

"Oh look, Tom," he interrupted himself. "What a fine shot from Imran. Splendid!" he applauded, rising to his feet. Imran had lofted the ball over a hundred yards back from the goal, and out to the left side of the ground, sending it fifty feet high between the posts.

"A good angled cut," added Tom. "Excellent!"

4–4.

As the teams returned to the centre of the field once more, Struell issued instructions to his players: "Mark your men, guys. Stay close to them. Don't let them take their shots."

The ball went in, and it was Hannigan who tapped it forward off the mallet. He followed it, pushing Tariq away to his right, his stick side. With Tariq locked out, the Irish number one took the ball down the near side of his own pony, one shot, then another, bringing it about under the pony's neck. Tariq's resistance now proved too much, and Hannigan began to buckle. Followed up by Michael O'Mahony, who called to the number one, "Leave it! Ride him off," Michael then struck the ball down the touchline, in rigorous pursuit. Barely evading Jalal's mallet, which the Lahore captain was stretching to hook Michael's, the Irishman moved closer to the goal. And then, in a moment of lost concentration, Michael missed his next shot, and Jalal swung a backhand which sent the ball directly into the chest of Wakir's pony; Wakir rode over ball. Struell was there, the ball struck through the goal and the Irish rode back to the centre as the bell rang. They made for the lines with the score at 5–4 at the end of the third chukka.

Hanif had not needed to warm up Cezar for the fourth period. He had already played once. Hanif knew that Cezar's best chukka was his second. Under pressure to close the game with a victory, Standing mounted Rashid's spirited steed.

"You're mine for the next seven minutes, you lovely lad. We can do this."

"Line up!" the umpire cried out, to commence the final chukka. He threw the ball between the players. It passed clean

54

through to the back of the line out. As the other six heads turned, the two number three players were onto the situation, clashing sticks as they both tried to strike the ball, Jalal on his nearside, Struell on his off. Neither succeeded, and they rode on beyond the ball. Wakim attempted to take the ball next, but Standing was right on him. He went for the hook, then rode him across the ball, and just managed to get his mallet to it, on his nearside, but not strongly enough; the ball moved just inches. Arthur's mallet then missed the ball, hitting the ground early, behind the ball, but no contact.

What could Desmond do? He cut the ball to the right, sending it a full sixty yards to the touchline. Imran Shin then took him out of the game, so he was unable to follow up his line. Arthur had moved up, and was first to pick up the play. He tapped the ball, turning it in the direction of the goal and waited for everyone to take their positions, marking their opposite numbers. The path to goal was clear. Was Arthur going to take a run at it himself, with maybe three shots to see it through? Always full of surprises, he had other ideas. Instead, he made one mighty hit, his millionaire shot, and sent the missile seventy feet high, from one hundred and twenty yards out to the left, clear between the posts.

"Wow, Arthur! Great shot!" cried Standing, Desmond and Struell.

"Great pony!" he yelled back, breaking into an involuntary falsetto. No mistaking Arthur's excitement. 6–4. The Irish percentage was restored.

Standing hit the ball first from the throw-in, through the legs of Wakir's pony. Imran moved onto the line and delivered a long high pass from his offside open backhand. Jalal had anticipated its direction and sent it towards Tariq who had moved up the field as his three and four attacked; two half shots and the ball was through. 6–5. The gap was closing again.

"How much time left, umpire?" Struell asked, as they lined up for the throw-in.

"One minute," Rashid replied.

"Mark tightly now, Ireland," Struell exhorted.

The ball in, Standing hit it forward, past the umpire, digging his heels into Cezar's belly. Imran rode him off hard from his nearside; Standing could do nothing. Imran then backed the ball around the tail of his pony, this time Wakir took up the play. Arthur was having none of it, and hooked his stick. Jalal had a clear run at goal, or so he thought. Desmond went for the ride-off on Jalal's nearside, and as he clashed shoulder to shoulder with the Lahore police officer, his own mallet ejected from his hand, catching his opponent's. The umpire blew his whistle. Time out.

Rashid explained "it was unintentional, but Jalal was foul-hooked, and I am awarding a sixty-yard penalty to the Lahore team."

The Irish team took their positions thirty yards from where the ball was placed on the marked spot, sixty yards out from and directly in front of the goal. At the same time as marking the Lahore players, who wanted to open a clearway to goal, the visitors were mindful of preventing the ball from safe passage, but not to cross the line of the approaching Jalal. He took his pony round, winding his stick into a practice swing as he straightened up on the final canter to the ball, the goal posts dead ahead. The Lahore Captain had been hitting the ball well throughout the game; surely he was not going to miss this crucial shot. If he scored, they would play extra time in a 'sudden death'. Jalal raised his stick to the sky, standing in his stirrups. He locked his arm straight, in line with the shaft of the mallet, and swung it down to meet the ball. The contact felt right, the ball soared high.

They all looked up; it was untouchable.

"No!" roared Imran. The ball had sailed wide to the right. The Captain had sliced it. The bell rang to end the game. The Irish were ecstatic. The players shook hands, and made salutary exchanges after a good game.

Back in the pony lines, Hanif said "vell done," as Standing dismounted Cezar.

"Well done, Cezar. I didn't do too much, but he rode with great strength. Thank you, Hanif. You looked after us well." Standing slackened Cezar's girth; slapping him on the neck, he told the chestnut what a "good, good boy" he had been. All the players made their way to the club room. Their bags were downstairs beside the bar. Standing remembered that there were no changing facilities, and he had brought a change of shirt. The evenings could get cold and the last thing he wanted was damp clothing as the temperature dropped. In December, the days were like the European Spring, with very little rainfall; the Monsoon rains would have ended in September, and even then Lahore district would not have had the deluge of precipitation that filled the drainage system of the Kush, boring down to the alluvial basin of the delta. In Winter it was the cold of night one had to anticipate. Everybody in the club room wore a fleece-lined quarter coat, some locals with pashminas and headgear, mostly Karakuls. Whiskey and tea were offered to the Irish players. The whisky met with approval, and the steward attended to them well, using two fingers as a measure.

Standing was introduced to Jamal Khan by Kublai Akram, Rafi's youngest son. Kublai had been watching the game with his three-goal friend Jamal. Jamal was tall, and dressed in a tweed jacket, and he wore a crimson cravat inside his open necked shirt. He spoke with a cultured British accent, and had come down from Oxford three years earlier, graduating with a two-one in Law. His career had taken him from London to Paris, where he was enrolled at the Sorbonne, hoping to complete his PhD in six months. Then he was off to New York to a post with the United Nations as a legal consultant on human rights to the Pakistan delegation. Six years older than Kublai, they had played with each other many times, in Pakistan. Jamal had played at Oxford, and at Harrow, winning the Independent Schools Championship in 1982. He had been asked to play for a high-goal French team based at The Bagatelle Club in the Bois de Bologne, Paris, next summer. The team patron, a Parisian businessman, played off a zero-goal handicap and he was bringing in a ten-goal and a nine-goal player from Argentina for the 1990 Season. Jamal had the required handicap to make up a 22-goal team, the maximum team handicap permitted under the European Polo Association regulations. Kublai invited him to play in the match against Ireland due to take place at the weekend, though he would need to discuss it with his father, the General. This made Standing apprehensive about their final match at the Lahore Club, which he already knew was going to present a formidable opposition in the shape of a General and his three sons.

Following their exhausting night on the train and then some vigorous polo riding, all the players agreed that it would make sense to return to their respective billets and turn in early, in preparation for the "International" match between the Lahore and All Ireland Clubs the following afternoon.

4

The International

The knock at his door came when he was in the shower. He dressed in his playing whites as he ate the toast left for him. His emerald green team shirt, which bore the number one in white, was made from fine cotton, and loose fitting. He placed a spare shirt in a bag to change into after the game, and sat to drink his tea. The match was two hours away. He opened his diary, a seven-day-per-page notebook to remind him where he had been. He relied on memory to fill in the details.

After placing the diary beside his bed, he moved the newly made mallets to the side of the wardrobe and thought of his friend Joe Henderson when he saw the two with his initials. Tom had recently visited Joe in California and they played a short tour down the coast. With Joe you always had to take the rough with the smooth; his mercurial friend, quick-fused and restless, kept everybody guessing. Experience had taught Tom never to take offense and always to be ready for the quick exit. He liked Joe, but he could be bloody hard work. In the two years he had known him, the depth of his troubled life distanced him ever further behind a constantly moving curtain of deception – who was he kidding, not Tom, but this was not about him. Tom did care – he felt a systolic thud serve notice that one day he would be compelled to write about his tortured friend. He picked up his bag and made his way down to the hall, where he found his boots; the ochre leather had been buffed to a high polish by one of Rashid's staff. He held them by their loops on his way out to the lawn to join Rashid and Meera, who were drinking mint tea.

"Good morning, Tom," they both said.

"Would you care for a drink?" Meera asked him.

"Thank you, no. I'll wait until we get to the club."

Standing's nerves began to build before a match, so much so that he would neither eat nor drink. If lunch was laid on, he would forego even the most sumptuous of meals, and then, ravenous, would later settle for the last of the dry, curled sandwiches at the bar. He sat between the master and mistress of the house, browsing newspapers. He read *Dawn*, the widest-read English-language daily in Pakistan. He had done some homework on the birth of Pakistan before leaving Dublin. First published in Delhi, India, prior to partition in 1947, *Dawn* was a mouthpiece for the Muslim League. Both the Congress Party and Lord Mountbatten, Viceroy of the British Raj, had pushed for Muslim inclusion in British India in preparation for the end of Britain's direct involvement. The latter had been agreed as a condition of India's continued military support for the British efforts in WWII. The strength of the position of Mohammad Al Jinnah, the founder of *Dawn* was predicated on the burgeoning Muslim populations of the Punjab, Sind and Bengal Provinces, which – albeit representing a minority overall – were pro-British, unlike their Hindu counterparts, represented by the Congress party. Jinnah spoke in terms of a 'Two Nation Theory' in the 1940 Lahore Resolution passed by the Muslim League. After the war, Jinnah proclaimed a 'Direct Action' day in 1946, which, it was alleged, he had intended to be peaceful. Not being a man of violence, Jinnah may have foreseen a certain inevitability to the outcome of the growing unrest between Muslims and Hindus, restrained only by the British presence, and a bloody uprising broke out throughout the state of India. Standing asked Rashid if he thought partition had been a good move.

"With hindsight Tom, most definitely yes. For too long there had existed racial and cultural tension, not to mention the religious issues. It was safer to divide the territory with a border. How do you say? *Good fences make good neighbours.* There is a mutual respect between us now, and this has bred a wider tolerance for each other."

Standing thought of the messier outcome of partition that had lead to so much hostility in the North of his own adopted country. Whether he came for a short family visit or for more prolonged periods, there was always an underlying sectarianism, both within the family as well as in the community at large, especially when given the trenchancy of some diabolical atrocity. His own encounters with either side of the divide were, even as an outsider (or maybe because he was one) generally hospitable, although the tenor of any situation could change instantly. He never could work out why, but with the 'honeymoon' over, he always knew when it was time to leave. There not being any personal explanation for the caprices of those he met, his only justification seemed to derive from his 'Englishness', which perhaps manifested itself not so much by his accent, but by what he said. He had been told that he needed to know where he stood, the inference being that it could be dangerous if he did not. For his part, he had never felt a strong affinity with that part of the world, hence no particular empathy persuaded him, and if he had a position on any issues, especially those concerning race or religion, his choice was to remain *on the fence*.

"And Kashmir?" inquired Standing.

"Kashmir? Ah! - The 'Disputed Territory'. It has its own dynamic. It is a confluence of cultures and territories, Hindu, Buddhism, and Muslim, and so it is a stand-off in perpetuity. In spite of occasional unrest, I believe it will remain as it is. I cannot ever see it changing," said Rashid.

The afternoon felt more vernal than wintry, the sun warming his face, and he stretched his legs and arms as a temporary torpor came over him. "Tom," Rashid said, touching his shoulder. "We must go now."

Ranjit drove them, uncharacteristically, in a fashion befitting royalty. Meera had told Rashid of her anxieties concerning his driving, and Standing was grateful for that. As they entered the polo club, they slowed to a halt as there were many cars waiting for direction. Standing sensed the occasion.

He had played many times on a Sunday afternoon on the Lawns Ground at Cowdray Park, in finals of club tournaments, as well as more recently in Phoenix Park. A feeling of pride mixed with nerves always gripped his stomach as he approached a big game, and this was no exception, despite the fact that the horses were provided without the urgency of responsibility. His own horses required his supervision in terms of feed, veterinary attention, travel arrangements, and tack. Jimmy, who lived near Phoenix Park, groomed the three animals he brought with him from England. Clusot, Pancho, and Marijuana were a formidable triumvirate: Clusot, a willful grey gelding; Pancho, a biddable yet powerful chestnut gelding; and Marijuana, a black mare as fast as any horse he had ever ridden. Today he would again be riding Cezar and Chiquita, and knew he was in good hands.

Rashid's car bore the membership sticker of the Lahore Polo Club, which Ranjit was anxious to point out to the boy directing the traffic. The boy waived them on, and Ranjit found some dust to announce their arrival, expressing total disdain for the serried line of military guards lining the route. Standing, impressed by the turnout, asked himself just why there was such a presence for a polo game. Everybody had referred to the contest as 'The International', and he had noticed posters around Lahore the day before. However, this much ceremony seemed over the top, especially as this was only a low-goal game, as defined by the handicaps. All the same, the attention heightened his anxiety, and it excited him.

Ranjit was out of the car and opening the door for Meera, but too quickly, as she dismissed him: "Let the dust settle" and he closed the door again.

"Why must he always do that, silly man?" Meera complained to Rashid.

"Ranjit is a terrible fellow. He can't resist posturing, especially to the horsemen in the pony lines. He thinks he has the best job in the world. I am sorry, dear. I will speak to him." Probably not, thought Standing. He knew that Rashid admired his driver, and had an affection for him as well. Standing's anxieties settled when he saw Hanif, who stood between Cezar and Chiquita, holding them with lead ropes. They appeared calm, and this was good. He pulled on his boots, and buckled up the knee pads he had bought in the Lahore saddlery earlier that week. They were a good fit, and would provide the essential protection needed when riding off an opponent. The strong bull hide would shield his knees, and the felt lining absorb some of the impact from a hard collision. To prevent a 'dead leg' as a result of being struck on the thigh, he wore padded protection on both legs, beneath his white jeans, and wore an athletic support to lift his genitals out of harm's way. He had not been wearing one the day he was playing Jester, a tall, skinny gelding with boney withers that belonged to Colonel Alec Harper, his first Polo mentor. Jester was a gentle old boy, but on this occasion, following another player on the House Ground, attempting to hook his stick, Jester jarred on the hard ground. Saddle met testicles, Standing met sky with a scream, and his right leg fell limp. He dismounted with a fall to the ground, and was carried off. He had torn his adductor muscle, severing the connecting tension required between thigh and pelvis. Six weeks later, following intensive ultrasound sessions and, when able to, walking in water (the sea preferably), he remounted Jester and resumed what became a life-changing summer: his first season of polo. Standing and Jester, along with his stablemate Torita played out the remaining two months of weekends, Wednesdays, and Fridays, mostly on the Ambersham grounds, sometimes the Lawns, and the perfect River ground. Happy days, he recalled. The upshot of this inception was his purchase of Torita, his first polo pony, from the Secretary of the Hurlingham Polo Association, Colonel Alec Harper.

If Jester had presented him with the challenge of a painful, debilitating injury, it was Torita who bore him the greater test, a matter of pride. The Wednesday in May when he had first arrived at the Ambersham grounds, was overcast and cold. A small gathering of players stood around the tea trailer, glancing each in turn at the newcomer whose arrival was far from subtle. Driving slowly through the pony lines, Standing noticed first their eyes, and then their facial expressions: *Who is this? Do we know him? Is he a player, or a patron?* The unwelcoming atmosphere turned to silent jeers, however, when the novitiate Standing rode Torita onto the field to play her for the first time. Gripping tight to the reins, his legs wrapped round the mare's girth, with one hand on the saddle. She had kicked off and Standing lost control. Torita was an old-timer and gave the new boy no quarter, carting him twice around the entire perimeter of the Ambersham Grounds, all its one hundred acres. Would this mare run him through the grinning gauntlet again? No. Torita eventually tired of riding the hundred acres and took him back to the lines. He dismounted, still clinging to the saddle. Colonel Harper's groom, Mandy, took the reins.

"I told you not to take that whip."

Not so much a matter of embarrassment, and not too late to quit, he began to have misgivings about his chosen sport. At the tea van he met the polo manager. "OK, young fella?" His reply, a whimsical smile.

"You city boys come down to the country in your fancy cars and think these horses are nothing more than legs. Best you don't come back until you can ride. Best for everyone." Well, that did it. *I can ride, damn you*. With his pride in a sling he drove home. Before checking in with the office, he had another call to make. When he hung up, he had arranged to stick and ball two ponies for the next seven days, morning and afternoon. Next he rang Peter in London.

"All OK up there?"

"All's fine here. How about you?"

"Torita took me racing. You know, the horse I told you about."

"Must be love."

On the first morning, he rowed with Torita about everything. Why wouldn't she do this, why not that, and when he asked her to stop the bay mare just yawed and rode on. *This bloody horse*. He tried time and again to get her to do as she was told. Once he managed to strike the ball cleanly and then, encouraged, raised the stick high above his head and wound it down with such vigour he missed the ball completely. "Hell!" He cursed his mount once more. Time out. He returned to the lines where he met a man in a cap who, without introduction, spoke softly.

"Have you been playing long?"

"First season."

"You see that shot you just made," the man said.

"Awful!"

"You might try playing a half shot — a bit like a dribble in soccer. Two, maybe three and the ball should go through the goal for you. Go back and try it." Tom rode onto the field and began to stroke the ball across the lawn with a gentler underarm motion, the way the stranger had suggested, and found that not only could he move it towards the goal with accuracy, he could now turn the ball in circles. A sense of solvency in the partnership growing, the stick and ball session at an end, they left their shared field.

"Where's that chap who spoke to me?" he asked Mandy.

"He left you this." She handed him a card which read:

Finesse in everything – Good Luck

He turned over the card to read:

Major Hugh Dawnay, Polo Instructor
Whitfield Court, Waterford

For the rest of the week Tom stroked and circled with Torita, practicing full shots from the standing position. Their morning and afternoon sessions were punctuated with ploughmans lunches and best bitter at the Black Horse in Byworth, or the Welldiggers, sometimes the Bricklayers Arms in Midhurst, sometimes with Mandy. Torita grazed well and drank fresh water. At ten o'clock sharp on the morning of the seventh day, he checked her girth himself, secured every buckle on the bridle, untwisted the double reins from the Pelham bit, and made safe the pony's bandaging around her lower legs, her cannon bones. Then he mounted her, unassisted. Helmeted, clean booted, stirrup lengths correct, the pair of them walked calmly onto the ground. From walk to canter they began to describe large circles. Balanced by subtlety of weight distribution and leg signals, they felt their way together. Moving to the side of the ground the circles decreased, making flying changes from right leg to left, then left to right, gliding through figures of eight, posturing giving in to serene prancing. Out of the turn he rode her straight for sixty yards, then sitting back, feet forward, light hands, her weight on her haunches, his weight leaning, they turned at right angles and rode on. They repeated this until the square was complete, then rode to where Mandy stood holding his mallet. He took it, and they resumed their graceful circling until the girl threw a ball ahead of them. When he brought the stick down to strike, Torita did not falter, and the ball skimmed true and quick over the ground. Two strokes later it crossed the back line, between the posts. *Result.*

Back at the lines, he stripped his pony's tack, and delighted in sponging her withers, running his hand along her neck, up and down the bristles of her hogged mane, her bay coat glistening with sunlight, vapour rising from her warmed muscles. She enjoyed his caresses; he thanked her for the manners she had put on him. Mandy produced sandwiches and apples and all three spent the afternoon on the ground beneath the high summer sky. When play resumed the following week at Cowdray Park Polo Club, Tom once again took his position in the lineout. And Torita? Well, she was always going to be his. He bought his second pony, Clusot, a grey gelding, soon after. The perverse push from the polo manager that day in 1982 had contributed to his arrival in Pakistan, representing Ireland. The brutal guidance of the polo manager had provoked his mercury, though it was the alchemy of his Irish mentor that had conjured his salvation. It was to be seven wasted years before he met this great man again, in Ireland, and it took a few more years for him to share his sense of feeling Irish when in England, and English when in Ireland.

*

The chukka bell rang, as Hanif beckoned: "Janab." Tom knew this meant 'sir' in Urdu, and that Hanif had the little black mare ready for him to mount. He put on his helmet, pulling the strap beneath his chin. He wore a glove on his right hand. This afforded little protection except to reduce friction, thus calluses, and give him an improved grip on the handle of the mallet. He carried a long whip in his left hand. This he used mostly to hold against his pony's neck, providing stability whilst the double reins were threaded through the same hand. The whip would prevent him from pulling back erratically on the reins; a further device to prevent pulling was to grip the neck strap with a couple of fingers, and this would also assist balance. Smooth, unimpeded movement by the pony would also lessen the likelihood of the mount square-footing, or jarring – the lesson he had learnt so painfully on Jester.

66

On the near side of Chiquita, Standing loosened the girth and re-tightened it, until he was satisfied that it would tighten no further. With his left foot in the left stirrup, and the reins in his left hand, he raised himself over the saddle, careful not to pull on the reins at the same time; this would only pull the pony around to the left, and away from where he stood, forcing a hop to catch up, simply an aborted attempt, or, worst case, being carted across the field in full view. All these things had happened during his period of learning, and he knew the curve was never ending. Every horse, just like every human being, is different, and each must be afforded respect and patience. Failure to observe this would nearly always result in breakdown. Once aboard, he reached down to the girth strap yet again, and tried tightening further the one, all-important piece of equipment on which his safety that afternoon might depend. No need. Hanif had tightened an over-girth, a surcingle, around saddle and girth as a final measure. All was secure.

"Ready," he said to himself, dug in and cantered towards the centre of the field. Struell called over to him.

"We'll meet at the side."

Standing turned his head to see that all the players were in front of the stand beside the club room. They lined up side by side, with the number one players beside each other, the number two players beside each of them, and so on, so that the picture in the photographer's lens was of the Lahore Polo Club to the right, and the Ireland Team to the left. Back well behind this line of competitors, two mounted umpires stood.

A regimental band strongly echoed its colonial forbears, high polish and gold braid, and a magnificent bass drum, struck up an unfamiliar tune. Struell guessed this was probably the best local rendition of the Irish national anthem, as he had been informed it was going to be played first. It was the cue, he had warned his players, for the number one to move out of the line and circle the team in a canter, and take up position again, from behind, in the original line. Number two was to follow when number one was half way around. Then numbers three and four were to follow suit. They had all performed similar drills in the past, and it went well enough, except that one of the umpires stood too close to their circling, nearly causing a collision. Spectators and players were all amused by the diffusion of pomp.

Next up, the LPC players carried out the same protocol, the band playing "The Sacred Land", the national anthem of Pakistan. No mistakes this time. The four riders circled with perfect timing, removing their helmets as they halted in deference to the chief guest, Benazir Bhutto, Pakistan's Prime Minister. She was accompanied by her husband, Asif Ali Zardari – himself a polo player, but not this day. He and his wife sat surrounded by bodyguards, in the centre of the stand which seated over one thousand spectators. Standing now understood the large security presence. The teams awaited the umpire's invitation to choose sides, chatting amongst themselves. They all knew each other at this stage in the Irish visit, so introductions were not necessary, and it was easy to forget that they were about to compete. All seemed civilised.

For Ireland, Captain Struell wore the number three shirt, behind him Arthur Murray at four, Brendan Hannigan number two, and Desmond O'Mahony sharing the number one position with Tom Standing. O'Mahony would play chukkas one and three, and Standing two and four. Desmond's father Michael elected to sit out the game. For Pakistan, represented by the Lahore Polo Club, Jamal Khan replaced Jalal Ounis as Captain, Rafi Akram number four, his son Genghis number two, and Rafi's youngest son Kublai at number one.

Desmond took to the field for the first chukka, while Tom warmed up Chiquita, first in a straight line a few times, pulling up with pressure applied from his legs, riding light. Then using the bridle he neck-reined to turn the pony first one way, then the other, and traced a circle, changing her leading leg from right to left, to describe a figure of eight. The exercises took less than two minutes, and Tom was satisfied that she was then ready to play in the second chukka. He mounted Cezar and cantered to the lineout.

The ball in play, Jamal had been quick to pick up the line, moving the ball towards the Irish goal. His team marked tightly, the Irish defence rendered ineffective in preventing him from scoring: 1–0 to LPC. Changing ends, Struell roared the odds, if only to wake up his team. The chukka resumed. This time Struell connected first and, under pressure from Jamal, tapping the ball towards his own goal. Holding their Captain on his offside, he lofted a high nearside backhander to the far boards. Desmond moved down the field, and Brendan took up the line. Arthur, backing him up, saw Rafi moving on him, and called him off the ball, yelling, "Man, man." Hannigan rode Rafi away from the ball, and Arthur went through to take it around to his right. The brothers Kublai and Genghis seemed to be more in conflict with each other than trying to engage Arthur, which left him a clear shot to goal, from about one hundred yards out. He wound up his mallet and hit the ball to within twenty feet of the posts. Desmond finished it off with a tap through: 1–1.

Both teams regrouped, the umpire took another ball from his pouch and threw it in. Kublai picked it up and moved forward, tapping, tapping, tapping, his team marking the opposition, leaving him an open goal. He went for a big shot to finish, but it went wide to the right. "Stay calm, Kublai," his Captain told him. With that, the chukka bell rang and both teams left the field for fresh horses.

Tom checked Chiquita's girth once more, mounted, and took to the field. He assumed the position as he lined up at the front for the throw-in. The ball passed between his pony and Kublai's, and Tom immediately moved on his opposite, shunting him into his own end. Jamal had the ball, but Arthur was on him. He hooked his stick, and the whistle blew. His hook was too high, and a penalty was awarded to Jamal from the spot. The umpire added the caveat that high hooking can be dangerous, and would always be penalised. Jamal circled, winding up for a big hit, his men marking the Irish keenly. He played a tap, Genghis broke free and moved up, ordering Kublai to take his man, and the second shot lifted over all their heads. One final stroke and Genghis had the ball safely between the posts. 2–1 to LPC.

Back in the centre, the ball rolled in. This time Hannigan met it, sending it back through the gap towards the umpire. He leapt his horse out of the way, and Struell told Standing to move up. Hannigan struck the ball, poorly, and Struell told him to mark. Arthur backed up his Captain as he raised his stick high to strike a long cut down the ground to Standing. Genghis took him by his nearside flank, while Kublai hooked his stick. The whistle blew. The umpire ordered a penalty to be taken from the sixty-yard spot by the Irish. He explained to Jamal that not only had two players engaged simultaneously on the Irish player, itself a foul, but that a high hook had occurred. Kublai protested, and the umpire moved the penalty decision up to forty yards. Kublai protested again, and the penalty moved closer to thirty yards. "If you say one more word, I will award a penalty one," the Umpire told him. Kublai turned to his Captain to ask him what that meant.

"It means a goal will be awarded without a further hit. So keep quiet."

Struell took the penalty, and the teams returned to the centre of the ground, the score then standing at 2–2. Thus was the recalcitrance of Rafi's youngest son rewarded. As the ball went in, the bell sounded; a further thirty seconds of play remained, unless either an infringement, a goal, or the ball knocked out of play ended the chukka. Kublai, still fractious from the penalty incident, hit the ball forward and made a huge lunge at it, looking for a hole in one. Not to be, the ball sliced off the mallet face, across the boards, and out of play. The umpires both called "Chukka!" as the players rode back to their pony lines for half-time.

The afternoon heat had taken its toll on some of the horses, and they were clearly finished for the day. The same could be said for one or two of the players, namely Hannigan, who decided to pull out, giving Desmond an extra chukka. Arthur, panting, removed his shirt, and poured a bucket of water over his head, drenching himself to his toes. They all drank copiously, and doused the white sweat lines from around the horses necks and tails. Half time gave everybody ten minutes to prepare for the next play, and those horses already played would be stood down. Tom had stretched Cezar in the same way that he had Chiquita earlier, and the chestnut was clearly eager to get out there. Peter was pleased with the team's performance, and if the brothers did not compose themselves, a win was there to be taken.

"More of the same guys. Mark up, and stay calm."

The umpire's whistle blew, and the players once more rode to the centre of the ground for chukka number three. Desmond had not ridden Hannigan's horse before, but his blood was up and he was not going to be fazed by anything. He struck the ball first. The pass gave Standing a good hit, and then Kublai pounced.

"Take him, Tom!" Desmond called from behind. He hit one, and was then hooked cleanly by Genghis.

"Stay with them," ordered the Irish captain. "Clear the approaches."

In the melee at the throw-in, Struell found himself marked by Rafi, and could see that Arthur was struggling with Jamal, riding him off the line. Rafi was to his left, as he swung to send the ball down the field. But he had underestimated the capability of Renegade, Rafi's best gelding, a 16.1 hands bay quarter horse from North America. In one move Rafi and his mount had pushed Peter and pony four feet off the line of the ball, winding the pair of them. Peter fell from his horse, holding on to the reins, and the whistle blew. "Player down," the umpire called. Peter bent over while he gathered his breath; Tom took his horse by the reins.

"We'll have to call you Ride-off Rafi," Tom said to the LPC number four.

"Make that Ride-off Renegade," Rafi said.

Once recovered, the Irishman remounted, and the teams lined up for a re-start. The ball was in, and it ricocheted from the mallet of Genghis under the belly of Desmond's pony. Desmond turned onto it, but Genghis was too quick and claimed the line, which Desmond crossed. The whistle blew.

"Foul," the umpire called.

Jamal took the placed penalty from the spot, and this time wound up the mallet three times with a full circle roll from his wrist, and then with a full extension of his arm, brought it down to meet the ball on its sweet spot. He found the perfect trajectory as the ball flew high through the middle of the posts. 3–2 to LPC. The crowd clapped loudly as they lauded the Lahore captain. When they rode to the centre, the bell rang and the umpires called "Chukka!"

"More of the same, Ireland. Mind the line," instructed Struell.

Standing was going to have to make a choice between one of Brendan's horses or taking Chiquita once more. She had played twenty minutes earlier, and Hanif had no problems with her playing a second chukka. She was cool and calm, and Tom decided he would play her. She seemed to ride him to the field, not he her. Kublai met the throw in, moving forward. Tom hooked and played a nearside backhand, sending the ball beyond the back of the line-up. Arthur played it, and Struell took out Jamal. Arthur caught Rafi approaching through the corner of his eye, and gave a short tap to create a new line. He tapped again and had Rafi dancing in front of him, avoiding the cross. Rafi was locked out. Arthur hoisted one swing, and sent the ball straight to goal. It bounced once before it went through. 3–3. *That saved my pony's legs*, Tom thought.

The first bell would end the final chukka, and the game, so time was of the essence now. Play resumed, Struell roaring for his men to mark – nothing else, just mark. "Open the door, just keep it open." They all knew what to do. The ball rolled between them, Standing took on Rafi, and glued Chiquita to him. Arthur sat on Kublai, one eye on the others to check any breakout - Desmond was with Jamal, and was his equal in riding off. This left Peter Struell to dispense with Genghis, and then do any scoring himself. Not an easy task, but Struell was confidently mounted on one of Rafi's own horses, a stout, biddable Arab gelding he had named Bedouin on account of his restless nature; this pony was level-headed but had to be busy at all times. It would take a good rider to get the measure of his capricious temperament. Bedouin was quick to respond when the throw-in deflected off the foot of Jamal's pony. Struell's leap onto a line that Jamal thought his own was aggressive, legal and clinical. His first strike was firm and accurate, straight toward the goal. His follow-up was equally direct, leaving him a final tap in. 4–3 to the fighting Irish.

Jamal's woes mounted as Struell began to repeat the move. The LPC captain swirled his horse to follow, and in two strides had ferociously hooked the Irishman's stick, right out of his hand. All Struell could do was to ride off his opponent's pony. As Bedouin moved hard against the pony's shoulder, Jamal swung back to send a cut shot out to the right. Breakout – Genghis picked it up and belted it down, stopping ten feet in front of him. All he had to do was tap it through. His pony sidestepped and he missed the shot, screaming in frustration. Not to worry: his pony got the job done, kicking it through with his off hind hoof. 4–4. All level, they both raced back for the throw-in, but too late. The bell rang. "What now?" they asked. The umpires conferred telegraphically, and called for a 'sudden death' to be played. The first team to score would win the match. Standing wanted Cezar. Chiquita had played her heart out, and could do no more. Hanif was ready with the sturdy steed, his head high as he danced on his forelegs. No time to waste, the player jumped from mare to gelding, turning about as he did so, and kicked on, back out to the ground. Standing knew he was fired up, and that was his warning that mistakes would be made if he did not check himself. He made time, in haste, as he saw the other players mounting to make their way out, to calm himself. He dropped his head, closed his eyes, and breathed deeply into his diaphragm, belly breathing. After a count of twelve slow seconds, he released the breath, at the same speed; he repeated the exercise. He could hear the sound of hooves rapidly closing towards him, and inhaled once more, holding it until the umpire's call of "Play!" forced a noisy exhalation.

The ball landed right on the head of his mallet. He was away to the boards, angling the line towards his target. Sweet spot, tap, sweet spot, tap, sweet spot, tap, and the goal was scored, the match won, to the Irish the spoils. Congratulations rang out, all around, players shaking hands with umpires, opposition, and team members, spectators on their feet, applauding the visitors. Tom dismounted, slackened Cezar's girth, praising him with a brio to befit his performance. Hanif, his face with the widest grin, said "Velly, velly, velly, velly, velly, velly velly, velly, velly, velly, velly vell done, sir!"

"Thank you, my friend, you've done a great job, Hanif."

"Go qvickly! The cup!"

He put on a dry shirt and blazer, and made his way to the stand. Both teams were facing the spectators as the President of Pakistan stood at the trophy table, smaller cups dwarfed by a grand silver cup with gilt handles. This was the perennial cup competed for by visiting national teams, ideally without professional players, certainly without 'hired guns' brought in from other national pools. This guideline attempted to ensure a standard of low-goal played in the Corinthian spirit. It had been a fair contest with a clear winner. When the club manager, Deepak Akram, had introduced all the players to Mrs. Bhutto, and she had presented each of them with their personal trophies, the victorious captain held up the cup. Peter Struell beamed for the photographers from nationwide newspapers and magazines as his team gathered around, arms about each other's shoulders, proudly posing.

5

Mona Depot

Ranjit was polishing the bonnet of the car as Standing appeared through the front door of Meera's house. Seeing him laden with sticks and overnight bag, the driver helped him load the car boot. Rashid spoke quickly with him in Urdu, giving him his instructions for the journey. Rashid wished Standing a good trip, and bid him farewell. Meera waived from the porch. "Good luck!" It was not until the evening that he considered the prescience of her departing expression. Could she have possibly known something he was to later find out, or were her words as innocent as he took them to be?

"Uh-oh!" mumbled Standing. "Here we go again." Ranjit drove with frenzied impatience, terrorising every other traveler on the canal road. He was on a mission and nothing was getting in his way. Struell had only heard about this maniac from Standing, and was yet to find out for himself. The car pulled into Imran Shin's entrance, its dust cloud in pursuit. Struell was seated on the lawn, drinking tea and reading *The Times*. "Where did you get that, Peter?"

"Imran gets the newspapers from the London flights arriving in Karachi. It's yesterday's, but better than nothing. It says here that the reunification of Germany is only a short distance away now that new border crossings are opening up between East and West. They are going to open the Brandenburg Gate soon. The street parties are still going on. Visa and currency restrictions are only being placed on Westerners. It's open season if you're coming from the East. What a turnaround."

"At last!" exclaimed Standing. "It's time for the healing to begin."

"Let's go, shall we?" Struell finished his tea. "Do we need to collect any of the others?"

"We're meeting them there."

Ranjit spun the wheels of the saloon from the gravel avenue onto the tarmac road to town, breaking again the still, morning heat.

"We'll get about twenty minutes of this, until we reach the other side of Lahore."

"What the hell's wrong with him?" Struell said.

"Braggadocio, old boy – think that's the word. He knows he can get away with it – used to drive for a general, don't you know? Hold onto your strap."

The next stage of the drive, clear of any traffic, the Irish numbers one and three loosed their grips and relaxed in the rear of Ranjit's carriage. Standing reflected on the evening he spent with Rashid and his young wife. They had invited him into their bedroom, Meera sat up covered to her neck with a counterpane of gold thread and silk, its hue reflecting the tiring light from freestanding candles placed to each side of the rattan headboard. If the scent of this night room, at ground level shuttered from the world with lined floor-length drapes, might have suggested an exotic invitation, Standing's judgement told him that this childless couple liked him, trusted him as a friend. No thought of any impropriety entered his mind as Rashid poured him a generous tumbler of whiskey, and lit him a cigarette. They neither smoked, nor drank, making their gracious welcome all the more generous, if slightly embarrassing – though he guessed he was the more gauche for thinking that. Meera's loveliness had not escaped him but the unique circumstance demanded that he should live up to their trust, as an Irish Ambassador.

For the best part of two hundred kilometres they sped through the Punjabi countryside, Struell and Standing exchanging biographies, Standing more so. Peter Struell, ever guarded, clearly shy, did open up about his ongoing discontent with the politics of the Irish club, blaming its recent decline in playing members on a regime of skewed standards that amounted to nothing more than snobbery. They would not advertise for new members, nor would they engage the homebred services of the number one instructor in the world.

"You mean Hugh Dawnay?"

"Of course. You must go to him. He will justify your handicap, probably even make it look cheap," Struell told him. *It would be mad not to.* For now though they were heading to the Mona Depot, a military remount centre which held up to sixteen thousand horses at any given time. A match scheduled there for three o'clock, to be played against the commandant's team, would prove challenging in ways beyond compare with the chukkas played in Lahore. Their chauffeur delivered them within the gates of the Mona Depot, where the flora remaining from the onset of the dry Punjabi winter filled the avenue with sweet fragrance of lavender and hardy 'dream weaver'. Ranjit slowed behind a white fiacre drawn by four grey horses as they negotiated the speed bumps, bloomless rhododendrons to the right and polo ground to the left. Gonfalons which moved gently behind the goalposts suggested this would be the match ground. On arrival at the officers' mess, two panoptic peacocks for sentinels, they were met by their host, the commandant, a small grey-haired man whose aquiline nose divided his wall-eyed glare. Behind his saccadic trompe l'oeil were concealed secrets hinted at only with a twist of his rictus grin.

The Irish players, once booted, were carried to the ground in the same horse-drawn carriage they had followed. An aide to the commanding officer escorted them across the hard, bleached playing field. Before them, tethered, stood forty ponies, their mounts. They quickly set about trying them. With little time to familiarise themselves with one, let alone four each, one thing was immediately obvious – every pony was 'green', inexperienced, and they knew they were in for a rough ride. "We'll have to take it real easy, lads, or people are going to get hurt" Arthur warned.

The look in the commandant's eye, which one he was not sure, had foretold how the cards would be stacked against the visitors. On the bank spectators had gathered, some seated at its foot, others behind them, and standing on top was a third line of young men, in white, carrying drums beneath their arms. They kept a drum each and shared out the spares amongst those already down the bank. Maybe one hundred and fifty drums now pointed across the ground, as Standing thought: *If they're for the commandant, then we're the target.*

A foghorn summoned all combatants to the centre of the ground, the Irish fighting to control their intractable ponies, the Depot team lined up awaiting the visitors. Whether from impatience or bias, the umpire threw the ball into play as the first of the Irishmen arrived at the lineout. It went straight to the commandant and, to an enfilade of driving drums, he took the ball through the Irish posts. Standing had barely moved from the centre when their host, a retired cavalry officer, arrived back, guidons about his chest, the tail of a large white turban trailing his wake. The ball stopped beneath his mallet, and he was away again, untouchable, as was his anomie. "We've got to do something here, lads," yelled Arthur.

"Send for Cezar!" cried Standing.

Arthur's pony reared, unseating him, and he hit the hard ground, badly. The goal scorer was all for playing on, as the drumming crescendoed on his approach to goal. Not until the ball went cleanly through did the umpire blow his whistle for time out. Arthur needed attention; with none forthcoming from the hosts, Struell and Standing dismounted, allowing their mounts to gallop back to the lines. Arthur's arm was sore, not broken, and with his shoulder intact, they lifted him to his feet. The team subsidiary Brendan Hannigan took his place.

"Not bloody likely. I'm not finished with this bastard yet!" Arthur muttered. 'Casus Belli' beckoned.

"Take it easy, Arthur. Remember the horse show – we got them that day," Tom said. Against heavy odds he and Arthur had reached the subsidiary final of the fifteen-goal tournament in Dublin, which was an achievement in itself given their paucity of pony power and the fact that Arthur was drinking heavily. Anyway, they made it in extra time, a first-goal sudden-death from a blinder of a shot by Arthur, stationary on the halfway line. They both knew it would take more than memories to encourage a result from this situation, but they weren't ready to quit.

"All of you check your own girths, over girths, everything, from now on," Struell told his team. "We're on our own here. I don't even trust the grooms." Both teams lined up, side by side this time. The ball went in – mayhem – sticks everywhere, Irishmen hit on their helmets, arms, legs, and backs. Desmond took a blow to his faceguard. The Irish Captain, face florid, protested to the Umpire, demanding that he blow his whistle to get some kind of rules observed, and maybe a little etiquette. The umpire could find nothing wrong with the game but assured him that he would be diligent. The despondent Irish left the field two goals behind. When they returned, on 'fresh' horses, the bellicose commandant had sat out. Play resumed and when the ball headed towards the Irish goal, this time the battlecry of the drums was silent. Some respite for the Irish, although the rough play continued. When the chukka ended, Ireland had scored a goal, the Depot a further two: 4–1 now. The halftime break gave them their only chance to regroup. Struell came up with a new tactic. "I'll go one, and the rest of you just try to get the ball to me. It's suicide I know. If it goes wrong we have no defense, but we don't have too much of that right now anyway."

"We have to try something," said Standing. He decided to play his first horse again, the others gambled on a change. When play restarted, Struell, at the front of the line-out, connected and took it with him, fighting his most difficult pony yet. He managed to strike twice, making half the distance to the Depot goal before capitulating, taking out a defender with a ride-off. Backing him up, Desmond swung when he was thumped from behind, and missed. A dangerous foul had been committed, his opponent having ridden over the haunches of Desmond's horse; luckily he had not gone down. Where was the whistle? Forget it, he couldn't even see the umpire.

Standing saw it all, but the goal was still there to be taken, and he did. Behind the goal, the ball boy, looking the other way, did not raise his flag to indicate the score, and the umpire, who had reappeared called for a hit-in from the back line. The Depot's number four tapped in, then smacked the ball one hundred yards towards the Irish goalposts. His three teammates cleared the way, winding the Irishmen with a series of fierce collisions. The Depot hitter galloped towards a certain goal, took a mighty swing and sent the ball wide to the right. The ball boy at the Irish end was alert, and his flag shot up to signal a goal. "What goal?" screamed Struell. "He bloody missed."

"Chukka!" cried the umpire. The Irish, demoralised, rode back to their lines. Whatever the governing laws of polo existed that day, the judgement calls of this umpire were living proof that they could only be as good as their interpreter. But then, they were only executing the will of a despot, the martinet of Mona.

"Look, lads. We can't win – that's obvious – we've been brought here for target practice. Well, let's just finish with some dignity. OK?" Arthur conceded. They checked their tack one last time, and took to the field.

"Let's try that again anyway," Struell told his troops. The drumming began as the Commandant rejoined his team, along with loud wailing from the embankment.

"Damn him," said Standing. The ball in, it went through the gap to the rear and Struell dropped back to defend. He picked up the line and hoisted, unhindered, a lofted backhand halfway to goal. Standing was on it. He moved as swiftly as he could on a horse barely backed. The gelding snapped from side to side, bucking and kicking, but somehow gave him enough space to swing. There would be no second chance, and a big hit was needed to cover the ground. He wound his mallet up above his head, twelve o'clock, eyeing the sweet spot on the ball. Just then a pony swung across his chest, and as he brought down the mallet, gasping, in front of him, its head reared up to strike his elbow. He blenched from the pain that seared through his arm, then slumped, the blood from his scored chest haemorrhaged from his torn shirt. He knew the player responsible. There beside him rode his trenchant adversary, and the drums beat louder than before.

When the final horn brought the conflict to an end, Standing rolled from his pony. He released the animal and walked to the bank, drums firing directly at him. As he approached, the frenzied timpani slowed to a single beat, then ceased as he climbed over the mound onto the avenue. He needed ice for his swelling elbow as it froze his arm into an L-shape. Unaccompanied, he made his way to the headquarters where they arrived, discarding helmet, mallet, and whip to the side of the road. *Bloody shower the lot of them. Cheats and hypocrites.* He found an attendant in the officers' mess, and asked for ice. Standing pointed to his elbow, which was by now pushing the short sleeve of his shirt towards his shoulder. The man filled an ice bucket. Standing squeezed his joint into the ice, but needed a larger bucket and the ice would need to be crushed. Another steward arrived with a peeling bucket from the kitchen, filled it with ice from the bar, and began to smash it down with the leg of a stool. The ten minutes waiting for his team and their victors to arrive surceased much of the pressure, and reduced some swelling, though he could not straighten his arm. He dunked his throbbing head in the bucket, and the steward handed him a towel when the players entered the mess.

"You alright, Tom?" Arthur asked.

"Getting there. Are we going now?"

"ASAP. I've put your things in Rashid's car." The Irish beat their final retreat, Peter Struell the only one, despite a lack of inclination, to shake the commandant by his hand. The rest of them had not so much forgotten their own manners as they recalled his.

"Where to now?" Tom said. "Lahore?"

"No. We're going to Tariq's hunting lodge. Have you forgotten?" Arthur said.

"I hope he has plenty of ice, and whisky."

*

The invitation had been to punt across Tariq's lake and shoot duck. Tom and Arthur were not in any mood for shooting anything, except perhaps a certain ex-cavalry officer, and they watched from the porch as the others cast off from the pontoon. Four punts moved to form a line in the middle of the water, disturbed only by the minimal moves made by the pilots as they worked their bamboo quants through the lake's muddy floor. Behind them, a backdrop of salt cedars and gum trees obscured the horizon's failing light, camouflaging their own silhouettes. From the surface on the east side emerged high bullrushes which concealed their quarry. To the rear of the rushes, beaters crouched on punts and more boys knelt on the bank with poles. The huntsmen stationed at the centre of the lake raised their barrels. A quiet settled on the scene, while all breath of wildlife hung in the bated silence. On Tariq's word, the beaters struck the rushes. There followed a terrifying cacophony of cracking stems and screeching calls from panic-stricken birds, fleeing, flying, and falling to the double-barreled retorts and the resonant pump from the cannons tholed on the gunawales of the prows of the punts. Flares lit up the flight path and the beaters held powerful torches high on poles, evading the line of fire. Further volleys followed from behind the huntsmen, where guns in waiting struck the trailing flight. Many birds hit the water, some made it clear of the rushes.

Barking dogs, kept quiet until then by their keepers, dived from the banks, racing to reach the birds before they sank. The dogs kept their victims proud of the surface as their plunging paddling stretched them to the bank, where they shook the lake from their coats into the flare light while their keepers secured the wildfowl. So many varieties – mallard, moorhen, widgeon, teal, and some moot swan – laid out on carts which would bring them to the cold house in Tariq's yard. In just moments a bucolic scene of tranquility had become a charnel cauldron. For what? A cull for epicurean cupidity? Now wearing an ice-packed sling, as good as any unction, Tom moved with Arthur to the pontoon to observe this 'son et lumiere' show. Cordite-imbued smoke rolling towards them reinforced the martial savagery. Arthur reached for his brandy. A houseboy had set up a tantalus, plenished with fine grain spirits from Tariq's drawing room. Tom gulped his malt, and again, as he looked out over a stage of unbridled carnage.

"Jesus wept, Arthur. I've never seen anything like it – this is slaughter, not sport." He fought back tears that dried quickly on his warm face, as he sniffed into his glass. The young boy topped it up, a full Muslim measure, and he drained it in two. Another, and Arthur the same, their spirits their balm. Sick to the pit of his stomach, Tom left the pontoon, wanting Roisin, her moon, missing Dingle, and he strolled back to the veranda of Tariq Thakral's summer house. A darkling nightfall now inhumed the backdrop, and the space of day would follow, as it always does.

The doors were opened by a tall, turbaned manservant in white djellabah and slippers with curled toes, his mojari. With a nod their eyes met as the doorman showed him towards the open fireplace. Dried branches some six feet in length lay against iron doglegs, arching the well-lit fire. As they burned, attendants would kick them into the grate, adding further lengths from the sides of the Inglenook enclosure, where they dried. Tom sat close in a high-backed chair, gazing into the crackling flames, lost in thought, tumbler in hand. He drank, this time his doorman replenishing, wasting not a drop from each rim-filled offering. When the others joined him, he had fallen asleep. After drinks, they sat for supper with Tariq, leaving Tom with two attendants who helped him to bed. They all retired soon after. The day had been long, and it was over.

*

Not from a dislike for Tariq Thakral did Tom Standing, now sitting on his host's lawn, sharing breakfast with him and the other Irish guests, begin to imagine answers to questions that troubled him. Tariq Thakral had neither wife nor children. He had many diverse business interests, fingers in many pies. He wore the cloak of a wealthy merchant, of green and black died silk thread, its sleeves hung from its elbows. His black moustaches curled to the shape of his blue eyes. At polo he would wear a blazer, whites and black loafers. He kept lasts at Fosters of Jermyn Street, where they made him boots and probably his Oxford brogues; his suits, bespoke from Savile Row, he wore with silk or sea island cotton shirts from the best of shirtmakers with royal accreditation. He did not speak of any of this, but Tom recognised the cut and did notice some labels. Tariq had attended Harrow from the age of ten, but skipped a place at Cambridge to explore business interests. Nothing wrong with any of this, Tom thought, except that the resumé stopped there. Nothing more could he find out about this international man from the Punjab. All he did know was that Tariq Thakral, a steward with the Lahore Racing Club, played polo, and had a life membership of the Punjab Club, most likely because his father had been a serving Officer in the British Army during World War II, prior to partition, and later a General in the Pakistani Army. "Today I invite you all to lunch with me at the Punjab Club," he said. "I hope you will enjoy it for its history – it is an archive of the Raj, and there is much to see there." He told Tom that he had played polo in England for a number of years and encouraged an exchange of ideas between the Pakistan and

Hurlingham Polo Associations. The Irish experience at the Mona Depot had been no surprise to him.

"This Commandant, he is from Gilgit. No rules, no manners there. I am sorry you were injured. I did not think he would have behaved so disgracefully. I would have expected some brinkmanship from a cavalry officer, but treating visitors in this indecorous way will be viewed poorly in the Punjab Club. I will insist that the incident is reported."

"Where is the club, Tariq?" Arthur asked.

"On the edge of Lahore, opposite the racing club."

While the Irish players travelled in Tariq's Rolls Royce, Tom recalled their lunch at the races with stewards of the Lahore Racing Club. Tariq had arranged the invitation. The boardroom where they dined provided a viewing gallery overlooking the finishing line. While Tariq held court, the other Stewards attention focused more on the final furlong. Water only was offered with Punjabi samosas, chapattis, and mildly spiced chicken. Tom heard frissons of activity from people on his side of the track, and their yelling muted the lunch conversation as horses galloped across the Finish. *If there's no drinking, and gambling is forbidden, what's all the fuss about?*

As they ate dessert, fresh fruit from an ice bowl, the fourth race on the card, for two-year-old colts over six furlongs, got underway. Peter Struell, a keen racegoer and part-time trainer, turned to watch the sprint. A jockey in yellow silk rode the leading horse as they turned the bend, a clear length ahead of the field. Then, on the final approach, the second horse, backed by a rider in fuchsia and black, shot past to win by half a length.

"How did that happen?" Tom asked.

"I'll tell you how it happened. The yellow jockey pulled his horse. It was a fix," Struell said.

Fine cheese and crackers were served with Arabic coffee, its cardamom aroma infusing the airless gallery. Meanwhile the final race of the meeting, a bumper over a mile and a half had begun. Struell scrutinised the finish even more keenly. The lead horse, clearly pulled, overtaken by its follower, itself by the next horse which ran ahead of both of them, reversed the order of what should have been a certain finish. Roars could be heard from beneath the stand beside their box. Standing looked out to see touts, bookies and punters exchanging cash, tearing slips, raising fists, jumping, throwing hats into the air. "Could be the Galway Races!" Struell said.

"Never been," Tom said. The larcenous activity here would only be tolerated beneath the noses of confederates in high places. He would have enjoyed wine with lunch, but that too would have been taboo. Struell turned to Tariq.

"Is there a representative of the Turf Club here? I've never seen such blatant race rigging as this."

"He must have been held up. I will be sure to tell him of what went on here."

*

Tariq's limousine led the convoy off the Mall through a gateway into a colonial throwback of acacias and manicured lawns, across a gravel conduit lined with white-painted stones, and delivered them before the grand portico of the Punjab Club. Established in 1884 (albeit poorly documented as a result of byzantine post-colonial restructuring, and a fire which destroyed many early records) the club remained, Tom Standing sensed, much as it had from its inception. Passing through its Palladian alabaster columns he felt the claustrophobia of its internal wooden structure, its oak paneling, oak and teak pillars, and furniture of walnut – solid, veneered and embossed, with carvings in ebony – all emitting waxy aromas of polish from their well-tended patinas. If this lobby resembled a mausoleum, its appreciation would have been mostly by those who had served as British allies, mostly in the Far East, against members of the Axis. They walked on through to a dining room as traditional as the lobby, though with a stained timber floor; the lobby's was marble with Kashmiri rug coverings which muted their footsteps. The maître d', in white, wore black shoes and a red satin sash. His turban, white with a long tail, met his beard where it had been tied over his ears. Recognising an English-speaking party, he spoke freely with them, discussing the menu, casually including some history of the club. He knew Tariq, who was happy for him to do this.

Their host enthused about the club's most celebrated past resident member, Rudyard Kipling, and Tom recalled the writer's house in Rottingdean, close to Brighton where he himself had grown up. Proud of its high wall of Sussex flint which bordered the rustic villa from the village pond, only its rust-hued tiles and tall stacks were visible. In his teens he would drive to meet friends along the clifftop road from Brighton, passing Roedean school, to drink shandy in the Loft Bar on the other side of the pond, and from there he saw the rural splendor of a fine English country house. The Elms faced him across its croquet lawn, edged by colourful borders, a weeping willow to the right surrounded by a white bench. Perhaps Kipling had written his 'Just So' stories from this very spot on fine days or from a study with the same view. Tales of derring-do had emanated from a memory of India while he resided in the Punjab Club, to be retrieved across an English country garden.

Seated at a nearby table two elderly military types ordered food. Their curt manner with the young waiter was abrasive, and one of them addressed him repeatedly as 'boy'. These retired officers – "generals", Tariq informed him – might well have been born before Kipling left India. Tom wondered if they had enjoyed his stories as much as he had as a boy. He leaned towards their table. Both men had long waxed moustaches: one twisted into curls; the other, straight as needles, pointed out across his cheeks. These looked as if they might droop but his constant attention ensured they remained horizontal. As caricatures of a bygone age they were impressive. When he heard them both order duck, he sat back. *Had the ducks from Central Park ever found their way to Rudyard's retreat or did they fly west across the Himalayas?* He excused himself from the table and wandered about the main lobby, entering the library, a military archive not just of documents but many weapons from nineteenth-century campaigns, along with paintings and histories of British and Indian leaders. What drew his eye was an oil portrait of Lord Roberts, whose resemblance to his own grandfather was striking, minding him of footnotes an Irish aunt had made on the pages of a biography of the Earl. She believed there to be a family connection with the field marshall, whose decorations included the Victoria Cross – in part because he had Irish links, his father from County Waterford, his mother Tipperary. Never taken too seriously by Tom, who understood that Roberts' posting to Ireland on his return from campaigns on the Indian subcontinent and South Africa, when he was made Commanding Officer of the British Army in Ireland, had been influential in establishing the Ulster Volunteer Force. His aunt had not suggested any familial line in Northern Ireland, and the trail seemed to run cold. Tom's gaze moved to the sketch beside it, Roberts on his grey charger Vonolel, and his memory nudged to a day in Dublin that summer when he visited the gardens of the Royal Hospital at Kilmainham in Dublin. When Tom noticed Arthur had followed him into the library, he said "look at this. Do you remember the headstone we saw that day in Kilmainham?"

"Lord Robert's horse?"

"Well this is Roberts riding him. They're both wearing medals," Tom said. Named after a Lushai warrior Roberts had fought in 1871, Vonolel, his small grey Arab, died aged 29 when the *Irish Times* carried the following obituary on October 21st 1899:

When the Queen awarded medals to her officers and men who had taken part in the Afghan campaign and in the expedition to Kandahar, she did not forget Vonolel. Lord Roberts hung round the animal's neck the Kabul medal, with four clasps, and the bronze Kandahar star. The gallant horse wore these medals on that day in June when the nation celebrated the Queen's Diamond Jubilee.

Vonolel's epitaph reads:

There are men both good and wise
Who hold that in a future state
Dumb creatures we have cherished here below
Shall give us joyous greeting when
We pass the golden gate
Is it folly that I hope it may be so?

Tariq invited the Irish Polo Team to sign the visitors' book. Beside it sat the club yearbook which listed rules and affiliates. Hannigan. a member of the Lansdowne Club in London, had not been aware of the reciprocal relationship between the two clubs. Standing, an alumnus of the City University London, delighted in its link. Vestiges of the Empire's reach remained on all continents; yet in spite of a sense of anachronism, Tom felt comfort in the strands which included him, no matter how tenuous. *We all have history.* The team drove into Lahore for one last night. Dinner at Rafis.

*

With Rafi, all of them felt more at ease. Some croquet with the family, more Muslim measures, their hosts, Fareeda, Rashid, Meera, Jalal with their families blunted the raw edges of Pakistan's wilder side. Life in an orderly cantonment brought with it a more civilised outlook, and with it pursuits which may have derived from days of warring horsemen, who tore live goats or sheep playing Buzkashi, a free-for-all for as many riders who turned up, which likely had spawned polo. Buzkashi was still played in Afghanistan, and the recalcitrant flouting of any modern polo rules, such as in Gilgit, had long since been marginalised. Polo in Lahore now thrived, Rafi told them. Tom perused the Kipling-filled bookcase. They were all there – the complete works. He took out an anthology of poetry and chose his party piece. *Oh yes, this is perfect.* Fareeda oversaw their Punjabi meal, punctuated with much toasting. Arthur stood.

"Now that's what I mean by beating the goat."

"You mean Buzkashi" Genghis said.

"I do not. So let's not go there." An atmosphere of friendship bonded East and West with laughter, storytelling, and polo hyperbole the dominant denominators. And more toasting of course. Tom stood to recite some Kipling, delivered with Cockney pathos:

> *There's a little red-faced man,*
> *Which is Bobs,*
> *Rides the talliest 'orse 'e can*

Our Bobs.
If it bucks or kicks or rears,
'E can sit for twenty years
With a smile round both 'is ears
Can't yer, Bobs?

Then 'ere's to Bobs Bahadur -- little Bobs, Bobs, Bobs!
'E's our pukka Kandaharder
Fightin' Bobs, Bobs, Bobs!
'E's the Dook of Aggy Chel;
'E's the man that done us well,
An' we'll follow 'im to 'ell
Won't we, Bobs?

If a limber's slipped a trace,
'Ook on Bobs.
If a marker's lost 'is place,
Dress by Bobs.
For 'e's eyes all up 'is coat,
An'a a bugle in 'is throat,
An'you will not play the goat
Under Bobs.

'E's a little down on drink
Chaplain Bobs;
But it keeps us outer Clink
Don't it, Bobs?
So we will not complain
Tho' 'e's water on the brain,
If 'e leads us straight again
Blue-light Bobs.

If you stood 'im on 'is head,
Father Bobs,
You could spill a quart of lead
Outer Bobs.
'E's been at it thirty years,

An-amassin' soveneers
In the way o' slugs an' spears
Ain't yer Bobs?

What 'e does not knowv o'war,
Gen'ral Bobs,
You cun arst the shop next door
Can't they, Bobs?
Oh, 'e's little but he's wise;
'E's terror for' is size:,
An' -- 'e -- does -- not -- advertize
Do yer, Bobs?

Now they 've made a blooimin 'Lord
Ou ter Bobs,
Which was but 'is fair reward
Wheren't it, Bobs?
So ell wear a coronet
W'here 'is 'elmet used to set;
But we know you won't forget
Will yer, Bobs?

Then 'ere's to Bobs Bahadur -- little Bobs, Bobs, Bobs,
Pocket-Wellin'ton 'an arder
Fightin' Bobs, Bobs, Bobs!
This ain't no bloomin' ode,
But you've 'elped the soldier's load,
An' for benefits bestowed,
Bless yer, Bobs!

"Bravo, Tom!" came Rafi's call, heard over the other plaudits. "Well read. A true Tommy!" Laughter filled the room.

*

Grounded in Ireland by his infected ear, a prescription of strong antibiotics and rest had taken ten days to break the fever, and he had

90

foregone the Irish team's trip to Barbados over the New Year. His mother, glad to have him about the house as his health improved, had established a routine with Kathy, her help from Virginia. She and Kathy would walk the dogs, shop in Kells, and take tea by Ramon lake. He remained restless and sought satisfaction elsewhere. He wanted to improve his play and decided to go to Argentina. Brendan Hannigan advised him to do the Hugh Dawnay clinic ahead of the trip. This would consolidate his ability from eight years of playing in England and now Ireland, as the Major knew how to improve players at all levels. Brendan had a good contact near Buenos Aires. He thought Tom might have remembered him when he visited Dublin that season. His name was Carlos Cormick and Brendan would contact him. Tom knew he could stay with Marcello so did not concern himself with Cormick. The Major's centre of operations, Whitfield Court, would be shut for the winter, and when he tracked him down to West Palm Beach, Florida, Standing booked a week's clinic in late January. When Brendan came back to him, Cormick offered to pick him up at the airport, and said he could stay with him at his home in Pilar, less than an hour from the city. There would be polo every day there. Tom agreed, he could call Marcello from there. His plan had shape, and he would fly directly on to Buenos Aires from Florida. When the day arrived, he hugged his mother and told her he would be back in a month. He called Sophie again.

"Has Joe come back?"

"There is no sign of him, Tom. We have heard nothing since he left. I even tried his ex, but couldn't find her. You know her, don't you – how to reach her?"

"Not really. I did have her address. Leave it with me. I'll put out some feelers. Are you OK, Sophie?"

"I am just so worried. If he is OK, how can he be so selfish? He knows how I feel about him. Anyway, how about you?"

"I'm heading to Florida soon, and then Argentina. Tell me, is Marcello still inCalifornia?"

"It's summer in BA. He must have gone back. I've not spoken with him since this happened. You will see him there if you are going. Please ask him if he knows anything, won't you?"

6

Malibu

Four Months Earlier

When bodies ceased their labour and spirits began their work, the night's candescence found earth through the lambent glow-worms in the dunes. The click of crickets syncopated the fall of the shore and Henderson lay back in the brittle cushion of dry grass, his thoughts awash with tone and colour, flowing without settling. Since checking out of the Valley Clinic, Joe knew at any time the impatience of his racing heart would propel him back to that musical landscape of his own making. Six weeks rehab had done less to modify his state of mind, and more to fuel the frenetic creative process that had driven him since his youth. In late September he had taken the beach house for two months, and installed a baby Steinway. The interviews for a new assistant had not gone so well. Only one of the young women had any potential. He was interviewing the third girl, a blond actress from Huntington Beach, when a vision passed his window. *The gates of heaven must be open. I think I saw an angel just walk by.* What lines would need to be drawn? Why had experience, weathered and seasoned by the disappointments of love in other places, constantly confounded his judgement as it again beckoned?

The laconic woman from Seattle, Sophie Santillian, handed him her resume. She was lithe, lissome, lovely, a brunette in a white dress with a European accent. She could give him three months. *I like the silence, but is she tender?* New in town, she asked if there would be a room for her, and insisted on the key. That evening his new housemate called him for drinks on the deck and they sat, listening to the caressing calm of the ebb tide, the sitting sun sinking beneath the ocean. He went to the cooler for frosted vodka. Empty. In the glass door he could see the girl moving before the Pacific backdrop, horizons converging. "Funny. I could have sworn there was a bottle here."

"I chucked it," she said.

"Who said you could do that?"

"My time, my rules."

For a moment he lost her in his own reflection. He heard her damp footsteps on the deck. A palm brushed his ear to cup his cheek. He turned into it, when, as if to a bruise, she pressed her lips to his, the way cold water might surcease a sprain. This voluptuary, not of pleasure but of pain, hunting for what she least dared to find. He tensed, flush, then froze when she said, "You think I simply want to make love? God, haven't we had enough of that?" He withdrew from her embrace, abashed by his desire, her rebuke. They retreated to their rooms, both wide awake, alone in their feelings.

At daybreak, sitting on the prow of his beached dory, looking back to the cottage, he questioned his motives as if he were still alone. If complementaries were not obliged to be lovers, could they co-exist, simply as part-owners of each other? What would it take to placate a sexuality he had always assumed. Just then, a broken accent called from across the water.

"I hired a boat." He turned to see the girl from the northwest approaching the beach. "Why don't you follow me out?"

"Sure, why not?" he answered.

At about two hundred yards, she dropped anchor. "This is far enough." She went back with him. They ate breakfast outside, discussing the album he had to complete before the end of November. His session musicians included jazz pros, a Celtic violinist and classical flautist. A generous advance covered the outlay. The studio time allowed would be more than enough. With fourteen tracks planned, the manuscripts and his annotations would be copious. He was ready. How did she feel? She referred him, again, to her resume:

Sophie Santillian
1955:   Born Montreal, Canada
          Father: Mexican
          Mother: French Canadian
1976-79: Conservatoire International de Musique de Paris
1976- : Singer
1982-86: Partner, Roussel Galleries

Henderson could not have known how, as a student, she had been drawn by the potency of the jazz and blues clubs of St. Germain and Odeon, the Latin Quarter. Her vocal range, developed at the Conservatoire, was her passport to the Left Bank. She would often sing three or four venues in an evening. From the first time she heard "Etudes de Paris", Joe's 'piece de resistance', her heartbeat fixated; collision was unavoidable. His compositions were complex, troubled, phrases constantly reaching for the thirteenth note, hung pauses, hinting at ending, never quite making it.

More than any musician she knew, Joe touched her, deeper than her heart. He found a place within her that no music, no Frenchman, had come close to. Her introduction to his music, two years earlier on the Island of Montreal, was by a pupil, a parting gift. She played it one last time before handing it to her teacher. The crackle of stylus on vinyl disappeared when the pianist launched into a tirade of riffs and power chords, not unlike Oscar Peterson, the 'Maharaja of the keyboard'. He scaled the octaves rapidly, caressing every note with a gliding touch. Its urgency then arced, pulling her, with its sweep, into a denizen of insight. Drained, she always wanted more. When he told her of the piece inside him he had struggled with for so long, she led him to the water's edge. They looked out over the Pacific, and she asked him what he saw.

"Err ... horizon, sea, bright sky, a paling moon. It inspires me. I just want to get started."

"Now look down to the water. What do you see?"

"I'm not with you."

"Just look, Joe."

"Well – I can see your boat."

"That's right, and you've already made it that far." His muse had found him.

*

The welcome tranquility of this new development was to change when his phone rang.

"Hi Joe, it's Tom."

94

"Tom! Great to hear from. What's up?"

"You were right, Joe. About everything." They had discussed their personal lives often, and when Joe learned that Tom would be in Wimbledon for a short stay that October he asked him to look out for his former partner. She had red hair, like Joe, was tall, pale with a birthmark on her temple.

"You sound pretty sure," Joe said.

Earlier Tom had driven along the road where Joe told him she might be. When he pulled up sharply to avoid a cat he looked left to see a tall woman digging a garden bed. She gazed his way. Her complexion was pallid, highlighting a blue ink mark, and when she wiped her sweaty brow she pushed back a scarf to reveal a shock of red hair.

"Where are you?" Joe said.

"London."

"I'll get back to you." Joe packed a small bag, and called a cab. He told Sophie he would be back in a week. She joined him in the back of the limo, and told him she also had unfinished business, in Washington State. They said farewell at LAX; she flew Northwest; he flew Delta, long haul, the red-eye into the beckoning European dawn. Before daybreak, a storm broke over the Atlantic, sheet lightning, booming thunderclaps shook the wings and the passengers into gripping tension, holding on, thirty-five thousand feet up, heading east at five hundred miles an hour, with damn-all protection against a prolonged aerial battering. The plane fought its way, roaring, diving, climbing. Babies cried, young girls sobbed, men gritted their teeth, crying inside. Some held hands, some their own, others prayed: Meccan chants, the Lord's prayer. How would it end?

It did end, as it was always going to, for good or bad, and activity resumed within the cabin; mothers soothing, attendants comforting, checking young and old and in between. Joe Henderson looked at the champagne nip before him, and chose to ignore it. That might come later; first, he had a mission to complete, and a drink at this stage would be of no help. His friend's call had triggered the denouement he had not hoped for, but now he had to see it through, with a clear head. He told the Heathrow cab driver to take him to Wimbledon. When he knocked on the door of his aunt's house, the young woman met him, shocked, in flagrante delicto."So, you've been here all along, the family covering for you while I went out of my mind, never knowing if we were finished – two fucking years of it, and all along you've been shacked up with this bloody cousin, the spineless little shit. Where is the son of a bitch? Hiding in the kitchen, pathetic wimp." Joe directed his anger at the cowering Nick and when he swung his fist, hard, cousin Nick went flying across the table, crashing to the floor, buried beneath gastronomic detritus, dripping fresh cream and desserts. "Just about sums you up, arsehole. Now my aunt's house really is a toilet. If I could flush it, I wouldn't waste the effort. You duplicitous fuckers just aren't worth it. Jesus God, who needs bloody family?"

Anytime he reflected on how it had all gone wrong, and his suspicions about those involved, such a paroxysm would have left him drained of hope, looking lost into the abyss. Yet this time, he felt charged with energy, empowered by his confirmed knowledge as he strode out of the house, taller than he could remember. He took a deep breath, and told the cabbie to drive up to the Common. Tom was staying in a house there, and had waited for his friend to show up since he made the call less than two days earlier.

"Joe. Well, how did it go?"

"Pretty heavy, but I feel better now it's off my chest. It's taken so long to get to the truth. They'd better not start contacting me now to say how sorry they are for what's happened, when I know they all knew bloody well, but nobody bothered to tell me. Except you. At last, I saw for myself – and I was right all the time. Thank you, Tom, for letting me know. Nobody else understood what it was like, just not knowing the truth. Just too many damn lies. It's clearer now."

"Come on, Joe, let's get a pint." They walked across the Common to the Crooked Billet.

"When are you heading back then?" Tom asked.

"I want to catch the night flight, so let's go steady on the beer. Can you to drive me to the airport?"

"Sure, we can talk on the way."

Tom, also torn by a destructive relationship, had resolved to the survival metaphor as an antidote to disappointment, polo. Joe, always needing more, plunged deep into self-abuse, neglecting mind and body daily. If he did anything right during his 'dark passage', it was polo, and what it brought him. Polo precariously juxtaposed his spiraling lifestyle with two exhausting seasons. In 1987 they pooled their prospects, forming the ToJos low-goal team. The results were mixed, but predictable, considering the lack of preparation Joe made before any game. It was a distraction, pushing back bitter memories for a few hours, and then a few more as an evening's drinking ensued, erasing too the match. His teammates would remind him of this moment, or that goal, complementing his own play, and now, travelling with Tom, he could still recall little of their two seasons in West Sussex. Carrying Joe, usually under the weather, the ToJos team, so-named after the joint patronage of Tom and Joe, was nevertheless more successful than he knew, and Tom told him of some of the brilliant shots he made, and goals he scored. "You were a natural striker. I don't know how but you were always in the right place."

"Divine providence, eh Tom?"

"Doubt it. Not you. I'll never forget a shot you played from the left, right on their goal line. You were galloping on Pancho, hit a backhand cut, and the bloody thing curved between the posts – a banana shot. Fantastic! You didn't even know you'd done it, and you asked me why we were all riding back to the centre. Such a plonker – all that talent, and you pissed it up against the wall."

"I know, Tom, I know. But you know why, don't you? All this shit on my mind just threw me off balance. But it's done now – I hope. How about you?"

"I'm not through it yet. But I'm sorry that your marriage has ended like this."

"My what? Oh yes, I guess you're right. Get me to the airport, Tom – I have somewhere to be." Joe felt for his friend, but he did not want to talk anymore. At the terminal, they hugged, and an urgency in Joe's eyes told Tom he remained steadfast, about something.

"Good luck, Joe. Keep in touch."

"Come and stay when you're ready." Four weeks later Tom received Joe's letter, explaining his need to get back to California:

Tom,

She was waiting for me on my return – I knew we shared that sense of nexus. She speaks little of her experiences of love so it was not yet her moment, nor mine, to reveal the past. It was more a point of salvation for the two of us, and we both felt it. How she goads me to the orderliness of her own life. Before her, the world was flat, night and day were the same, but now night follows day, follows night, round once more. Get this. My life has become an open book as she picks me up on everything, especially all my weaknesses. We went for dinner last week on the Boulevard. Coming home, I noticed a pretty girl walking casually on the esplanade, and turned my head. Sophie's gentle hold on my hand loosened, and that chill of abandonment set me adrift before I quickly put my arm around her shoulder and gathered into the softness of her satin neck, inhaling the blend of warm sea air in her hair with the natural feminine perfume she wore, as if from a bottle. She has a warmth I have almost forgotten, and she knows me so well. She is incredibly strong.

She overwhelms me. I guess I'm beguiled. But, what do you do? This might be a gamble, but it feels right. In the evenings we walk along the shore, gazing out at Santa Catalina, that fecund mammary that sits so proud above the ocean, touched only by wind and waves. Lingering, on our strolls, our conversation ebbs and flows between the chaos of unstructured fragments that went before, mostly mine. With little in common, our first kisses sealed a bond of opposites, predicating hope, and the happiness only it can bring. Her kindness is expressed in the timing of her touch, when I least expect it, when it means the most.

Some moments are without measure, mere solutes within a solvent of memories that only a creature so unique, not of a kind, can dispense. I can say I love not only her name. I love her, Tom, but 'I love you' is still to come. It will, even from such an inextricable place. I hope you have been able to resolve some of the difficulties that faced you when we met briefly, that night after Wimbledon. I will always remember your friendship. You and I have similar histories, and we understood each other when we first met. I have found 'closure' after a lifetime. If I can ever help you, I will.

I have extended the rental on this Malibu house, and should be ready to record the new album in about another month. Anyhow — when are you coming over? Plenty of polo here, all year round, if you are interested. I have not played yet, but heck, we could put the ToJos together again. What do you say?

Come soon.

Love, Joe.

As tempted as Tom was to board a plane, his friend's progress had thrown his own demons into relief, and it was time to confront them. He caught the last Saturday flight to Aldegrove, Belfast, and hired a car. The drive across the Ulster countryside was winding in parts, dark, and less familiar than he remembered when he left over two years earlier, when he might have been travelling home to his waiting wife of nine months. Perhaps not at two o'clock in the morning though. Then he was twenty-four, she seventeen, both babies, yet capable of inflicting pain from the spirit or the heart. He, naïve, still found difficulty in reconciling the fickleness of a free spirit, when he had always believed that at the centre of the senses is the heart. He had been wrong, and maybe that was the hardest part; either way, he was tortured, and it somehow had to end.

From conversations with his cousin Paul, he understood that she was living in a caravan, in a field near his aunt's house. He guessed this was a front, as Paul's brother, David, lived in the former family home where his own mother and her two sisters had grown up – the Lodge. He made straight for the field. When he rapped the door, she appeared in a black see-through baby doll negligee. *Christ, she never wore that for me.*

"Looks like you're busy."

"Come back in ten minutes," she told him. He went back to the car, and sped fifty yards down the road, jumped out, and ran back. Out of the caravan emerged the offending cousin, the upright farmer and all-round 'good sort', fourteen years his elder, a stealthy predator of married woman. That was all he needed to know. His nocturnal foray into friendless terrain could now bring down closure on a painful episode and, as charged as he had been on leaving

London, he was done; fatigue had dissipated his appetite for recrimination. With all his questions answered, he drove to the airport to catch the first return flight. The following morning he called his lawyer.

"End it, Jonathan, a.s.a.p.!" he instructed.

"Need anyone cited?" Braithwaite answered. *All I wanted was the bloody truth.*

"Nobody worth mentioning."

*

Tom stood by the baggage claim, and saw his friend through the barrier. It was late September, warm, and they were going to play chukkas in Santa Barbara that afternoon – "if you're up to it, old son?"

"Damned right I am. I never felt more like it- and less of the old."

"What do you think of the wagon?"

"Nice wheels, Joe."

"Sophie's. She got her settlement – I love it."

"I'm looking forward to meeting her."

Leaving L.A. behind them, the grunt of the Daytona eating up Pacific Highway, they soon reached the Colony. Barney greeted them at the gate.

"Wotcha' got, Barney?" Joe asked the security man.

"Well, I just don't know, I really just can't understand it. I just can't understand it at all."

"Barbara Stanwick?" Joe said.

"Oh! You know that one. How's about this one? - You ain't gonna learn English 'cos you have to read – 'cos if the good lord had wanted it you'da bin born knowing how…that's why!"

"Got it! Walter Brennan," Tom called out.

"Hey Joe, who's the wise guy?"

"This is Tom, over from London. He'll be staying a while, so be nice!"

"The hell I will! Damn Limeys!"

"And that's The Duke?" Tom told him, recognizing John Wayne, as Joe put his foot down. Sophie was by the shore when they

100

walked onto the deck. "Let's go see her." Joe led his friend across the sand. Her obvious appeal became clear as they approached, but it was the allure of her obsidian pupils within those lustrous, insightful eyes, that revealed the charity of her pathos. *Joe's in safe hands now.*

"Hi, Tom. I've been hearing a lot about you. Is this your first time on the coast?"

"I was here a few years ago, in Portland and San Francisco, and then later I drove down Pacific Highway from Oregon through California – just loved it, had a great time. I was with a friend. We stayed in San Diego, and then one night at the hotel Del Coronado."

"Funny you should say that. Joe was hoping you might play a couple of tournaments, one on the beach in Del Coronado, and then the San Diego Club at Rancho Santa Fe." Tom recalled visiting Rancho Santa Fe, near Del Mar. Four grounds on a flood plain, inland from the race track, were overlooked by haciendas on the heights, and he thought then what a great place it would be to live.

"Well, that's where we'll be staying, right above the number two field. I have a girlfriend with a house there. Her name is Mariette – French, like me. I think you'll like her." Sophie was Joe's muse, polo manager, and now matchmaker to his friend.

"Tom, there's a three-goal Argie guy called Marcello at the Santa Barbara club, not far from here. He's organising ponies, and a high-goal player to join us – don't know who yet but he tells me he'll be cheap, his handicap that is. So, what do you think? It'll be great. We'll stay at the Del, play on the beach, you know, where Tony Curtis impersonated Cary Grant in *Some Like it Hot.*"

"Of course: Duty, duty, duty. That was a great film Joe. And don't forget the restaurant - The Prince of Wales. Apparently Edward VIII met Mrs. Simpson there, or maybe they just ate there. Anyway, I'm definitely up for it. When do we go?"

"Tomorrow. We need to get to know these horses, and we can do that at Santa Barbara – go up this evening if you like – stick and ball a few. Oh, and by the way, Tom. This is my shout."

They all swam, and Tom lay by the shore, while Joe ran a few riffs on the Steinway. Sophie, in yellow bikini and diaphanous sarong, took off in the Ferrari to buy lunch from the store on Ventura Highway. When Joe rejoined him, they spoke of London, the outcomes of their relationship breakdowns, and how their difficulties had left them. Tom asked him "Where to next then?"

"Right here suits me well, Tom. I'm on the ground, so if I do walk through any windows, I'll live to make it out to Rancho Mirage – you know, the Betty Ford Clinic. Can't think of a better place to dry out than the desert. The writing is going well, thanks to my lovely luminary. Getting to grips with Wimbledon is a lot easier with her in my life, rather than dwelling on it perpetually in my head. Filling and sharing my time is the best way to deal with a fait accompli." A low-passing pelican squawked, and Tom had not heard the last part clearly.

"What was that, Joe?"

"Oh, just that we can never fully undo what is done, don't you think?" Tom's sense of having shut the door firmly on his own mess had left him without any notion of perpetuity, and if he was curious about Joe's continued preoccupation with the past, he chose not to dig further, not then anyway.

"How about these ponies, Joe?"

"I'll call Marcello, tell him we'll be up when Sophie gets back."

"Did you play much this year, Tom?"

"Sure did. In Dublin, at the All Ireland Club, Phoenix Park."

"What was that like?"

"Feet didn't touch the ground for six months. Between chukkas, tournaments, drinking and parties, and a few balls, I met some great people. Only thing is, they put up my handicap, so now I'm one goal. I know it doesn't seem much, but playing off zero gave me more value and with a higher rating it's going to weaken the vigor of any team I'm in."

"Probably won't make a huge difference. Is it all low-goal in Dublin?"

"Except for the Horse Show Tournament. It's fifteen goals – played during Horse Show Week, early August. High-goal players came in from Argentina, the US, and UK. I went half-patron with a

102

guy called Arthur, and we brought in two five-goalers, an Aussie called Derek Ryder and Oliver Dawson. Between Arthur and me we had just five ponies, so we had to borrow and rent a few extras."

"How did you make out?"

"Not great, but it was good fun, in and out of the Horse Shoe Bar in the Shelbourne Hotel, dinner parties, the Horse Show Ball in the club house – a good weekend. Bloody exhausting, but I can't wait 'til next year. They really know how to enjoy themselves."

"Do you think I'd like it?"

"You'd love it."

"That's the trouble – I'd probably love it too much."

"They'd love you too."

"Maybe I'll come over and we can play that tournament next year. I'll talk to Marcello. You should get to know him. He's a cool guy – from Buenos Aires. Knows everybody!"

Sophie arrived and they ate a feta salad with pastrami and warm bread drizzled with olive oil. For dessert they managed to lay back and laze the afternoon on the deck, until it was time to leave. Sophie took the scenic route, Pacific Coast Highway, the ocean to their left, and then inland on Foothill Road beside Los Padres National Forest, home of the redwoods. She did not ride, her preferred thrill putting the roadster through its paces, and she could drive. The men were wide awake when she brought the yellow bomb to a crunching halt beside the clubhouse, cutting the engine with a final tap on the throttle. As they piled out, Marcello left the ponies to greet them. He was tall, slim, tanned, with long black hair, Latino. "Hola, Sophie, Joe, and you must be Tommy – how are you?" Marcello shook his hand.

"Great thanks. Good to meet you."

"Will you stay long?"

"A few weeks I guess. We're all going to play the tournaments down near San Diego. I'm looking forward to playing with you, Marcello. Joe said you're bringing in another player to join us. Is that right?"

"Si, si, he from Cordoba, six goals, very nice guy, Pablo Mendoza. Muy bien, rapido. I went school with him, Christian

Brothers, BA. We have same age, twenty. He been playin' in California this year. November he play Argentine Open."

"Wow!"

"They make him eight goals after, maybe nine."

"Sounds like he'll be ten one day."

"We hope. But later."

"Six goals makes him a steal right now then, Joe," Tom said.

"For sure. He's going to play the ten-goal at Rancho Santa Fe with us. The Del Coronado weekend is only three-a-side, up to four goals, so that'll just be us."

"Pablo might come tonight. He say me he leave message at the club," Marcello told them as he walked them along the pony lines, giving the ponies backgrounds and names. Although most were American quarter horses, Marcello had brought some from Argentina.

"Tommy, you try these four," he said. The ponies were ready, girths tightened by three blonds in bikinis tops. They were all calm and well turned out. *First things first.* Tom checked himself. He mounted and moved to the field. He headed down the ground alongside Joe, towards the sun, tapping balls to each other, here and there taking a full swing, changing gait, then leg, pulling up, using their legs to change down through the 'gears', easy on their ponies' mouths – their 'brakes'. Brakes failed on horses, as with cars, they all knew, and the more they were used, the more likely they were to break down. The girls had bandaged all the ponies' legs; they had seen the results of oversights, when cuts, painful bruising, or worse had occurred during play, and no groom ever liked that on their watch. Even for a gentle 'stick and ball' practice session they brought astringents and ointments to rub down and soothe limbs and muscles after a workout.

The players brought their horses round in circles, each tapping a ball as he did so, stroking to the offside, then bringing it around to the near, reaching from right to left, over the ponies neck, to stroke the ball on that side. They changed ponies after about ten minutes. Tom's girl, Rebecca, made a note of his comments on each pony. The first, Mariposa – bay, agile, responsive – turned quickly, and was true to the line he rode, did not deviate. This correctness about her would save having to make adjustments when concentrating on other players, or fouling, maybe missing a shot.

Next up, Becky held Romero, a pinto with a keen eye. Tom stepped up from the stirrup, holding the double reins loosely with his left hand, fingers gripping the curve of the saddle's cut back pommel. His right leg over the pony's back, and his foot in the right stirrup, he adjusted the stirrup length and double-checked the girth. The reins were new, a little squeaky, yet supple in the hand. The top rein of the pair he held between his thumb and index, the lower through his index and middle finger. He made sure that the lengths of leather were equidistant on both right and left sides of Romero's neck, and that they were not pulled tight, but slack enough for comfort, yet with scope to rein-in if needed. The saddle was suede-topped, with leather sides. Mariposa's was the same, and also with a cut back pommel which removed the high front end rise above the ponies' withers. The saddles were short, low-backed and light, and the rider felt secure despite the lack of size. Tom was more familiar with English saddles; they tended to be longer, and so often higher-backed, which he had found sometimes could eject him forward into a high pommel or worse. He liked these smaller saddles.

Marcello had brought sticks for them to try. He produced a bag of more than twenty, differing in length from fifty to fifty-two inches. The mallet heads were painted white and bore the manufacturer's logo, *Casa Villamil, Hurlingham*. They were light, pliable, would bend with natural spring through the cane length of the shaft, and were initialed MB. Marcello had brought them with him to California, along with four saddles, girths, overgirths, and mutlicoloured hand-woven blankets. Their 'look' gave them much appeal among the Californian fashionistas, and Marcello's order book was swelling daily. The local saddlers were displeased with his arrival, and his contacts in BA were quick to tell him who had tried to circumvent his endeavours. He did not really care, as he was locked in by agreement with all the manufacturers he represented, and found the whole business a bit tiresome. But business was business, and one of the girls working with the ponies was keen to act as his agent, so he was working on a contract with her.

The three players rode the field in formation, backing each other up, trying some ride-offs to get a sense of how effective their ponies were in physical contact. No problems in that department with Mariposa or Romero. Becky took the gelding from him as he slid from its back, holding another mount, a dappled grey gelding, Ruben, fine boned and tranquil as he climbed over the saddle. Intuition told him that Ruben, using the same fifty-one-inch stick he had used with Mariposa and Romero, was steadier again. The horse enthused confidence in him as he practiced penalty shots from as far back as the halfway line, one hundred and fifty yards from the goal. He had never lofted place shots like that, not on any horse in the eight years he had been playing. Sure, he had made some memorable shots, like those he reminded Joe of back in London. The measure of those was the frequency with which they could be made – could they be relied on? If he could depend on them for their regularity, then he could live up to his handicap. Ruben was a platform for a golfer who had never ridden, to plant a ball from tee to green. Maybe he could play him first and then last. To play him twice would be a feast. One last time, the ball on the sixty-yard spot, he circled Ruben in a gathered canter, winding the stick around his wrist, in reverse, as if preparing a backhand, once, twice, three times, all this a prelude to the forehand, first with a forward warm up from the wrist, followed up by a full overhead swing. The mallet met the ball, his eyes glued to it, and lofted it towards the Pacific horizon, landing thirty yards behind the centre of the goal posts. "Peachy."

Becky took Ruben, as Tom raised himself over his final mount. He changed stick, down to fifty inches, for the 15.1 hands black mare, compact, gathered, and very fast. He kicked on and Bridget sent him off the back of his new saddle. He scrambled back on board, and went through the same routine of circles, figures of eight, tapping half shots, winding up his big shot with two or three rotations, sending the ball more than half the length of the field. As with the others, he played the ball under the neck, from the offside, then the nearside. He tailed the ball, around the rear of the pony, from off, from near, and backed it away with open shots, again on both sides of the pony. She stopped and turned on a sixpence. *This*

106

baby could hurt herself she's so good. All this, and she could ride off with courage.

Back in the lines, Becky was hosing down Ruben, sponging from his neck along the length of his strong, sleek back, up over his muscular rump, and down to his hocks. Mariposa and Romero were already cooling in the ocean breeze. *I'd love a bit of that myself.*

Becky turned the hose on Tom and a shower plumed above him. He lifted his face to the sparkling zest, refreshing his sun-baked complexion. He opened his mouth, the spray splashed his tongue, washing down dust thrown up by the horses.

"Becky. That was really good. They're all beautiful ponies. But I've never ridden anything with as much pace as Bridget. She had me out of the saddle at one point, and she does everything. And Ruben is an absolute gift. He'd make anybody look good. I feel really spoilt. We're all gonna have a great time, especially at the beach."

"I ride all of them every day, but I don't play, so I guess I see them differently. You are right though. They're all lovely animals, sweet natured. They're easy and good-hearted, plenty of spirit. Marcello says they have a nice life here, very relaxed. I love them, my babies. Marcello has sold them to Pablo's boss, Henry Williamson. So, look after them, please, please, please!"

"I will, don't worry. Are you coming to the bar? We're eating there this evening."

"Sure. See you in about an hour."

"Marcello, do you want to put the sticks in my bag, or keep them with you?"

"Is OK, Joe. I keep them with me. We go clubhouse now?"

"Yeah, sure. I'm starving. These ponies are superb. Did you bring them from BA?"

"Si, si. They from estancia in Gualeguaychu. My family."

"Say that again."

"From the family in Gualeguaychu."

"Wally what?"

"Gualeguaychu."

"Wallywhychoo – what a great name. Where is it?'

"Entre Rios. Is north of BA."

"You have many horses?"

"Not too much. Less than one sousand, mas o menos."

"Jeez, Marcello, what do you do with them?"

"If they no good, polo, then salto. Sorry, jumpin'. Rodeo. Or they go Brindisi – meat."

"Do you have many like these?"

"Si."

"D'ya hear that Tom? Plenty more where these came from. We'll have to go down there, check it out. What do you say? I've never been."

"Me neither. I'd love to go. What do think, Marcello?"

"Si, si. You stay me.'

"Wallywhychoo?"

"And BA," Marcello told him.

"Let's eat and talk about it."

*

The team showered; Sophie went to the bar. When the men joined her, spirits were high.

"Who do we play, Marcello?" Joe asked.

"San Diego we play eight teams. On the beach we play six."

"Any big hitters?"

"How you mean?"

"Patrons?"

"Not really. Just club teams."

"Where's Henry, the guy Pablo plays for?" Joe asked.

"He pull muscle, so he go Barbados, lay in sun, walk sea."

"That should sort him out."

"He say Pablo, he no ride, sex hurt, but he take girlfriend with him. He no trust Pablo, I think." As Pablo entered the club room, every head turned. Some were familiar with the blond, richly tanned, strong limbed number one with La Espadania, the five times victorious 'Open' team. Those that knew his charms, were happy to see him, and those that did not equally so. Pablo cast a smile about the room, keeping his distance. Marcello greeted him.

108

"Que tal?"

"Bien, Marcello. Como le va."

"Bien, bien." They shook hands. "Pablo, I want you meet Joe."

"Hi, Joe, how are you?" said Pablo gripping Joe's hand. "We play some good polo together."

"And this Sophie, Joe's girlfriend," said Marcello.

"Hola, Sophie." Pablo's hand gloved hers, as he lightly kissed her on both cheeks. Standing and Henderson exchanged grimaces. Tom had the same thought, as Joe said: "We'll have to watch this guy. Henry was right."

"Pablo, this is Tom. He just arrived from Europe," Joe said. "He'll be playing with us."

"Hi Tom, how you like Los Estados Unidos?"

"I love it."

"You like Henry's horses?" Pablo asked.

"Really good!"

"Who you ride?"

"Mariposa, Romero, Ruben, and Marucha."

"Aah! Ruben,' Pablo smiled, raising his fingers to his lips: "Fantastico!"

"Absolutely!"

"Habla Español, Tommy? I mean, do you speak Spanish?"

"No."

"Do you know polo language, in Spanish?"

"No."

"I teach you. Many players don't know, and is good when I call you, you know. I say you 'cola' for 'tail' and 'abierto' for 'open'."

"I like it. We'll have to try it." The girls entered, laughing, moving quickly to the bar.

"Hi, Becky, all the horses down for the night?" Tom asked.

"Yes, they're all fine, fed and watered. Now it's our turn." The length of the BBQ was smoking in the gazebo as they moved to a table nearby. Juicy sirloins, crispy onion rings, French fries, steaming crustaceans, garnished with butter and garlic, and cold seafood, floating on ice. Bins held bottles of Mexican beers, their tin crowns breaking through the surface ice. And wine, from Napa, Chile, Argentina, red, white, and rosé. Then there was Clerico.

"What's this?" Tom asked Marcello.

"This! This Clerico. White wine, fruit, sugar, and limonade if you like."

"Hmm. I like." Marcello brought three large jugs to the table, and Tom poured the white sangria from Argentina.

"It's like Pimm's, only white," Joe said. The three blonds from the yard sat opposite him. Becky he knew. She introduced Conzuela, from Rosarito in Mexico, and Nadine, from Orleans, France. Nadine looked after Pablo's ponies. *No surprise there. She's the prettiest.* She was just a little girl, with plenty of spirit, and handled the string with firm care. Despite Pablo's reputation, polo was business and he could not afford to mess up. He and the horses all knew she was the boss, and behaved themselves on her say so, except one perhaps, Rosso. This Argentine gelding, 15.3 hands, was taking his time adjusting to a girl's control, but she told Tom, "I will win. You will see." She stood to raise her glass. "Salut! Horse riders from Europe. Welcome here." Conzuela, demure behind her limited English, felt at ease with Tom as he struggled with his lack of Spanish. His knowledge ran out after anything salutary. He could hardly add 'cola' or 'abierto', so he didn't.

"Salud!" he said to her as their glasses met over the table.

"Gracias," she replied. Conzuela had travelled with Marcello from BA, where she had worked in a high-goal yard for two ten-goal players. She knew her stuff, and with her on board the team would operate like a well-oiled machine.

"Marcello, Conzuela must be a really good groom."

"Tom, she the best pedicera in all the world – I love her. Yes, I love her. I adore her. Really." He hugged and kissed her on her cheek.

"And I love him. Te amo, Marcello." They embraced warmly.

"She a vet. One day she look after me in every way. Eh Connie, carino?'

"Me gusta!" She held him yet closer.

"You like my Mexican chica, Tommy? Come to BA. I find you muchas chicas en Buenos Aires – the best." The thought of a trip to BA was looking better all the time.

"Just one thing, Marcello. How welcome is an Englishman in your country right now? You know, after the Falklands war and everything."

"No hay problema, Tommy. You have Irish passport, si?"

"Good point."

Pablo sat to his right. "You havin' fun, Tommy?"

"Absolutely, Pablo."

"This a very nice club. Everybody simpatico. And is a good polo. You will like. You see."

"Pablo, I'm looking forward to playing in San Diego next week."

"Si, Tommy. We play the ten goal. You play ten goal?"

"A little." Pablo poured more Clerico from the pitcher.

"The first time I play tournament at Association in BA, it was ten goal. I was one-goal, and my job was mark number four, a seven, Rodrigo Lula. He never keep the ball and tap forward, he always hit hard, long way. So, I think mark him no good – he always beat me. Better I go up, maybe mark number three, or two. I more use there. This Rodrigo, his weakness, his big hit. He play it every time. I read him, you know. He think he strong, but he not so much. He like himself too much. Anyway, we win. Ha Ha! Tommy, when we play, think fast, look good the players, maybe they have weakness you don't see straight 'way. Study your mark, and try be more clever than him. Marcello, no entiendo esta jerga, por favor, me lo podrias explicar 'sacar ventaja' en ingles.'

"Tommy. He say you must 'get the jump'."

"Yeah, yeah, yeah! I got it."

"Read the game, he say you. Make defense your attack."

"Like chess. You play, Pablo?" Tom said.

"Chess? Not so much. No now." *To outplay an opponent, first you have to read, and anticipate his every move.* He understood.

"We play a practice tomorrow, guys. OK, Tommy, Joe," Pablo said.

"Can't wait," Joe said.

Sophie stood to announce that Joe was invited to play the club piano, and he left to take his place before the drinkers and diners in the bar. He enjoyed composing, and wanted to produce a good album before the end of the year, but his first love had always been performing, especially in intimate night clubs, cabaret. It was his comfort blanket. Only one time had he faced a difficult audience, when a table of Germans heckled him, calling out for rock and roll. On that occasion he turned up the tempo, when his rage spurred him into a paroxysm of arpeggios and riffs, after his lifelong leading light, Oscar Peterson. When his outburst was done, the offenders sat riveted, beguiled. A moment of epiphany had prompted their apologies, and their conversion.

*

Joe was comfortable in a room that cloaked him, more than one he dominated, just happy to be part of the décor. He played until late: Brubeck, Garner, Peterson, his favourites. The Bechstein upright stood against a wall, draping a shallow recess. He hit the opening bars of Erroll Garner's 'Misty', the audience at once captive to its plangent mood. If the piano held them, it was the sonorous female voicing that trawled their emotions. As Joe played the closing cluster of chords, Sophie emerged, dimly visible from the candle on the piano, the words taking her where they would. Sophie had the soul of Billie Holliday and the delivery of Sade.

Joe broke into the opening riff of "The Long Goodbye". Sophie picked up the Johnny Mercer lyrics, the footlights radiated the gloom of a black backdrop, and the diva, in inky gown, lifted them out of their seats. More plaudits when Stevie Brown, a former Chess Records session man, played in on alto sax. The Goddess fronted her troubadours. A swarthy young guitarist, Django, stepped up as Joe moved to keyboards. The trio warmed up with some twelve bar, "Breakin Out", and the Gitano plugged in his Goldtop, bristling with sweeping arpeggio fills across its neck. In the grip of the valve-warmed Humbuckers the revelers abandoned any care of the dawn when night fell into "What Kind of Woman is This?"

Django's full, moist lips voiced a range of stentorian base tones and felt falsettos, as he sucked the syllables and punctuated endlines with the sounds of sex. He finger-picked through every sense. If you were happy, you probably got lucky, and if you were lucky, you were happy. Conzuela, warmed earlier by the taste of home, the asado, BBQ, whispered: "Estoy caliente, Marcello."

He squeezed her hand. "Me tambien." Everybody felt it. Love was the drug, dance the natural selector. Django opened with an A-minor blues lick, as he slowed it down with a closing B.B. King number, "The Blues Come Over Me." Partnerships were galvanised, couples became one. Lovers were making the night theirs. When he laid down his guitar, the dancers continued to shuffle, in intimate embracing, oblivious to the musicians. Django's alchemy had worked.

They all left the Santa Barbara Polo Club. Becky and Tom climbed into the back of the yellow roadster, holding hands, kissing. Sophie pushed in a tape and fired up 'her twelve wild horses, in silver chains', Joe's hand on hers as she moved assiduously through the ZF gate of the gearshift. In understated husky tones Chris Rea sang his paean to the 365 Prancing Horse. The gurgle of the throbbing V12 stallion aroused mares and geldings. Holding back the pull of four hundred horses, the chanteuse slowly slid onto the highway. Joe lay back his head and gazed up to the October sky, bathed in moonlight. He changed the cassette. "Moondance", Van Morrison. Perfecto!

*

Joe and Sophie slipped away, leaving their guests to the night. The zest of the ocean a prelude to their point-event, Tom drank in the Clerico essence of Becky's breath. She stroked his contours, as she had the gelding's haunches earlier, exploring between his thighs, whispering those sweet things lovers love to hear, calling him 'darling'. Moaning and moving in all the right places, the night places, he was hers, all she had was his. Spent, their love-making liberated, as freedom is afforded by friendship. They were friends — a good way, he thought, uncomplicated by passion or desire for anything more. Prone, she laughed, and joked about a 'good chukka'. "Your handicap needs to go up."

His thirst slaked, he lay face-down to slumber, unresponsive to her straddling limbs, both basking in their body warmth. Before her suggestion found expression, tranquility replaced ardour, waves losing their seahorse posture, still delicate, sensuously innocent, falling to the shore, brush-stroking, draining, flaccid, to the sea floor. She slid from him, collected her clothes and called a cab to meet her at the Colony gate. Her other charges needed her now. Leaning over him, she whispered "I doubt we will ever do this again, sweetheart. I'm glad we have."

"Me too, Becky. Until the next time." They kissed. She left.
She moved through the mist as a cool breeze wound into the cobweb catenary of pleached hawthorn. If the predawn hinted promise behind its hoarfrost as candlelight might an aniseed drink, and birdsong replaced night calls, it was the crystalline path that sealed her amourette.

*

When Joe, Sophie, and Tom left that evening, they drove into a sepia gloaming cast by the descending sun. Tom had little sense of the unknown that lay ahead. Sophie, herself lured them to another flame, taking the freeway around LA and found Pacific Coast Highway. She lived every gear change as it would echo against the cliffs, then dissipate towards the ocean, different again as its howling muffled to warbling by zestful crosswinds as they passed over the high bridges that joined the outcrops on either side of the ravines. These controlled conduits to the great ocean a drain for the precious California waterways balanced the capacity with a need for sustenance as well as wildfire emergencies. Sophie dropped gears, swung the roadster left, roaring up the hill road to Rancho Santa Fe – The Ranch. They were heading to Mariette's. Fresh from the drive, the friends met their hostess in her doorway.

"Pablo is with her at the Cedars-Sinai," she said immediately.

"Who? Who is he with?" Sophie asked.

"You don't know? Oh my God – nobody told you. It's his girlfriend, she's been kicked – about three hours ago, at the stables."

"Nadine! That bloody horse finally did it. What happened?" Joe said.

"Pablo said she was getting him ready for the trailer, and he just kicked out. She was hit in the stomach and the head. When they found her she looked dead. Another girl turned her and she opened her eyes. An ambulance came and she is in intensive care right now."

"I'll go back," Sophie said, kissing her French friend on her cheeks. "Joe, you stay here, look after everyone."

"I'm going with you," he said. Only when they disappeared beyond the crest of the hilltop at the end of the road, did Tom see Mariette, again silhouetted in the door of her home. He introduced himself.

"I know," she said. "I'm Mariette."

"Yes, I know." The crisis had conceived an instant bond of emotion. He felt he knew her as they began to share the evening. She linked his arm when they crossed her threshold. As Mariette tended to her guests Tom made his way through the small gathering, meeting her son, Henri, a recent European literature graduate from the Sorbonne, planning his Masters on celebrated ex-pats living in Paris between the wars. Gail, his English girlfriend, in her second year of literature at Cambridge, had joined Henri to fish the Pacific from Lincoln City in Oregon, and do some whale watching. Her youthful impudence did not avert his thoughts from Mariette, moving with grace around her soiree. His yearning intensified each time he caught her eye. Her peignoir trailed, revealing then concealing her elysian figure, embonpoint, crested with waves of lush black curls.

The circle decreased and, resolution approaching, he went to her observatory. It looked out towards the beach at Del Mar. The moonlight over the Pacific drew a line, neither a rule nor a wall – a meeting point where only people could cross without breaking anything. When they kissed, the lids closed over her deep brown eyes...as she lay beside him, the light gave tenebrism to her face and he wondered at its radiance.

*

Mariette sat at the edge of the bed where she placed a tray of toast and tea. She poured for both of them as she spoke softly: "Events moved quickly last night, Tom – from Sophie's description, I expected a well-groomed Englishman with good manners. You are all that, I can see. She did not say I should expect a man with feelings, and I don't just mean muscular." She laughed. "You are that as well." Tom became aroused as he listened.

"Come here," he said as he handled her to his side. "I want more of you, now."

They stroked and gripped, thighs between thighs, arms about shoulders, in a divine contortion, sighing, licking, feeling every point of pleasure. When she held his head in her thighs, tightening on his ears, arching from the small of her back to dig into his, she uttered, with her mother tongue, "Je t'adore, cherie. Je t'adore, je t'adore, Tom. Cherie, je t'adore," her orgasm reaching, reaching out, reached its climax, all the time his tongue working her clitoris, throbbing to a second, and then another, each release more intense. Her womanhood moistened its lips as she drew him to her consuming embrace, when their tongues exchanged an intimacy as they had done beneath the stars. As then, his loins spurred further by the taste of lust, craved fulfillment. His French woman wanted him in that way and, as she tasted his member, he opened her vulva, savouring her inner perfume. Her hand now firmly around his strength, she moved him in, then out, drawing blood through its veined length, thickening to its head. They shared the taste of him now as she turned about to face him, his hand and hers on the vigorous erection as it found her. She rode him on top, then he her, and every time she came, he came, each time reaching deeper. Their abandon occupied the morning, and continued throughout the afternoon. With fevered kisses, she held him to finish, as their tension spilled, the couple now limp on the daybed. Skin still touching, they slept, overlooked by Mariette's oil canvas, Centaur with Woman, a statement of her cynosure.

116

*

The phone rang, and Mariette took the call in the kitchen. It was the hospital. "She is going to be OK. Nadine is out of intensive care, and wide awake," Sophie told her friend.

"That's great news, Sophie. I don't know her but give her my love," she said with salutary generosity. "When will we see you?"

"Pablo has gone ahead to Del, so why don't we meet you there. You are coming for the match, aren't you? With Tom, I mean."

"Yes, I will tell him." She preferred to stay but Tom had to play, so she would go.

"Great. We'll see you at the hotel. Dinner at eight, OK. And hey, you like Tom?"

"I feel like the Queen of England, darling." More tea, more toast.

"What was that about the Queen?" Tom asked. They stayed in bed until five, then shared the wet room, joking and playing with each other, happy that Nadine would pull through. She washed him to his groin where her rinses once again aroused him.

"Steady, old girl. We'll miss dinner."

"I prefer hand food."

She wrapped her thighs about his rump. Standing, at attention, gave all he had in a taut, torrid exchange of muscle pulse and sweet surrender. The essence of this woman, upright on his erection, her back against the wall as he drove in hard, exuded from gap-mouthed moaning. That final thrust of humanity, spending, sighing, spent, she held on until she felt his time was done, for now.

*

A warm breeze filled the green Cutlass as he drove Mariette's classic '66 Oldsmobile south into San Diego County, with the hood rolled back. Through the quiet evening streets, the lull of pre-night balmed the lovers' respite. When they crossed the bay via the Coronado Bridge, its long S-shape took them to the peninsula, where sweet scents from perfumed gardens rose over wattled thickets, and through white pickets, the lazy smoke from BBQ beds lay across their lawns. Mariette's fragrance mingled in the still air, and he longed for the Ranch once more. He reached across the seat to find her shoulder, and she moved closer. They checked in to the Del Coronado Hotel, and were taken by buggy to their chalet, leaving the Cutlass with a valet. Joe had arranged a place for them to be alone. While Mariette used the bathroom, Tom lay on the king-sized bed, Joe's treat. He rested in thought while he waited. When a thing stops, the vacuum needs to be filled. So it had been with his English partner, nearly his wife, when she would not join him in Ireland, after seven years. He made busy with his new life and its regime of polo from March to September. All the time he believed she would come to him if she missed him too. When she did visit, once, in July, she turned down his proposal and left him, one last time, crestfallen. His immediate reaction? Nights in London, cricket at Lords, watching the British Open at Cowdray Park, The International at Guards. All helped shore up his failing will, but each only for their duration. He was smoking again, and drinking madly, falling down. A year without partnership, polo had been half the antidote to his desultory direction, and as his burgeoning desires intensified, sex would become the best substitute for love. Neither polo nor sex would be avocations any longer, as the dynamic of a triune developed into a triangle of desire. He lived for polo and he needed sex.

"How are your muscles?" she said, deshabille. What form she had. What a friend they both had in Sophie, who had recognised where kindred forces might work so well.

"Sweetheart, we're late. They'll be waiting for us." He rose to hug her and they held each other's heads to kiss. "Come on. We need to go."

Minutes later, they walked across the lawn. She wore a viridian silk dress, low cut behind, gathered loose at the edge of the flow of waves of her thick black curls. She carried her shoes to the path. The high-gloss Pigalle patents gave her three inches, when their eyes leveled. She linked with his arm in its white tuxedo, and thought how handsome he looked, and he her. Heads turned as they entered the Prince of Wales restaurant, through the hush some thinking 'goddess' as she graced the room, endimanché in 'Fuck Me' heels.

118

At dinner, they spoke of Nadine's accident. She had entered Rosso's box to wrap his legs with travel protectors when he lashed out. He had not kicked her head, as everyone first thought – her head hit the side of the timber cladding after a hind hoof struck her in the stomach. The initial shock dazed her, and she could not stand. The paramedics took her straight to A&E. It might have been a spleen injury, or some other organ damage. Her bloody mouth had come from a tongue-bite after the collision with the wall. There had been no internal haemorrhaging and all tests were negative. The hospital just wanted another day for observation, and her prognosis was good.

Sophie's account of Becky's report outlined the scene, as Tom's imagination filled in the gaps, the thud on the plywood as Nadine's winded body recoiled as she released her painful exhalation when the pony's toe had caught her solar plexus. Momentarily out cold, she could only have collapsed into the shavings as Rosso bolted through the yard. How many times she would have entered that box, to muck out, feed, or brush his roan coat, pick out his feet, that very foot which he had used on her. When she spoke of getting the better of this gelding, her only challenge in the string, her bravado had merely hidden the fear she felt when he first looked her in the eye.

"Thank God she's going to be OK. I told her to stay with us at the beach while she recovers – as long as it takes," Joe said.

"And Rosso?" Tom said.

"He's gone." Beneath the table Mariette's hand gripped Tom's for a moment, then let go.

"So we play here tomorrow – on the beach – ten o'clock. That suit?" Joe said.

"A bit early."

"It's too hot to play in the afternoon. We might play again in the evening."

"Four chukkas?"

"Only three. And they'll get a good break to cool off in the ocean," Joe said. Mariette took Sophie from the table and they walked outside, around the pool, chatting about Mariette's time with Tom.

"He is very attentive, in bed I mean. I think it was a Frenchman who told the world that the English are lousy lovers. He touches me with passion. He makes me happy, Sophie." Their arms around each other they walked on, Mariette humming, Sophie then thinking of her friend's difficult past. She had been brought up in a Parisian suburb, Ris-Orangis, by loving, professional parents. Their avid protection was breached by her uncle, when he violated Mariette, aged fourteen, beside the wall around the family garden. Years of therapy revealed little of a young girl's internal struggle with that memory of the wet spring morning when she sat at the foot of a wall, mortified in a fixed stare. It was nearly ten years before a man from Montreal relit any light in her eyes. Any emergence from her saturnine teens was short-lived however, when Jules Dubois dispelled all hope of her second chance. Three years of marriage to a bully and philanderer were no match for the psychological damage she had already endured, and she walked out. His attempted subjugation had strengthened an overdue resolve which launched her into independence, in every way that could mean. Her successful publishing business set her financially free. She lived alone, by choice, yet welcomed many houseguests, some long-term, though none outstayed their welcome. Dark places still drew her; her therapy, painting the Pacific, bringing it to her observatory, harnessing its void. Sophie had met her at an art class in Seattle when they both had issues to resolve, and their friendship grew over three years of shared marital breakdown.

"Have you fallen for him?"

"Falling – yes, for now. Fallen? I did that long ago."

Joe and Tom had moved outside the restaurant bar. Sundowners stood on the table, where they talked about Becky. Her only concern, while Nadine convalesced, was her replacement. Pablo, ever demanding, expected a high standard from his grooms, and Becky's opinion of the locals was that they were usually 'goof-offs'. Each player needed a groom for his ponies, and there was very little time to find one. They need not have concerned themselves, as Becky would always do her own thing.

*

She spent the evening with Conzuela and Marcello at the Ocean Bar, beside their motel. Eating nachos and calamari, they drank cold beer and watched the football game. The San Diego Chargers were playing the Tampa Bay Buccaneers at Qualcomm Stadium on the mainland and the bar erupted when the Chargers scored, or sank with despair when the Buccaneers touched down. The noise of the place forced many on to the street, and there Becky met Luis. The Costa Rican, with a mouthful of bright white teeth, long black hair, and a smooth mahogany complexion, could laugh for Latin America. When he finished with his laughter and their love-making, around dawn, he told her he had arrived ahead of his team, and the patron had pulled out, so he had time on his hands. Becky had presumed he played polo, and when he said "soy un novio," she did not understand and he clarified.

"Pedicero – how you say, groom."

Before he could say groom, she already understood 'pedicero', and that was it, a done deal: she had a full crew and a weekend lover.

*

At the hotel Tom returned to the chalet with his new interest, shoes removed on the lawn, his hands beneath the fall of her dress line to feel the small of her back, and beneath where it opened. The taste of her had lingered beyond the dining, as post-prandial promise lured them closer to their night feast. Barely over the threshold, their savouring impatience threatened a loss of control and there was much to be done. Premature climax might cut short the pleasures they anticipated throughout dinner, when he had fought back the rushes of nature with polite discourse, good food, and water, his only lapse from abstinence one small nightcap of brandy.

And then he stopped thinking, as a trail of clothes followed them to that massive bed. His fetish had tantalised him through the evening: her silk dress. He still did not know for sure if anything lay beneath it except for the warmth of her flesh and feel of her hair and the moistures, textures, purpled plicatures that wanted him about and between them now. The requited erotica that attracted them was symbiotic. They wanted the same thing. They wanted sex. Bent over their white playground she lifted her back with a firm push from her hands. Her legs followed, raising the roundness of her high action rump, launched now from those black heels up on the chalet floor. Definition enhanced the fleshy shape of strong thighs as he wondered at the fold of the join with her calves, and she poised on the balls of her feet. He stroked her ankles, licked her joins, stretching his hands around the rise of her thighs to tightened buttocks that now relaxed from the caress of his tongue as he divided them. He tasted afresh the sweetness of her intimacy, and she wanted him on her, in her. From the left side of the bed, her legs stiffened astride its corner, he mounted her. A silky frottage of contact sensitised every part of her he touched, his thighs against hers, and his right foot on the bed brought his calf to her cheek, his right hand at her hip, his left gathering the fall of her locks in a light grip, gently pulling back her head. He eased between her, and as the points of her heels dug into the rug, he raised his left foot to back his raven-haired mare, then from his amplexoid posture he kicked on with his heels and pointed in the saddle of her womanhood. They found resonance and she began to writhe and rear with his rhythm. When he changed leg, her left hand took the strain as he threw his weight into her right flank, impaling her to his hilt as he gripped her hips.

In the width of the window, he saw their bodies reflected as the moonlight moved with them, at one moment bathing them, then withdrawing them from its gaze. From light to dark the drama filled the stage as they rode with athletic equipoise. She spasmed with short breaths, pulled hard at the sheets as her thighs tensed on him, then again, and he continued his sthenic thrusting to his own surge of release. Still erect, he poured them water, and she wanted more. He stood at the bed where she leaned to take him. Her hand worked its head, tracing her tongue down the shaft to his sack, and mouthed her stallion's balls. She moved between them, rolling them, all the time masturbating the strength of his cock. His priapic pride throbbed to her touches, their nerves shared a currency of energy, on fire, as she slid the turgid member in and out swallowing its long swelling. There would be no return when she gripped his balls back between his thighs, drawing his glans with a suction so intense, fervently wanking him to ejaculate into the back of her throat. Still gripping his penis tightly she moved her hand rapidly up and down its length, releasing a spewing spasm of jism. They rolled free then, supine, spent.

*

"We're on in twenty minutes," Joe said when Tom picked up the phone. Beneath the hot bright sun, the ToJos (Joe Henderson, Tom Standing and Marcello Barolo) rode onto the sand to face Two Blonds and a Mexican. That was the name of the opposition – one blond from Germany, Renata (one goal); the other from France, Celine (one goal), and a four-goaler from Cancun. The ToJos wore pink, buttoned to the waist; the opposition wore white and gold, unbuttoned to the navel. *That's unfair.*

After three chukkas in the blazing heat, the ToJos conceded a 6 –3 defeat. When the ponies were stripped down, the players and grooms, in trunks and bikinis, rode them bareback into the warm Pacific surf. Mariette, already in the water, spilling her fecund curves from a tiny black bikini, waved to Tom, and he pushed his horse to her. He hoisted her aboard, her legs strode the strong shoulders of the black mount. "Like that, Tom. Just like that, darling. I live for this – my moment with my centaur." Their black hair flowed, back muscles moved through her thighs, beneath her groin. She felt her mount and man move as one behind her rump. They held an unclipped tuft as they all rode together, loins open, out of the spuming foam, their hooves sonorous sucking in the holes they made in the water. At the lines they left their black friend to turn for the chalet.

She wanted him as he smelt, horse sweat in their groins, on their thighs. They buried themselves in genital lust. "Fuck me, my stallion. Fuck me. Lay me out like a sacrifice. Fuck me till you're done with me." His fuck muscles on fire, he was ready to ride again. He thrust through her furrow, his nostrils flared from the perfume of steamy horseflesh, and she could taste him on the sheet from earlier.

His gyrating stretched her, and she wanted more, something else when he withdrew to offload a fecund volley over her breasts, and she again drew the gushed remnants from within her cheeks. This time she did not swallow, but lubricated her sphincter with it. She guided his erection into her muscle as its pulse at first resisted the intruder, then relaxed in sweet surrender, as she exhorted a puling sigh. "Yes, yes, Tom. Push - deeper, deeper, darling - fuck me hard right there". This new virility consumed him. He worked with her and as they relaxed, his involuntary lunges eased in and out of its passage. When he exploded, she collapsed. As his swelling subsided he relived the memory of an act so intense, so delicious, when he climaxed his thoughts washed from him as he was delivered to an elsewhere of surrender. They embraced in a loving kiss. If Mariette's liberation from taboo happened long before Tom's, they now shared in a tender bond. Beads of perspiration rolled from him as he left the bedside. He showered, and it continued to stream from his forehead. His vision blurred, he toweled himself.

"Mariette – I can't stop. Look – it's pouring from me."

She wrapped him in her own robe and found more towels. She filled a bucket with ice from the cabinet outside the chalet door. She cooled each foot, his neck, and his head. She talked with him until he had calmed. She monitored his pulse and closed the heavy drapes to darken the room, and lay beside him until it was time for the evening game. The second match began at six p.m. Much the same as the first – sandy with a beach ball, not quite as hot – and then cheered by the arrival of Nadine, yelling her support, bandaged but ambulant: "Vive Los ToJos!" Alas, too late as the chukka bell rang. Nadine, surrounded by her friends, had to be restrained from tending to the horses.

At this stage everybody was exhausted. Clerico provided the 'pick moi up' and they drank around wood fires beside the shore. They stayed on the beach for the BBQ and ate beneath a thatched shelter as dusk closed in. Mariette asked Tom if he followed F1 motor racing because she had a boyfriend she went with to Brazil to see the race in Rio. The boyfriend told her how he preferred the Interlagos circuit in São Paolo because of the final bend, called

124

Junção. He had told her how a driver had to get the power on early to maximise the ascent of its long rising curve, and when it reached the top it straightened out for the drivers to launch into a final surge at full power. Tom got the picture. *She's relentless.* At the chalet they sank into a Clerico cloud in the soixante-neuf position, to sleep ménage-a-deux.

Day three the ToJos made a fist of it, to avoid the wooden spoon, and came out winners against a sixty-year-old billionaire patron who could have bored for the entire Northern Hemisphere. What he did not know about was mostly what he talked about, and for a beginner he was on a mission. *Heard it all before.* These guys throw money at the game, no bad thing, but they are rarely the hardy perennials and their careers are usually short-lived, if only because of their age. The patron homed in on Mariette, but she went home with Tom. They had their own remit. When they returned to the ranch Tom had said goodbye to everyone as he was flying to Europe the following day.

The lovers drank wine, then lust, and love again beneath a night full of stars. In the morning they drove to Los Angeles. The warmth of a dry California breeze followed them to the check-in. She would miss him, but not yet. She lead him to the Ladies rest room and pushed the bolt of the cubicle. She stood on the lid of the bowl to help him upend her. Her thighs rested on his shoulders, her dress fell loosely to her face, he kissed the purple folds of her labia, rolling the bud of her clitoris between finger and thumb. His lips to hers, his tongue flicked the point of her sex. She gripped his hips to hoist her thighs further on to his shoulders, smothering him, all he could breathe was the essence of sex, and she tasted his virile thickness. He rotated her feet to the floor, where she held a hand grip to push against him with reverse thrust. As he reached quiver point, someone entered the next cubicle. Too late, he bit his finger, the pump of his heart, the flow of his ejaculation – all that moved in the convulsion. Then it was time to go. She pressed a small book in his hand when they kissed at the departure gate. On board he removed his jacket to hang it and pulled out the book to see her parting gift. A 'billet-doux' fell onto the tray before him. It read:

Tom my darling satyr,

Your vade mecum - to remember all that is known to you, and what is yet to come.

Grand bisous.

Love,
Your nymph Mariette, XXX

7

Florida

January, 1990

Whether it was wanderlust, an inability to settle, or a sense of 'carpe diem', after his post-Pakistan recovery, Tom slung a bag over his shoulder and took a departing look in the cheval glass in his bedroom in Virginia, said goodbye to his mother and drove to Dublin to take the midday flight to New York. He flew to JFK then shuttled to a motel beside La Guardia where he flew on to West Palm Beach, Florida, in the morning. He was fully functional and ready to play. On the first evening he left his room at the Beach Inn to find dinner down the street. A row of retail outlets gave onto a square with parasols above tables of diners. Not expecting to see familiar faces, he sat at an empty table to read the menu. He liked American food, and decided on a cheeseburger with all they could put in it, with a side order of onion rings, French fries and a small Waldorf salad. He ordered a pitcher of beer. He picked at the nachos left by his smiling waitress. He looked about him and the square, filling rapidly with diners, and anticipated a demand for the three further seats at his table. When he heard the Antipodean voice ask if they could join him, he looked up to see a face he knew from Sussex - Alan Flint, eight-goaler. They had never spoken.

"Feel free. It's Alan isn't it?"

"That's right. I know you don't I?" Flint said.

"From Cowdray. Tom Standing." They shook hands.

"Of course. You played with that maniac Henderson. The ToJos wasn't it? What are you doing here?"

"I'm starting the 'Polo Vision' clinic with Hugh Dawnay tomorrow. And you?"

"I was knocked out of the Open today, so off to the beach with my wife for a few days." Alan introduced Julie to Tom, and they sat for dinner. Friendly, the pretty blond did not sound like a Kiwi.

"I detect an Ulster accent," he said.

"People rarely get it, you know. Do you have connections over there?"

"Apart from my Mother. Oh, and I was born there."

"Where?"

"Portadown. Lived in the South of England all my life though. Now I'm living in the Republic."

"I'm from the North Antrim coast, near Ballycastle. Do you know it?"

"No. I left the North before I was a year old and I never made it north of Larne."

"Tom," Alan interrupted, "that's brilliant. Dawnay's Clinic. Everybody should do it. It should be compulsory. Too many people think because they can hit a ball and ride a bit, then they're good enough to play but most of them are dangerous, always causing accidents, people getting hurt, getting hurt themselves. Gotta be careful what I say, though – we professionals need their money. Anyway, did you do the clinic before?"

"No."

"Your mate. I saw him, here, just the other day. Are you not with him?"

"I'm here alone. But Joe, you mean Joe? Where did you see him?"

"Well I think it was him. He played piano one night, had a cute Latin girl with him."

"Do you know if he's still here?" Tom needed to know.

"No idea. Sorry, Tom. Tell me where I can contact you, if I see him."

"Here's my room extension number – I'm at the Beach Inn, round the corner."

"We're there too. So why now? The clinic I mean. You must be playing ten years."

"I'm going to Argentina straight from here, so I want to be sharp."

"Dawnay's clinic will set you up. But those Argies – watch yourself. Stay in the city, rent a car, and keep the key in your pocket.

They drove me out to the country and left me. I was marooned for God knows how long" Flint told him.

"What's the point in that?"

"Two reasons. One, they keep you to themselves so no-one else can find you – that's about horses and money of course. And secondly, it's just their bloody schadenfreude - they've always got to have the final joke, so watch your back. " Julie left them at the table when she saw a girlfriend arrive.

"All the same," Alan said, "I'm jealous. The girls are great – cheap, you know. They'll drive you wild and fuck your brains out. You ride all day, then ride all night."

"But seriously," Tom changed the subject, "I need to find out more about Joe. He went awol about two months ago, and everyone's really worried about him. His girlfriend's nearly out of her mind, and he has commitments. He's supposed to be on tour now."

"Wouldn't worry about him. He looked as happy as a pig in shit – that Latina babe was really hot. They came into a pole dancing club one night and she stripped to her waist – just gave it all she had, and she left with her knickers full of cash."

"Was he drinking?"

"Didn't notice. I'd say he's taken off with that little bird and headed for São Paolo or wherever she came from, to find some more like her. Lucky bugger, eh Tom?"

"If you say so."

"You'll love it down there, so don't begrudge him. He'll be fine. He'll turn up." Tom's anxiety increased as he thought of how Joe might turn up, and knew it could not end well.

*

When he arrived at the West Palm Beach Polo Club, arrows pointed to the field where Major Hugh Dawnay's Polo Vision Clinic was just beginning. Tom thought of the major as a friend at this stage. He had played in his home tournament at Whitfield Court, Waterford and it had been the Major's advice nearly a decade earlier that had really given meaning to what he was doing. For years he had scored goals from his finessed half-shots. Now he wanted to up his game. The first day he learnt how to turn attack from defense, using tail or open shots, to turn on subtle taps and pick up the new line himself, or make longer passing shots to the next player. He learnt to leave his backhand shot to let the next player move the ball onto the new line and he would be there to meet it. He began to understand the art of playmaking. And in the evening he took dinner with Hugh Dawnay, the Major.

"Good to see you, my boy. Come in and have a glass of wine." Relaxed, they spoke of Ireland and England, India, and Argentina. Hugh spoke about Cormick, who had worked for Eduardo Moore, some said the greatest ten-goal player ever. Tom told him of his conversation with Alan Flint. Cormick would look after him, the Major reassured. The following day the clinic moved onto tactics. They learnt about 'hitting in' using the 'Diamond' formation – the four players described the points of a diamond, which would contract into a straight line (four, three, two, one) when the ball was struck forward from the back line, cutting through the opposition. The 'Crushed Diamond' formation flattened the structure and this gave scope to tap and strike, not into the diamond but at an oblique angle, presenting number three with open space to clear the ball ahead, his number two then backing him up (four, two, three, one). Against an unsuspecting opposition these tactics would be devastating. The 'Diamonds' could be moved to any part of the field where a set play resumed a chukka. As Tom practiced with his group, the prospects of these new dynamics excited him. The combinations became more fluent with each attempt and the team engaged as a tighter unit. When their group played slow practice chukkas with another group, they played as a team, helping each other with clear calls, setting up their next move. They would shout "tail" before backing a shot around the rear of their ponies, or "open" when playing a cut, away from them. When Tom called "cola" the Major said "you're learning."

The clinic had begun for the 'teams' with the use of a rope which the four players, on foot, held equidistant along its length. Using short foot mallets they tapped the ball along the line and if the

130

ball skewed, perhaps pulled to the left, they would regroup, adjusting to the line which the player following would establish. It was crucial to turn, look, see what was happening, and the greatest tip of all would be to know where your number three was positioned at any moment, and where he was in relation to the left goal post. Why? Number three, the strongest member of a team, usually captain, would anticipate and read; and if numbers two and one, ahead of him, could link him to the goal, then they would be on target as he passed the ball, or called them to ride off opponents, clearing the way. And the left post? Well, a player must hold the mallet with his right hand, so the stick side of the pony created the best shots, tapping or otherwise - aiming towards the left you had the entire width of the goal as a target from your dominant side. "Simple" said the Major.

He explained how the trajectory of a shot could best be described by the shape of a wheel. The arc of the wheel should project the ball, when struck cleanly, in the same direction the wheel was turning at the moment of impact. He went on to say how the 'follow-through', a posthumous swing, would reduce the energy of the shot, allowing the mallet to once again settle back in the rest position, its weight balanced upright in the hand.

Tom did not dwell on how he might have avoided repeated mistakes and mishaps had he been more attentive in the past. He was heading for Argentina and hung on to every word of his insightful mentor.

8
Buenos Aires

Carlos Cormick waited in his rented Peugeot for the Aerolineas Argentinas flight from Rio de Janiero. Tapping his fingers on the dashboard he whistled through his teeth. Brendan Hannigan told him he met Tom Standing in Phoenix Park that summer, but he did not remember him on this temperate fall day, mid-February . Only when Tom walked out of Arrivals did he recognise the Englishman from the All Ireland clubhouse.

"Hola, Tommy."

"Hello. You must be Carlos."

Tom did not recall meeting this man with freckles and dark curly hair, ginger, wearing a check shirt, sucking and blowing through his teeth. On the drive from Jorge Newbery domestic airport, as he looked left towards the vast estuary of the River Plate, he perceived Cormick's countenance as neither warm nor cold — more matter of fact, controlled. Mid-whistle, Cormick asked "how's your Spanish?"

"I don't speak Spanish."

"You must speak some?"

Tom thought about it, for the first time since deciding to travel to Argentina. It had not occurred to him that language, or lack of it would present any difficulty, and Cormick's English was good.

"Si – there's a word. And non – yes and no. That's a start, OK?" Tom said.

"Don't worry. But no is no. Non is French." Cormick quietly blew the same indecipherable tune all the way into downtown BA. He pointed out the polo grounds as they drove through Palermo, where the Argentine Open is played in November.

"Is there much polo now?" Tom asked.

"The Opens are over, and in high summer the big tournaments are in Uruguay, Motivideo, Punta del Este across the river. Now we have country polo on the farms. If it rains we play at Zorro's." *Now*

132

there's a name. Cormick pulled into a filling station. "I only need enough to take this car to the rental garage." He put in one thousand Australs, according to the pump, and when Tom thought he had returned from paying, Cormick asked "do you have dollars? They only take US dollars."

"How many do you need?"

"Just two."

Tom gave him the money and they drove on. Cormick changed the Peugeot for a Renault Doce, for no particular reason it seemed to Tom. Of course, Cormick had planned that the new rental would be in Tom's name, as he would be benefiting from its use, whichever of them happened to be driving. Unfamiliar with the geography of Buenos Aires city and its province, Tom let Cormick take the wheel, and settled for a peripheral position in Cormick's daily schedule. This 'tour' of the city, the first time Cormick accompanied him there, did reveal its busy, brightly-coloured streets within its European structures of Parisian mansion blocks and Italian Renaissance styles. Its people, the snapshot this drive-through allowed him, exuded elegance with the overt vibrancy of youth. It was not the sun that warmed him now. He wanted more, he wanted to fit in. He wanted to be here.

"Do you live far from here Carlos?"

"Not far. Maybe half an hour." They left the city, and drove to Pilar, an hour north on the concrete Pan-Americano Highway. They had dinner in the town centre, a simple chicken salad with papas frittas. The café had no cellar, and was out of beer.

"Any chance of a drink?" Tom asked, as Cormick made the sign of the cross when he drove by St. Francis church. When they arrived at the Golfers Country Club, on the other side of town, night was closing in, and he could see little of this drab, sparsely inhabited gated community that lacked a gate. Cormick showed him his room – it had three bunk beds, beside it a wet room. Neither had windows. Although the single storey house had been empty when they arrived, a smell of humanity hung there, especially the bunk room. Tom sat at a communal table and watched a noisy tv chat show featuring a lot of gay screeching from transvestite celebrities. He opened the bottle of Johnny Walker he had brought from Miami. Cormick declined and placed a carafe of water on the table. When the show ended, he finished his second glass and decided to go to bed. Just then the door opened and five men in their early twenties burst in, making rapid and excited conversation, laughing in hispanic banter. They seemed friendly at first, though surprised to see him. Cormick spoke with them and they each introduced themselves then to Tom. He offered them whisky, and poured a third for himself. As noisily as they had entered they now departed, to their bunks. The remaining bunk was his. *A bit like school.*

After a period of inurement, confined in a bunk room of human gasses, he managed to sleep a while, with his head deep in a pillow. How he hated sleeping face down. If he was to suffocate he would rather not know about it. Meanwhile, Cormick slept soundly across the hall in a double bed, his window open to the cool night air. Early, around six o'clock, with a clatter of boots, buckles and belts, Cormick's 'gauchos' exited. Tom opened the door, and the front door, and left them open. When he dressed Cormick had gone out. The fridge had no milk, and he could not find tea, and the only bread he could find, stale. He ate some muesli, dry. *Too early for a drink, 11.15 a.m.* He took a ten-pace stroll around the uncut lawn, and saw a swimming pool through a bush. He pushed aside some branches to find the small pool empty apart from a mound of fallen leaves. Cormick had mentioned on the drive that he might fill the pool on account of his coming to stay. But then Cormick said a lot of things. When he arrived in the red Doce he had croissants and fresh coffee. A small bag of groceries contained milk, fruit and dulce de leche, the staple confection of Argentina. Tom found it too cloying for his palate, so he ate croissants, drank the coffee and took more muesli, with milk. *Just in time.*

"Today we can go to Hurlingham, if you like?" Cormick said.

"Yes. I would like that." Tom knew that Cormick meant the Hurlingham Club, celebrated for its clubhouse and English sporting facilities, including golf, tennis, cricket, and polo. What he did not know was the town that had grown around the club, influenced more by polo than any other sport, which had developed into a service centre of craftsmen. Bootmakers, saddlers, mallet makers, lined the main street, muddy in parts; the only thing missing were cowboys on horseback, a saloon, a stagecoach, and a few gunslingers. At city prices he passed on the Merlos saddles, a bit top-heavy at $400, but he ordered twenty mallets from Casa Villamil, and could not resist the double-skinned buffalo hide boots from Fagliano. Top quality, top price. The ten-goal Mexican Carlos Gracida had ordered a pair the week before, Senor Fagliano just happened to mention. He bought another pair to take away, hand-stitched from knee to toe with a floral design. He was hungry again. They lunched at the Hurlingham Club, where they ordered croque-monsieur, and drank Coke. Cormick had arranged chukkas at Zorro's for five o'clock, and he needed to go somewhere on the way. No time then for Tom to look around this old colonial house, no time for discovery of any possible ancestors. *Another time perhaps.*

Back at the Golfers the boys were in their bunks, taking siestas. Cormick gave them work and expected them to ride a lot of horses, maybe ten each every morning, and if there were chukkas, to organise the pony lines. These horsemen were more than grooms, most of them played, and might become professional, in Europe or the United States. Mostly, all Tom knew about them were the noises they made, and the odours they left. As they headed back to the yard, Juan Fernando arrived. Fair-haired and jolly, Juan carried a lot of weight, uncharacteristic within the equine community. They were all 'flaco', skinny. Juan Fernando was 'gordo', and he spoke English well.

"Come on Tommy, let's get a drink somewhere."

A short distance on the road from Golfers towards Pilar they stopped at a tack shop, Polo Plus. They looked at saddles, suede, hide, some with both, racks of mallets, from forty-eight to fifty-three inches in length, their heads painted, some blue, others red, or yellow, white, or simply varnished. Foot sticks hung diminutively above those of the adult game.

"You have sticks Tommy?"

"I need some. I ordered some from Villamil."

"Shuh!" Juan placed a finger to his lips.

"I need a whip, two sticks, fifty-ones, and I like the look of that helmet." He would be recognized by its turquoise. He had all he needed to go with his new boots, and he already had good knee pads from the UK.

Juan took the hat and said, "Unbelievabubble!"

"What?"

"Unbelievabubble! A great hat" he said again.

Tom smiled. He liked this guy. Juan Fernando Alvear played off three goals, and lived nearby on his brother's estancia, where they had an indoor arena for schooling. When even Zorro's ground was unplayable, chukkas might be played there. Juan told him there were two hundred polo grounds around Pilar but most of them out of use this late in the season. Horse deals mostly gave impetus to this pre-Winter period. They could play two or three-a-side at any time in the arena, and players came from all over to try the horses that he and his brother Luis bred and made for polo. "Luis, he play Los Etados Unidos and brings clients to try ponies. They like come for the Open and the chicas. You like, Tommy?"

"Sure, I like."

"You come BA with us tonight?"

"You bet." They left the tack shop and took the farm lane to Zorro's field. Ten players stood in a group at the end of the pony lines, some twenty animals in number. The field had the edge on so many of the others on account of its gradient. From goal to goal its incline of ten feet over a two hundred fifty-yard length gave it drainage. The leaf cover, mostly to the lower end of the field, would have been a challenge had Zorro not taken Cormick's advice to shorten the playing surface in favour of a longer run-off. If play was slower than they might have liked, it would be dry on this bright autumn evening.

"You play with me," Juan said. He looked forward to that. Cormick met them. He had Tom's boots and knee pads.

"Ah! You buy sticks from Polo Plus – good. I know them well." The shop, owned by Alfonso Pieres, a ten-goal player and brother of Gonzalo, himself a ten-goaler, may or may not have looked after Juan, or Cormick, when they brought customers, but

136

Tom did not care. This was their living and he understood that. To be in the company of one of the best players in the world, who with his brother had won the Argentine Open five times playing for La Espadana, was the greatest kickback he could have wanted. The brothers would go on to win again that year, with Carlos Gracida and Ernesto Trotz, both ten-goalers – the perfect forty-goal team.

Cormick walked Tom to the lines to show him his first ride. Blanca Flora stood calm, nonchalant at 14.3 hands, aged twelve. He mounted, then pulled her girth one last time, and adjusted his stirrups by two holes. "OK?" asked Cormick. He rode onto the giving ground and made circles, first one way, then the other. The little grey mare was responsive to his touch. He then stroked at a loose ball and made clean contact. If anything his fifty-one-inch mallet may have been a little long, and he moved his hand down its grip. He stroked another ball – better! As a practice game, they would not play under match conditions, without an umpire, and a 'hit-in'or from the spot would restart each play.

"Listo?" Juan called, then "Huego!" He cantered his chestnut from the bottom end and struck the ball, sending it up the left to fall before the halfway line, where his number two tapped on and sent the loft shot to goal. Tom had already placed Blanca Flora on a path from his number three player and the left post, when the ball landed ten yards before him, dead straight, on target – a sitter. One stroke, then one more did it. He slapped the little mare on the neck, and they turned to move back down the field. When Juan cried "Huego!" they were ready. This time he moved out to the right and the number three took it on. Tom adjusted his position on the post, and the ball came again, and he tapped it in once more. "Chukka!" He rode to the lines. Cormick took his pony, when he removed his helmet.

"Got a towel?" he asked. "It's hot out there."

"Sorry. Use your shirt." Cormick held La Luce, a chestnut mare with a white flash. Tom could only see that her hinds had white socks, her forelegs bandaged. She was small, also twelve. After his checklist, he turned her in circles and made as if to tap. She was biddable and agile, and she took him where he needed to be. Another sweet chukka, another two goals.

"Nice ponies," he told Cormick, who thought so too. "Who's our number three?"

"That's Rodrigo. Rodrigo Ruerda. He plays off seven. You are playing well together."

They were ready to go again and he remounted the grey mare. Still calm she gave him another good chukka, and when he finished his fourth, he dismounted La Luce, at least a kilo lighter. Rodrigo thanked him and they shook hands.

"What's your handicap, Tom?"

"I'm one from this season, in Europe. "

"You're better than that. Do you have a rating with the Association here?"

"No."

"You should do this. If they say you are one, then you are two in Europe"

"I don't want to move up too quick," Tom said.

"I know. But if you play one there, this year, then they move you up next year. So you'll be cheap this season. Do you have horses here?"

"I'm trying some with Carlos right now."

"These two?" he asked. Tom nodded. "You should take them. They are good with you. He has more, so try them. Anyway, you are coming to dinner with us this evening, so we'll talk then. Well done, I enjoyed playing together."

The horses were led from the field, some grooms riding with two either side of them. Following this phalanx of horse power, Cormick at the wheel, Tom caught a deplorable stench that whipped up through his open window.

"That's disgusting." A mound of organic detritus sat at the side of the road. "What is it?"

"From the hen house," he said. Tom saw the broiler house. Unhatched eggs had been dumped, and Cormick had never known who cleared the heap, apart from vermin. *From broiler house to bunk house.* "We have dinner with Rodrigo a few miles from here and then you go with Juan to BA."

Rodrigo had played in Europe and North America, and enjoyed both equally. They ate chicken, Tom had steak, with fries

138

and salad, washed down with a pitcher of Clerico. Their discussion moved from play to horses. Did many players in Ireland look for ponies from South America, Rodrigo wanted to know. He told Tom that Argentine ponies were not expensive and there were plenty of them. Did he have any he might try, Tom asked.

"I think Juan will be waiting back at the house for you so we should go," Cormick interrupted. When they arrived, Juan, Zorro, and Nico, who had played number two with him earlier, were leaning by Juan's car. As they hit the Pan-Americano it was the red rental that carried them to the centre of town, Nico at the wheel. Midnight began the bewitching hour, they told him as they passed beneath the motorway bridges where short-skirted hookers peddled their wares through wind-rushed blouses. They laughed – these were not ordinary streetwalkers, they were 'travestis', whose androgynous deviance relegated them to the outskirts – they were sex lepers.

"You see a girl, but is not a girl. Cuidate, Tommy," Zorro said.

"What do you mean?"

"Take care," Juan translated.

"They really do look like women," Tom said.

"They think they are," Juan said as he described a voluptuous female outline with his hands. "Like chicas, but with three legs," and they all laughed again.

"Zorro, thank you for the chukkas today. You have a great place," Tom said.

"Thank you Tommy. Tomorrow we have asado in my garden." Tom liked BBQ.

"Sounds great."

Nico parked the car outside Athos. Tom followed the other players through a cool breeze into his first nightclub in a city that woke at midnight. They all found second wind. Athos was a good place, they told him, and he would meet pretty girls. There were anterooms on either side of the hall and the bar was brightly lit and filled with large circular tables. They sat facing each other, drinking Fantas and Cokes. Girls sat at some of the tables and from the small bar one, a blond, young, pallid, and lips blood red, wearing a short white tight dress, came to theirs and slowly circled them. In turn they looked at her, then each other. *Would she* (and he glanced below her waist to check) *sit down?* Tom thought. *Should he invite her?*

"Momento," Zorro gestured. As she moved to sit at another table, a comely brunette began her tour of the table. Sex oozed from kissable lips and brooding eyes as she scanned and stripped each of them. That got things going. Zorro took her arm to sit her on his knee. She sat and whispered and he nodded approvingly. They made an attractive match. His boyish charm, more hispanic than latin, gave him the appeal an outsider might have. Tom hoped he might have it too, with one proviso – that he did not share Zorro's dental neglect. When his ravishing date, buried in his neck, could not see his mouth open, in that instant, Tom was shocked by his lack of teeth. What he saw were black stubs and gums, incongruous within so handsome a face. He could only guess what had caused the deterioration, and that there would be no kissing.

The blond returned and sat with Nico. His short dark hair contrasted with hers, and their ages compared, nineteen maybe, both of them 'muy flaco'. They laughed and smiled and touched each other with modesty, teasing, caring. They would be lovers soon. Tom looked up at a black girl. She wore a pink tulle suit, arabesque coin head band and gold mojari on her feet. Her mesomorphic contours were those of a belly dancer, and he offered her his knee. A clean mustiness descended around him, and he sensed the promise of an exotic encounter. Juan Fernando had his mind on a larger, red-haired lusty woman in her thirties, one hand somewhere on one of his legs, the other elsewhere. The party was complete, and they left. Zorro and Nico escorted their friends down the street, while Juan drove Tom and their girls to a motel he knew, not far from Athos.

In the dim light of their small tryst, they were gentle as they felt each others' arms, hers brown through her draped veil, his tanned, high-veined and muscular. The hold of the voile to her aroused nipples brought his hand to her breast. Beneath the warm flesh he felt the race of her heart, when they kissed, their lips at first pouting, then, apart, they licked their tongues, and their loins braced together. No more than twenty, he thought, this young woman made love with the tenderness he knew from past girlfriends. With them

140

he would have spent entire weekends, sharing intimacies, hidden, private, never discussed beyond the bedroom, for their memories alone. In this moment he was there again, savouring the thighs and fragrances of a young body. She did not rush, even as they lay in post-coital calm.

When Juan called from the front desk, he knew it was over, and they dressed. She did not return to Athos, and they dropped her near her apartment, where his night in Arabia ended. Driving to pick up the others, Juan asked him "What was she like?"

Reluctant to share the experience, he replied "she was beautiful."

"Maybe I try her next time." *Rissole.*

The boys were waiting on the street. In the car they became animated, talking more quickly than they had all evening. Not understanding them, Tom, within his own thoughts, did not get involved in their lurid exchange, swapping notes for future encounters. Zorro asked him if he had fun. When he said he had, Nico put his clenched fingers and thumb to his lips in approval. Their banter continued, and he was content not to participate. More excitement ensued when they passed beneath the motorway bridges, jeering and gesticulating. Tom wondered how their evening had been. At three o'clock in the morning the bunk house more rank than ever, he put his head down with his memory intact.

*

The next day he told Cormick he would buy the two mares, and asked him about moving out of the bunk room. Cormick told him he had more horses for him to try, and he had arranged a trip to the country for two nights. He hoped to do something about his accommodation while he was away. Then they drove to Luis Alvear's farm. Juan was riding in the arena when they arrived. Riding into the corner boards he schooled the pony to stop. As Tom looked from a viewing step, he saw Juan, leaning forward out of the saddle, standing, as the pony tried to scramble over the top, and he let him, even kicked him on until the pony gave up. When Cormick walked Marucha into the arena, Juan left.

"Your pony OK? " Tom asked.

"Si, si, bien, bien. Is OK now." Marucha, 14.3 hands, black, strong-boned and stocky, did all Tom asked of her, in the arena. She would be brought to Zorro's field that evening, and he would play her then. With bad weather forecast the chukkas had been brought forward to four o'clock, and they went directly to Zorro's, passing the growing poultry pile on the way. The daily accretion attracted swarms of flies, making Cormick wind up his window with his left hand, while his right held his nose. They hit a pothole, with a thump and a bang. *That had better not be a blow-out. This is the last bloody place I want to stop.* They drove on to the field and checked the wheels there. They were OK.

Players arrived from the city and outside provinces such as Entre Rios and Cordoba, hours away. Zorro's provided a horse-trading venue for players going to Europe to play the summer season there, and they would have order books to fill. From Chile Tom recognised Gabriel Donoso (nine goals). He remembered him from the British Open. Santiago Gaztambide (eight goals) turned up to play – selling, buying, both maybe. Tom remembered him for a fierce ride-off, when Gaztambide's pony's haunches welted him hard on the thigh. The dead leg lasted only minutes, the deep bruise for months. *What was that for? This is only a practice. Bastard.* Riding Marucha at the time he worried for her welfare too. Had the impact affected her? He rode her to Cormick, standing in the lines.

"She's OK. She looks sound," he told him. Until then Marucha had moved him over the field quicker than any of the others. From standing she took off with a surge of energy that launched her from a quick canter to a gallop before he could catch up. He slid off the back of the saddle onto her haunches. Her lack of withers gave lift to the saddle where his fingers gripped the pommel as he scrambled to recover. He had dropped his mallet. Nico put his own mallet's head through the loop of the grounded stick and returned it to him. Meanwhile Marucha had stopped as fast as she had taken off. *You're a flying machine, baby.* With stick in hand he assumed the position the clinic had taught him. The checklist: on the balls of his feet, pushing away, knees on, half seat, reins not tight, yet in touch with the bit, equidistant, whip to balance, mallet vertical, at rest. *Ready.*

In the next play Juan roared "Huego!" and sent the ball one hundred feet over the field to land close to sixty yards before the opposition goal. Marucha took off - it was Tom's for the taking. They overrode the ball. When he pulled up the little mare, she turned so fast he headed back to the ball, backed it to his open side to turn once more in attack, with time to spare. He scored.

"Bravo," some of them said. It had been a ninety-percent pony moment. He had been a mere passenger. When he dismounted, his leg ached. All the riders left the field and chukkas had finished. The ponies were taken away, back to the yard, and Cormick drove him to Zorro's house, beyond the line of trees at the top of the ground. They drank Coke, sitting on the unkempt lawn in front of the single storey dwelling of the phlegmatic roué, Zorro. Despite his toothless grin, his handsome countenance, financial independence, and own polo ground made him an attractive catch. Blanca must have thought so, although his insouciant lifestyle did nothing to placate her irascible nature. As the players enjoyed the evening sun, Blanca could be heard from within the house, responding to his supplications with voluble outcries. Cormick explained that Zorro's return from BA the previous evening, at around three a.m., wearing the fragrance of another, had vexed her, and the rest of them hoped they would get invitations to the forthcoming wedding.

Tom liked Zorro. He had suggested that he remove his boots after chukkas if they went into town. Polo boots might serve too much as a reminder to the less fortunate of the binary nature of Argentine society. Tom also recalled the only time until then he had driven his Doce into BA. Following Zorro into the centre, he ran a red light. Not wanting to lose him, Tom did the same. A police officer stepped into the road and flagged him over. Language being a problem, Zorro came back to help.

"He wants $200" Zorro said.

"Sure, and I know where that's going."

Zorro spoke again with the officer. "He says he'll take the car instead."

Tom dangled the keys towards the officer. "Tell him he's welcome to it." When the officer spoke again, Zorro told Tom he would be arrested if he did not pay.

"OK so long as I get a room of my own." He began searching the pockets of his jeans. He knew he had about $300, but when he eventually 'found' $20 the officer took it and warned him. "He'll eat well tonight."

They headed back to Golfers Country Club in Pilar, quiet as always, except for the sound of rain as it fell on the tin roof of the lean-to garage, the little house once again Tom's venue for a solitary evening of TV soaps and chat shows. The burgeoning austerity measures of Menem's government had subjected the majority of the country to a regime of penury and there would be more to come as increases in fuel and food prices were imminent, the ten o'clock news announced. Tom's dictionary helped, and a few drams of Mendoza malt. He went to bed before the stampede began, the storm still raging. Tomorrow he was going to Las Heras.

9

Las Heras

Cormick drove them to the University Law School in BA. His friend Estefan Dominguez met them at the foot of the Faculty steps. His sister Manuela joined them, when Cormick left. Her blond hair hung down the back of the seat, she rested her feet on the dash. Standing noticed her tanned thighs. They went to a friend's apartment in town. Matthias was coming with them. He offered them tea and they went inside. Matthias' brother, Guillermo, wearing fatigues, greeted them. He spoke some English and was interested to know Tom. When Tom saw the photograph of Guillermo in full battle dress carrying an automatic rifle as he stood before a large sign (*Las Malvinas son Argentinas*) he mentioned only his Irish background.

Matthias drove the dull red Peugeot to Hurlingham. They needed to collect tack from Merlos. Estefan drove on to the country, Las Heras, the studlands fifty miles northeast. The level land, mile after mile of pale grass, grazed by a million cows, stretched to a treeless horizon. Here and there, a solitary hawk watched from its catenary watchtower. Mapmakers must have struggled to find variety in such a monotonous landscape. The road, concrete, was hard on the car, and it succumbed to its unrelentng punishment; two punctures within as many miles. They carried two spares luckily, then crawled the last few miles. At the gates of the estancia, the recent storm had destroyed the clay avenue, a half mile long.

The boys left Tom and Manuela to get help from the farm. Manuela's English was good enough to discuss politics, polo, and places she knew in Europe. Her favourite, though, was Australia. The riding, like Argentina, was open. She had ridden for days and seen nobody except her boyfriend. She had been twice to the outback with her boyfriend. If he was going to share anything with her it would be the mosquitoes coming in through the driver's window. Humid conditions, the muddy lane steaming, produced a surfeit of rapacious bloodsuckers from its swamp. Tom shut tight the entry point. As they made for cover swatting, the creatures, driven by blood lust, persisted in their onslaught on the blond and Tom even more. His blood offered a novel foreign sweetness. One taste and the little devils were delirious. They killed maybe fifty of the tiny foe. An open bottle of Merlot, from Cordoba, attracted its own thirsty beggars. Where did they come from? Red wine always resurrected these minute midges to take a last drink.

Without signs of injury, they remained in the car, unventilated. Manuela did open her window, with a towel placed over the gap, but the humidity was as uncomfortable, airless, so she closed it again. When Estefan and Matthias returned, with a tractor, the steamed windows said nothing of what had happened during their absence. They amused themselves at what might have happened, though. Manuela was quick to put them straight, pointing to the smudges on the seats and dash, streaks of bloody entrails.

"Tommy, you are a gentleman, si?"

"Siempre. But that's all I'm telling you." They laughed, and the boys hauled them out of the sucking loam of the floodplain. By the time they reached the house (a large, ornate, timber chateau) the crunch of its graveled approach set to memory the earlier entomological encounter. They took their luggage from the car before it was towed clear to clean its airways. Estefan's mother greeted Tom in English and showed him to his room, large and high-ceilinged on the ground floor. Lucia had taught English in BA, and as a lover of horses had moved to her husband's family farm to rear foals. For forty years Manuel had run the stud, broken two-year-olds, ridden rodeo, and lived the life of a gaucho. Señor Dominguez would not have slept in the bunkhouse however. Over dinner Lucia translated for Manuel. Had Tom bought any horses? Three, he told them, from Cormick. She explained that their stock was young, not ready for play. They had more than one hundred and fifty foals and many more older horses at various levels of training, all broken, awaiting selection for different sports – rodeo, polo, show jumping – or they might remain on their farm or elsewhere to be used for rounding up cattle, cutting.

146

Lucia held his interest throughout cena (dinner) as she introduced words to him for the first time. Some he wrote down. She asked him if he would like more wine.

"Queras tomar algo?"

I'll have to remember that, he thought. When they finished eating, Lucia said that in the morning, 'mañana a la mañana', he would ride the farm with the others, and she bid him goodnight. He sat with Manuela, Estefan and Matthias, watching *Lawrence of Arabia* in Manuel's study, and they drank Merlot from a carafe. The film, in English with Spanish subtitles, was both welcome and instructive, unlike the popular shows he had watched in Pilar. The wine suited his palate better than the Mendoza grain. When the credits rolled Estefan showed him to his room where he lit a scented coil that would repel mosquitoes. A net also hung over the bed. He slept until dawn.

As he stood up from the bed, brushing the net aside, he could see the ash from the burnt coil. Looking at himself in his bathroom's mirror he saw large bites, red and purple, five or more. They throbbed to be touched and bled if they were. He did not shave, and could only rinse the night's residue from his face. As he dressed he noticed a second unused coil beside the table lamp at his bedside. Should he have lit that during the night? How could he do that if he was asleep? Lucia knocked at his door and said, "Desayuno." He opened the door and she was shocked at the pustules, one on his nose, another on his eyebrow, and three on one cheek. She lead him to the kitchen and, from a first-aid box, found unction to soothe the ugly swellings. She gave him a repellant to wear for the day, and an electric plate with tablets which would last the night.

The morning air fresh, still overcast, he followed Estefan to a coral with forty or more horses, where he told him to choose a mount. There would be no time to try any of them. Whatever he liked the look of would be his partner for the day ride. The first benign eye he saw, he selected, and a groom attached a leather head collar to the bay mare and led her to where a rug and saddle sat on the coral fence. A Pelham bit with single rein was fitted and cloth girth fastened the saddle. Estefan gave him a leg up. The mare was responsive through the seat and he moved his weight forward. Her mouth was sensitive to the bit; he would need to ride light. Estefan, Manuela and Mateo were joined by two grooms, Julio and Franco. The men wore black berets, except Tom. Manuela's blond hair lifted from her neck as they cantered the path into open countryside.

Tom's mare, still lively, gave him a sense of oneness as they followed the group. The men spoke quickly in Spanish, laughing with familiar laughter. These friends had shared many equine experiences, growing up in families that had done the same before them, for generations. The Dominguez' estancia had one hundred and fifty thousand hectares, a vast tract of Buenos Aires Province, split between cattle breeding mostly, separate from the family-run stud. Julio and Franco worked the stud as their brothers and their fathers before them. Tom envied more the weekend 'gaucho' lifestyle, but he admired the dexterous handling of the grooms, checking their horses mouths and teeth, fitting shoes, pulling tails, fitting bridles with gentle assertion. The healthy condition of the ponies reflected more than diet; they were well tended.

The jacaranda avenues had lost their bright summer colours, the acacia more brown than green, the thickening pile of the fall floor covering crinkled as the sun dried it. They stayed mainly to the pathways through this vast farm, flat, little grazed for the first two hours, the sun on their backs. Preoccupied earlier with the insects of the night, now far from his thoughts, a sense of mission narrowed within the tree cover as the six riders, some seated, some, like him, forward in their saddles, cantered over leaves and twigs with a tamping timbre. A susurration of disturbed dead wood harmonised with a growing syncopation now, as they turned to see foals following.

"Have they come from the yard?" Tom looked at Manuela.

"Yes. They are beautiful. They will stay with us all day."

There must have been ten or more young ones, as they rode alongside, intermingling with the bigger horses. As if there was a spirit common to all, they rode on out of the woods onto the plain, the horizon ever distant. For the next hour they passed just one house, timber, painted pale blue with veranda and a tidy lawn. "This is the house of Carlos Basualdo. He is a friend. We will see him on the way back," Estefan told him. When they stopped at a dry copse, they dismounted and removed the tack from their ponies. They let them roam freely, with their foals at foot when they went to a narrow stream to drink.

Julio took a haversack from his back, and began to gather small twigs into a pile with leaves, which he lit with matches. The heat rippled from the flames, beneath the shelter of a small jacaranda tree. From his bag he pulled a flat, round steel plate, about eight inches in diameter, and placed it on the burning wood. He handed dust to the edge of the plate to stop flames licking up onto it. Then he placed three sirloin steaks on its surface. The sizzle split the quiet in their lunch place. Franco had bread sticks, plastic plates and goblets, and the picnic was set. He opened a bottle of Merlot, and they shared the pale Pampas beef, their 'asado'. Tom lay on his saddle rug beneath the branches, basking in the midday warmth. He heard only the foraging of the horses. Manuela stood over him when they had finished their 'siesta'.

"Now we go to see Carlos."

They tacked their horses and remounted. He had not experienced such tranquil animals, but they did not yet know the rigours of a sporting life. They walked a while, then cantered the track to the house they had passed. Carlos stood in his garden to greet them, and they hung their reins over his fence, slackened their horses girths and brought them water in buckets. Carlos had played high-goal polo in Europe, but it was in the Argentine Open, five years earlier, that his horse fell and rolled over him, breaking his arm. Worse, his concussion hospitalised him for six months. He had an eight-goal handicap at that time, and rising. He retired, aged twenty-two. Tall, dark haired, his blue eyes were denied the gaze of a champion, and any further admirers, but he was happy living in provincial solitude with his French wife Marie-Rose, and their three-year-old son Bruno. Marie-Rose invited them for tea, and they sat in her garden, bordered with late blooming roses and rhododendrons. Carlos kept some horses for Bruno to ride in time, and to one side of the lawn a manicured playing field was prepared. He would still 'taqueo' (stick and ball) or play if his brothers or friends visited. Tom could see Bruno holding one of his father's mallets. He handed him a foot mallet, but that had no interest for the blond-haired boy. He swung at balls here and there on the lawn in scythe strokes. When he made contact he yelled out. Tom remembered the first time he had that feeling, when was thirty. Bruno was hooked at three.

His mother brought a pony from its stable, a placid palomino with a child's suede saddle. Carlos lifted little Bruno onto the horse and his mother held him by his left leg with her right hand. She held the pony with the reins in her left hand, and they moved slowly forward. Carlos lit a joint and the men smoked as they watched Marie-Rose lead the horse around the perimeter of the field, Bruno barely astride it. He had not let go of the long mallet, and began to swing at a ball his mother had thrown down. He used both hands to gain momentum with his stroke, and when he hit the ball his excitement made everybody clap. He hit it again, further, and wanted more. "Rapido, Mama! Muy rapido." She held him tighter still when he leaned out of the saddle to hit a ball under the neck of the pony. He hit the ball at least a dozen times before his daily lesson finished. When he toddled over to the lawn, he lay in the sun and slept, both his hands around the stick. *So that's how they have so many ten goal players.* Marie-Rose grew apples, pears and olives, and when the band had remounted, they moved to the track, with foals in tow, and Julio and Franco's packs hung heavy on their backs.

When they cantered the dust swirled up as they disappeared. To their right a lake reflected the sun, and silhouettes of animals moved around its edge. As they rode closer the capybaras continued to graze on semi-submerged shoots the lake offered. The creatures' nonchalance captured the serenity of the late afternoon. It was a mile beyond the lake that Tom looked down and saw his jeans were covered in mosquitoes. He brushed them away, leaving smears of blood on his hand. The insects had injected their proboscises through the thick denim into his flesh, sucking while he rode. Flies swarmed about his blooded legs as he fought them off with his whip. His horse, used to the flies, did not alter from the homeward course, unfazed. The gate to the coral open, they rode inside, with the foals,

150

removed their tack, and thanked Julio and Franco. They left the fruit with them, taking some of the olives for Lucia. Tom made for his bathroom.

The swelling on his legs seemed more superficial and did not itch the way his face still did. It was his back that concerned him more. Not feeling their injections at the time, he could not have known how many must have covered his shirt as they feasted through the thin cotton. From his shoulders to his waist were countless reddening mounds, some erupting, others with secondary bites upon them. His back was a mass of ugly festering. When Lucia came to him, she scolded him for not applying the repellant.

"I did, but not under my clothes" he said.

"You have the sweet skin of a gringo," she told him, applying ointment everywhere she saw a vile growth. "Your blood is the best they have ever tasted." No comfort in that he thought.

"Bloody vampires."

"Estefan is leaving for the City, soon. You should stay and I will treat these things. Who will help you in Pilar?" Lucia said. *Who indeed*, he thought. "Tomorrow Manuela drives back in her car. You can go with her."

"OK, Lucia. I'll do that." He drank water with dinner, avoiding anything sweet, eating dry bread, and no fruit, and definitely no dulce de leche. Manuela told her mother about their ride with the foals, and their picnic, and then Bruno. Carlos hoped that Bruno might one day go on from where he had stopped, Lucia told them, to continue the Basualdo dynasty. She and Marie-Rose had become good friends, and she loved her olives. After dinner they bathed Tom's back, and he cleaned his legs one more time. They applied copious amounts of cream from tubes and jars and wrapped him with a loose covering of cotton towels. They put him to bed, tucking in the net at all corners. Manuela plugged in the repellant and placed a tablet on its plate.

"This will stay on the whole night," she said. Lucia lit two coils to fill the roof space. She took the whisky glass from him, his nightcap, which held him until he slept.

"There, Tom. You will sleep well tonight. Buenas noches."

Manuela drove through the grasslands of Las Heras with more care than Estefan, and they did not have to stop, although he wanted to. Would he be rejected if he placed his arm on her shoulder? Maybe she felt the same way. The evening before she had soothed his wounds, at his bedside, and it had been difficult to tell if her care had been entirely medicinal, but he would have liked it to have been more. He stroked the nape of her neck, and she warmed to him, but she did not pull over.

"Sorry" he said.

"Me gusta mucho." He ran his fingers through her golden hair. She moved to his hand, then said "para Manuela. Stop, Tom! I have my boyfriend. He is in Buenos Aires. He is waiting. I cannot, with you."

Tom opened his window and sighed. He understood. "Entendo," he said. At the end of the Pan-Americano, she drove through the leafy suburb that gave onto a wide avenue. "Where do you want to go?" she asked. Here, he thought, then reached for his wallet.

"I have to make a phone call." They stopped beside a café on a tree-lined sidewalk.

People were having lunch in the sunshine as they asked to use the phone. Manuela dialed the number he had written on a napkin. One corner of it read *Santa Barbara Polo Club*. As she pressed the last number she said, "This is near here, this number." When somebody picked up at the other end, she asked Tom who he wanted to speak with.

He told her "Marcello." The Barolo family apartment was a short walk from the café. Tom said he hoped he would see Manuela again after kissing her goodbye. Marcello met him on the street. They shook hands and held shoulders.

"Is good see you Tommy. Why you no call me before?"

"It's a long story, Marcello" he said.

They stepped up from the paving through a plate-glass double doorway. Marcello held one door open by its palm-sized brass knob. He introduced him to the concierge, Fernando, so he would know him at any time thereafter. They took the lift to the fourth floor.

"Conzuela? Is she here?" Tom asked.

"No. She in Mexico with her family. She go there in January, after California. But she coming here soon. What you been doing in Argentina?"

"Did you meet a guy called Cormick, Carlos Cormick, from Pilar?"

"No. I don't know him," Marcello said.

"I've been staying with him. Somebody in Dublin arranged it. We play chukkas most days, and I'm getting really fit."

"Come, meet my family."

They walked from the vestibule into a drawing room which overlooked the main street through Recoleta, Avenida Alvear. Marcello introduced his mother Julia. Her fair hair curled about her pallid complexion, her light blue eyes smiled an apology that had lost the hope of youth for some time. He hoped she liked him. Marcello's father, Lalo, probably responsible for Julia's demure retreat, exuded the enthusiasm of a salesman. His dark features, woven eyebrows hung like lynchets over lively penetrating glares, gray highlighting the thick waves of his black hair. In his late fifties, he was in good shape. His English was more Malaprop than poor, and when he told Tom that he had been at the 'stocking change' that morning, soon to be followed with a proposition that the two of them should go to Montevideo, pronounced 'Monty' and 'video' as in videotape, the visitor understood that they might be going to try on nylons at a video shop, or something. *Unbelievabubble.*

Marcello's brother Eduardo heard his father.

"It's OK, Tommy. He means Merill Lynch. He spends some mornings looking at the stock market in their offices on California Street." Lalo liked to go to Uruguay as he was not so well known there as in Recoleta. He could play out his fantasies anew, with greater success, in a town he rarely visited, and Tom would make a perfect front. All this before we've even broken bread, Tom thought. They went through to eat. A place had been set for him beside Lalo, where the erstwhile boulevardier of Recoleta continued to make references, sotto voce, to 'stockings' and 'changes' and 'Montyvideo' and "vos y mi" - you and me. Lalo had a new mate and he would have to come to 'Wallwhychoo' to stay at the estancia. Tom liked Lalo's thinking. He knew he had to extricate himself from Pilar, post haste. How though? He had horses now, and equipment, all with Cormick. And a car.

In the afternoon he talked with Marcello about a strategy to get him into the city finally. Marcello said he should get the car so that he would be able to return to Pilar to play the chukkas. There were none in the city, and when they finished, and he returned to Europe, he could leave his ponies with Marcello on the farm. Marcello showed him an apart-hotel on Parera, a side street opposite the Barolo apartment. He looked at a room with shower, foldaway kitchenette, dining area, TV, and a matrimonial bed. From the window, he looked out to see single, pretty girls strolling in the sunshine.

"OK, Marcello. Ask them to reserve a room for me for twenty-four hours, maybe forty-eight."

"It's not a problem. Now is winter. They have rooms." Marcello wanted to show him the parks and street life of the district, but the prospect of living there had excited him so much, he could not bear the disappointment of something going wrong now.

"Take me to Pilar, Marcello. I've got to get out of there."

They drove up the Pan-Americano, Marcello pointed to the Tortuguitas Country Club. He told him they play an 'alto-goal' (high-goal) tournament there before the 'Open' (Abierto) at Palermo in BA.

"You must come, Tommy. It's the best in the World. 40-goal polo. Is fantastico."

His car was not there when they arrived at Golfers. Inside, Marcello, offended by an acrid aroma and lack of facilities, wondered how his friend could have found himself here.

"This place is shit, Tommy. You must leave now, with me."

"No, Marcello. I have to end this properly. Remember, he has my horses, and that bloody car."

"Do it – then BA. Rapido, Tommy. BA is waiting." The thought tightened the desire within him to break out.

"There is no phone here. I will arrive when I arrive. Is that OK?"

"No hay problema, Tommy. Cuidate."

They shook hands and when Marcello left a sense of abandonment gripped him. *Stay calm, keep busy, stay calm.* He took a shower, mindful of the many bites still on his back and face, the run of the water over them freshening and cooling. Cleansed, he picked up his towel to dry. When he put it to his face, the miasmic odour shocked his nose, and he could see the stain of excrement scraped into the fibres of the colourful beach towel. *Some bastard's wiped his fucking arse on my towel.* Incandescent, he screamed.

"You shits! You bloody shits! Where's my bloody car? Get me out of this fucking hole."

When he dressed, he walked around the road of the country club. Then he could see that Cormick's must be nearly the only one occupied. He walked back towards the small house, and could see Cormick at the front door. He was carrying things he had unloaded from the car. Tom sheltered from sight behind a shrub. Cormick turned on the lights of the house and could not have known that Tom had returned. Tom waited and moved to the wall outside the bathroom. The wall was thin and he could hear the shower, then he heard Cormick whistling. *Not so stealthy now, you fucker.* Tom crept in and through to the bunk room. He gathered all he had, and when he looked into Cormick's room he saw the car keys on his bedside table. He grabbed them.

For the first time, he turned on the ignition, then the lights, and decamped, without regret, from the bad hours, those solitary evenings of watching local TV channels, and painful swallows of gut-rot whisky from Mendoza. Passing the empty municipal buildings, he noticed lights inside, mindful of Cormick's remarks about the extravagance of administrators, able to flagrantly waste resources, when the community was subject to overbearing austerity measures and penury. He would say this every evening, returning from chukkas, while signing the crucifix beneath the entrance to the church of St. Francis.

Inflation was running at twelve-hundred percent. Tom had seen women, with young children, returning basics from supermarket baskets, when price rises of twenty percent were announced over the Tannoy, across the board, with immediate effect. They had sat in a half-mile tailback one time queuing for gas, prompted by a government-declared increase in pump prices, thirty percent from midnight. The petrol gauge showed half a tank. *Thank God.* Everyone was in need, hungry for something. Crime had soared, and corruption was rife. The worst offenders? The police. He needed to break out, realise his wanderlust for the city, Buenos Aires.

He turned right at the Pan-Americano, an ambitious concrete freeway intended to reach from Tijuana to Tierra del Fuego. The fortunes of such a project, subject to the protean nature of a continent devoid of federacy, was reflected in its state of disrepair as well as, up-country, its abrupt stoppages, where road and money just ran out. Its uneven sections, ridged and fallen, from edge to edge, pocked with potholes so large the tiny French car made crashed landings on entry and crunched collisions on exit. Concerned as he was with punctures and broken wheels, it was looming shadows of mobile megaliths in the shape of carcass-laden Frigorificos, and cumbersome trailered horse lorries, heading for the European meat boats, that began to box him in, the three-lane option reduced to the confines of a gauntlet. For twenty miles, within its corridor, the convoy beat the approach; all he could do was hang on and trust his Doce not to break apart. Blow after blow hit his seat, his spine absorbing the after-shocks, repeatedly ejecting him into the roof. *Just keep it level, boy, keep it straight. Hold on. Hold on, little one.* He needed to open the window. The smell of oil, the overheating gearbox beside his right leg, turned the aroma of tack leather from new saddles, bridles, boots, to a cloying clot, stifling the cabin air. He held the steering wheel with both hands and, in pain, he gripped harder. No respite. The charge continued to carry him and his wheels for a further hour. Lights dawning in the distance, he caught sight of the city exit sign. Before it disappeared beneath the leading truck, he read it.

Buenos Aires
Centro de la Ciudad

Made it. At bloody last. Well, nearly. He pushed down his indicator. Would they let him in? He waited, longer, how much longer? He'd miss his turn. *Come on, come on.* The trailing truck eased back, lights flashing. He pulled across the lane, straight down the exit road. *Jeez! That was too damn close.* Their farewell, a cacophony of claxons, his fanfare. Maybe they had his interests at heart. Maybe this was acknowledgement for the sport he had given them? *More latino schadenfreude.* The channel through the parkland of the city limit, a braking zone of choking chicanes interfaced the power drive with the truckers from the tranquil gaucho hinterlands and the throbbing center of a sleepless city.

Out through the trees, Avenida Libertador presented a thirteen-lane tarmac option. Window down, he heard birdsong, circadian fricatives, caught glimpses of fading bloom, coxcombs, and felt a rush of zest from a cool breeze. The freedom he quested after on the struggle down survival alleyway now fell on him and his battered automobile. They both took in the air, easing towards the traffic lights. He threw his hands through his hair, and wiped his brow, blood beating hard in his temple. The short time it took for the lights to change was enough to form a serried line of autos, mostly black and yellow cabs, either side of him, engines revving, clutches riding. On green, an enfilade of missiles was launched across the start line, and they all roared the distance to the next phase, a two-lane pipe into the first barrio. After the frustration of the Pan-Americano, he now expressed his own kind of aggression. He hit the floor, valves crashing at the top of each gear. God knows where he was going; he just had to get there first. He did, twelve 'Fangios' trailing in his slipstream, charging down the throat of Recoleta. At the end of its drag, Libertador slowed to a street of cafés and evening promenaders. Tom Standing had found equilibrium with the city's pace, now he was cruising to the promise of its pulse.

10
B.A.

The disdainful countenance of the aging courtesans seated by the boulevard hinted at what lay behind the Parisian architecture of Buenos Aires' prestigious residential district; a trompe l'oeil pastiched these dames, cruelly sneering, as twisted monsters. If the vignette retracted them into a blockhouse of lost youth or broken hearts, their resolve was most typified by subtle flickers from inertia in manual mannerisms. Hands drawn across upper lips underlined desultory gazes, followed with dismissive strokes by the back of the hand from the neck through the chin line, closing with a raised roll of the eyes, put distance between them and any admirers. Not inelegant, the ladies of Recoleta would not be seen in the barrios where they would not be seen. Maybe their time was up, and the most they could manage was to out-look their competition as the sun went down on their cocktails. They were not what he was looking for, he thought as he crawled Avenida Alvear to meet his friends.

At the desk of the Alvear apartments was a younger man than Fernando who called the Barolos, and when he pointed to the lift, Tom went straight up. They had dined with some English guests, who had been trekking in Patagonia. The two men, both former Guards officers, saddlesore from long days on the trail, declined Marcello's invitation to go clubbing. "Can't dance even when I have legs," said one. *Who said anything about dancing?* The other man Tom recognised, and asked him if he played polo. He did, and he remembered a match against the ToJos on Smith's Lawn, Windsor, two seasons earlier.

"That musician maniac here with you?" he asked Tom.

"Yes, Tom. I see him two weeks ago. He was here, in Recoleta. He say me, he stay the Alvear Palace Hotel," Marcello said.

"Why didn't you tell me, Marcello? He disappeared months ago. The last I heard he was in Florida with a girl," Tom said. "Where's the hotel?"

"He no there. I look him, but he gone. I don't know where."

Another trail, no sooner mentioned than cold. When the English left for their hotel, Marcello, Eduardo, Lalo, and Tom went to the street for a stroll and a nightcap. He would stay with them that night and move into the 'apart' in the morning. The night was cooling quickly when Lalo sat outside behind a shrub in a blue flower box. He ordered two Cokes for his sons, and two Americanos. Tom did not remember drinking Campari before, but this drink with soda refreshed him with its rush of bitter effervescence. The boys saw a friend two tables away and went to talk. When Lalo saw a friend, she came over and they kissed on the cheeks. He introduced her as a family friend, and when she left, he said "diosa". Tom pulled out his dictionary. "Goddess". Two younger women then caught Lalo's attention. "Mira, mira!" he muttered. Tom looked at them, and as much as they tried to conceal the attention they attracted, their modesty capitulated to laughter. This Tom wanted.

Lalo placed a hand on his arm. "Tranquilo, Tommy."

Eduardo came back to the table and Lalo left with him. When Marcello said, "Now we go le club," something in his manner told Tom this would be the main event. 'Le Club' on the corner of Parera and Quintana, would be less than a minute from the 'apart'. Behind a black door the dimly-lit entrance, manned by two tall bouncers in tuxedos, had its cloakroom to the right. A girl with long brunette hair, dressed in black and white, showed them through a curtain where they stepped down to a bar on the right. Two barmen worked the intimate atmosphere of the small bar which had one stool to the left, where it met the wall. Entrance had been free, and Tom thought it might be expensive to get out, if it was anything like a French club, which its name suggested. He asked Marcello what he would like to drink, and he told him, "Café is libre." - it was free.

"Dos cafés por favor" Tom said. They laughed and Marcello introduced Jorge, their barman, in a black waistcoat and tie. "Sometimes give him tip, you know, gratuity. He look after you." A group of girls now stood at either side of them. They were friendly and polite and did not expect drinks. He noticed that girls drank very

159

little alcohol in Argentina. If two glasses of red wine with the Barolos and one Americano had made much of a difference to the evening, their effects were behind him. Something else held him now as he sensed a growing attention from the girls at the bar. Glances and smiles competed for response, and one girl held his arm, not to restrain him as Lalo had done. He looked to Marcello and asked, in a whisper, "putas?" Marcello shrugged in that Latino way, lifting his shoulders, opening his hands, with his mouth dropped.

"Maybe." If Marcello didn't know, how could Tom? Marcello knew all the staff, he must know how things worked. "Most si, but not all."

The girl at his side looked Italian, or Greek. Her brunette hair hung down her back. She was not 'flaco', nor was she 'gordo'. There was only one way to find out, he decided.

"Cuente?" he asked.

'Libre' she told him, but he would need to pay for a hotel. He forgot about feeling wretched and gauche when she asked him if he was American. He told her he came from Ireland, and she thought he said Holland, and told him she could speak some English, but not Dutch. We'll speak English then, he decided.

"What time should I return to your home?" he asked Marcello.

"Is OK. Stay with her and I see you tomorrow."

"But your parents? It's very rude."

"My mother expects it, and my father is jealous. They like you, Irish!" They laughed.

Tom's global landscape was expanding by the hour, from exile in Pilar to Dutch, Irish, American, with a Porteno woman who looked liked Nana Mouskouri. The couple took a cab out of Recoleta to immerse themselves in each other's flesh until dawn, when they slept and woke to want more – and they did, until she needed to go to work. She lived in Recoleta with her elderly parents and young sister. They were strict Catholics, but she had her needs, and she chose him. Her unashamed admission seemed to complete the release she sought so rapaciously when they met. He did not speak of his needs. They were the same, prurient, riggish, and he liked her for her honesty. She worked in the financial district around Calle

Florida, and they caught a bus. When he recognised Avenida Alvear, he squeezed her hand and kissed her on the cheek, said "Ciao" and stepped down to the paved street. He looked back. She did not.

"Buenos dias, Fernando."

The concierge acknowledged Tom with a "señor" as he took the lift. It opened directly onto the hallway of the Barolo apartment where Eduardo read a morning paper.

"Good morning, Tommy. Have you had breakfast? Come, there are croissants and coffee in the kitchen. And how was Sophia Loren?"

Tom shook his head and tutted. *Marcello and his big mouth.*

"Que tal? Como lo va Tommy?" Marcello greeted him. "Sophia is muy hermosa – beautiful, si? What her name?" Tom did not know, and quickly made one up. Carolina.

"Pretty name."

"How is your mother? I feel guilty about last night."

"It's fine," Eduardo said. "She understands. Marcello told her about Pilar. She is out now, with her sister for the day. Lalo has gone to Florida – you know, the 'stocking change' – he wants to meet us for lunch. Tom showered and could shave over the swellings on his face. The sap had gone from them as they dulled and flattened. He flannelled his back and washed the shampoo from his hair to rinse the suds from the remaining lumps. They too had settled. He wore a clean polo shirt, blue, inside a pair of pressed chinos, moccasins, with a white sweater tied loosely around his neck. Then he checked into the Apart Callao. Clean sheets and towels on the honeymoon bed, warm running water, a TV with thirty channels, a telephone, and an open window. It felt like home.

They talked of Gualyguychui as they walked to Lalo's office. The Barolos spent much of their youth growing up on the family estate. Then they had half a million hectares, grazed by half a million head of cattle, and a few thousand horses. The boys learnt to ride with their father and the gauchos who lived on the farm. Some might job from farm to farm, others settled to raise families, and they had built houses from timber and brick, and corals for livestock and kept horses for rodeo, their 'diversion'. They lived off the land and shared mate through copper straws from the wooden bowl of a hand pot. For the brothers it had always been hard to leave for the city, their education – the pull of mackerel twilights and eating beef from the herd having drawn them again into that simple world of childhood. The more they learned, the more their hearts wanted to return there. They would be going there at the weekend, and he must join them, as he knew he would.

Lalo sat behind a partner's desk, his back to the wall, two telephones for company. The office was poorly lit, by sunlight from a high window. He appeared to be doing nothing, yet anxiously tapped his fingers on the desktop. Maybe he had been waiting for a call, or a caller, and had forgotten their rendezvous. He stood up, distracted as though he had been caught out, and lead them all out onto Florida. They walked the short distance to the offices of Merrill Lynch, the Wall Street brokerage where he would get his prices. *So this is where he changes his stockings.* Marcello introduced Tom to a young broker. He only heard his family name, Merlos, and it was later that afternoon, when they watched a match on the infield at the Hippodrome Race Track, that Marcello reminded him of the Merlos he met at Merrill Lynch: Pite, nine goals.

Lalo's fortunes had contracted throughout his life as he sold large tracts of his inheritance to support the family. The only way for them to cling to a fading childhood had been his offloading, until then, pieces large enough for towns to be built and, with little background in finance, he entered the investment world. Tom knew that world, as he knew the look on Lalo's face when his confidant told him he had taken a hit on a line of stock he had been placed in the previous day. He did not say how much, but Tom guessed it had been substantial. Lalo excused himself and the three of them went to the San Isidro Country Club on the northern outskirts of the City. Green, well-kept lawns, tennis courts, and an eighteen-hole golf course surrounded the Tudor-style clubhouse. They ate ham and cheese toasted sandwiches.

"I know these – jamon y queso."

"Hey Tommy. Your Spanish is good now" said Marcello.

"And I can order: tres cocas, por favor" he told the waiter. They watched the game at the race track, and saw the young Merlos take a fall, but he was OK. They drove back into town and met friends, whose girlfriends all wanted to practice their English. *Great to be popular, whatever the reason.* On their return to Alvear, they found Lalo in sparkling mood. The stock had turned around in late trading, and he had taken his profit – Champagne time! Tom knew those times too.

"Vos y mi, Le Club esta noche, Lalo?" Tom asked.

"Shhh! No, no – Monty Video."

They dined well. Pork with crackling, fried chicken, and in the hearth a joint of beef sizzled above the embers. More champagne. Lalo carved the beef. It had been a good day after all. He broke into song.

"Start spreading the news...." He knew all the lyrics.

When Marcello, Eduardo, and their brother Ricardo, who had arrived home from Rio that evening, sang the chorus, Tom joined in. The insanity of the moment captured the zeitgeist of a former time – his own time, 1986. When the party ended, Marcello wanted to go to Le Club. "Buenas noches, Jorge," Tom said as they stood at the bar. He poured two coffees, and Tom left ten dollars.

"Gracias, señor."

"Where is Sophia Loren ?" Marcello said to Tom.

"Not here." They were in frivolous mood after their good supper. Girls appeared from recesses at the back of the room. Brunettes, blondes, short, tall, slim. *Like a sweet shop.* They made Tom feel as if he was the confection. Andrea had raven hair, shoulder length, and wore a tight cocktail dress, black with low-heeled stilettos, also black. Her eyes said she wanted to know him, and he took her arm as he gazed slowly towards Marcello, smiling back at the smiles along the bar.

"See you tomorrow then" he said.

"No problema, Tommy. Have fun."

She held his arm as they walked along Calao, kissing his neck and cheek, speaking quickly. He understood everything she said, except the words. He kissed her. He did not know her perfume, but it smelt good, and she was good to feel. Her curves excited him, and when she looked him in the eyes, his resignation became involuntary. He said goodnight to the concierge, and by the time the lift doors closed, his embrace had reached between their thighs, the kiss a potent aperitif, sustained in sexual suffocation. They fell from the lift gasping for breath, laughing, enjoying the consensual freedom of lovers.

As he opened the door she wrapped her legs around his waist and kissed his ear. He felt her hand on him. With the intimacy of two as one their energy absorbed them, their flesh, until their coup de foudre embedded. Tender strokes about their arms and shoulders, little kisses where their lips were, her fingers in his, she guided him to her, and whispered "cajeta" and licked inside his ear and blew. He slid over her flat taught stomach, and his tongue stroked her mons venus to find her clitoris. She tensed, gripping the sheet, arching to him. He opened her, savouring her womanhood. He worked deep within her, and she held his head and moved his mouth again to that point of excitement: "Estoy caliente." He stroked its swelling. She sucked her breath. He sucked her softness. Her muscles held the fingers now inside her, while he moistened her little tongue. His licking continued, and when she gasped to hold her final breath, she gripped his hair with both hands, and still he worked until she found second wind: "Fack mi!" – and he did, and when he had, she took him the way he had her, then bestrode him. One hand to his chest she played his nipple, her other hand behind her fondling his genitals, stroking strength into his erection, and as he ejaculated she took him in hand to masturbate his flow. He moaned and moved to her touches, as she moved hand to mouth to taste and swallow the semen. With brio she gasped, "Estoy liberal."

Andrea might have been twenty-four, as she had informed him when she wrote the numbers on a pad. She needed to leave, which he understood when she said "bebe" and showed him her stretch marks. She dressed to leave. He could not let her go out alone in the cold, in the middle of the night. It was four-thirty. So he drove her, somewhere near Palermo. He learnt more words: 'derecho' (right) and 'izquierda' (left), 'para' (stop), 'coger' (to fuck), 'te amo' (I love you). She did not let him walk her to the door, and they said goodbye in the car. Leaving the district by its cobbled streets, a landscape of trees and European buildings emerged through the clearing dawn, the world his alone, in a city of eleven million inhabitants. Where had his friend Joe gone after Marcello saw him? Had he left BA, or was he close by? Tom slept late. At midday his phone rang.

"Hi, Tommy." He had given little thought to Cormick since his move to his apart-hotel. *How the hell did he get this number?* "We play chukkas today at five o'clock. I thought you would like to know. I have a new horse for you."

"Like the others?"

"He is a palomino, a little bigger than the others. I think he will suit you"

"OK. I'll see you at Zorro's," Tom said.

"Wait, no. We are playing at Pando's."

"Who?"

"Pando. He has a field near Pilar. If you pick me up we can go together," Cormick said.

"Just tell me where the field is and I'll see you there."

"You won't find it."

"Let's meet at Polo Plus then, and I'll follow you."

"You don't need to come that far." Tom knew that Golfers was further than Polo Plus, so what was Cormick's game?

"Meet me in town then."

"OK, Tommy. At the Cantina, you know, where we have coffee sometimes." He knew the place and said he would meet him at four-thirty. He followed Cormick from the centre of Pilar heading north into the country. They turned off the main road, taking a single lane dirt track through a gorse common until it reached a plateau. Pando's field had been well-kept by a set of five gang mowers. In spite of its exposure to wind it did not drain so well as Zorro's and was used more during the summer months. Pando was a steward of the Argentine Polo Association, and Tom could expect an umpire to enforce the rules. Tom pulled up beside Cocine, Cormick's groom. He was wrapping tape around Blanca Flora's tail. This would prevent his mallet from being caught up if he took a backhand shot around her rear. The others already had theirs taped. Cocine turned them out to as high a standard for practices as he would matches, and the pretty mares, with the new saddles (monturas) Tom bought from Polo Plus stood ready to play two chukkas apiece. The tan-coloured fourth pony, Bandido, stood 15.1 hands, his head, higher than the others, he was alert to all about him. He looked intelligent and handsome, and he would need a fifty-two-inch mallet. This game would decide for him if Bandido would join the mares who would be his hardy perennials. His mares had not disappointed him at Zorro's and neither did they at Pando's. Bandido had a higher action than them. If at speed the girls flattened their backs to give their rider a level platform to strike from, Bandido launched more into rock and roll. Steady and true that he was, it took Tom both chukkas to adjust his balance to the higher strides and lunging reaches of a gelding he could get to like. Absorbed as he was in getting on equal terms with this fine animal, he could not ignore the irate outbursts of another player. Tom had seen him at other games, and he played well. His name was Serge, and he liked to lead from behind. He was angry with his horse. She did not respond to his signals, and he began to lose patience. He whipped her repeatedly, screaming Spanish expletives.

"Puta, mierda, bastardo, boluda, condom." When the chukka ended Tom shouted to him to stop. Serge scowled.

"Fuck off, Gringo".

Back at the car Tom sat and watched as this four-goal player galloped the bay mare from one end of the field to the other, pulling hard on the reins to drive the bit into the back of her mouth, to stop her, all the time whipping. He turned to repeat the three-hundred-yard gallop to the opposite end, whipping, screaming, whipping all the way. He pulled her hard again and turned. This time he aimed at the corner where Tom had parked and, thirty yards away, he pulled up using both his hands, blood pouring from the mare's mouth, her lips torn. Her snorting nostrils flared to the size of her bulging eyes. Her breathing, loud and erratic, the sound of her panic, was terrifying. Tom hit the car horn. Serge raised a fist and roared.

"Shit you, Tommy."

His whip, broken now in three places, he threw down, and as he turned her, began to use his fist on her neck. She took him to the end of Pando's field one last time as her heart, broken, failed her and she fell to her elbows before rolling onto her back. Serge stepped away as onlookers shrugged to open their palms. Cocine knew to say nothing as Tom wound down the car window to make his protest clear to Cormick.

"That bastard's a bloody disgrace. He should be banned from the game, and never allowed near a horse again."

"Serge just tries to make a living. He is a fool. Now he can never sell this horse" Cormick said.

"That's it, is it? He just walks away from this and we're supposed to feel sorry for him."

"No, of course not. It's life."

"If that's your idea of life, you can keep it, and your bloody horse." The irascible Serge had impaired his own judgement, and he hoped Cormick would not take it out on the big gaited Palomino. *Do I have to buy every horse from these whores, to keep them safe?*

He put the car into gear and when Cormick tried to stop him he told him to "go to hell." He floored the Renault from the field, and tore, as before, to the city. His memory of the drive was a blank until he hit Libertador and raced the guts out of the car, beating all to Alvear, and he threw open the door outside the apart. He did not hear the girl at the desk, who had messages for him, as he went straight to his room, poured four inches of scotch and lay down. The phone rang, he ignored it. It rang again. He picked up and put down. It rang again. This time he left the receiver to one side. How could he deal with these people? How could he disabuse a culture so inured in its lack of standards to be not merely savage but venal. He felt impotent. He took a second four-incher with him into the shower. The powerful jets of hot water filled his loofah, and he sponged over the last of the insect swellings as he felt them less and less. He could not expiate the guilty, and he was no martyr, but the shock of whisky chased his flushing douche. As he dried, a knock came to the door. It was Marcello. "I been ringing you. Where you been all day?"

"I went to Pilar for chukkas."

"How was it? You OK?" Tom told him what happened, and when Marcello understood his point of view, his spirit lifted from the nadir of his first time in the country he was falling in love with. To love a city first you must love someone there and, before that, be lonely there. The difference would be the backdrop to an affair still more potent than anything he had known. His messages had been from Marcello, except one. Andrea hoped to be at Le Club later, and would call him tomorrow. He would go there anyway. First the two friends went to the Barolos for dinner. They talked more of Gualyguaychu . Tom would travel with Eduardo and Marcello in the family Peugeot on Friday afternoon. Lalo and Julia would take the second car, a 1959 Chevrolet Corvette convertible, a classic, Lalo's pride and joy. They were all appalled at Tom's account of the equicidal Serge, and Lalo assured him that it would be brought to the attention of the eminences of the Polo Association. Tom told him that some officials had been there and seen everything, and did nothing. Lalo knew people and he would insist that the incident be investigated. The Americanos went some way to settling his ambivalence, though he could not deny his voices, and with some nonplussed resistance, he accompanied Marcello to Le Club. They drank Jorge's strong coffee. Tom took his black and sweet, throwing back the small cups as they cooled. If he was not to drink more alcohol, he would need an antidote to sustain him through a long night. It began as a girl with big Afro hair smiled.

"Hola."

She looked like Tina Turner. Her complexion tanned olive, she had a striking countenance with pronounced cheek bones, lustrous red lips, and stood level with him, and he understood her when she told him she was from Mar del Plata. Fuchsia stilettos launched her tanned legs to muscular thighs where flesh disappeared beneath the leather of a tight black mini skirt. He knew how he would bury the day's iniquity. He would fuck his way out of it. He looked to Marcello, whose grimace, top teeth on his lower lip, beaming a grin of approval, told him what he already knew.

"Wallywhychoo mañana, Marcello."

"Goodnight, Tom."

Tina Turner mounted the steps from the bar ahead of him, and as they made to leave Andrea walked in. She might have been surprised, but the girls knew each other and their conversation was not hostile. They took an arm each and lead him down the street. The night porter gestured with a nod of her head "Buenos noches" as the trio disappeared into the lift. When the door opened his arms were around them while he moved from Tina's lips to Andrea's. Their ménage a trios had started without the matrimonial bed. Perhaps a spirit of competition now gripped the two Latinas; Andrea livelier than even the night before, she did what she could to occupy him solely. She pleasured his loins with her tongue, her thighs astride his face. He could not see her in the dark, and could not hear. His lips felt her inner flesh when he had kissed and sucked on the softness of the thighs about him. His hands moved on the roundness of her rump. Her responses gripped him in a wrestle hold. He breathed her essence when he sucked her sweet spot. She let go a brief cry on his penis. Tina held him and began to stroke it while kissing inside his thighs, then running her tongue over his cojones, quickly at first, then slower, her lips now engulfing them. She massaged his cock into Andrea who made busy with hungry sucks and even when his juice hit her throat, his lovers held the intensity, until he groaned his priapic paroxysm as it died in its final throes. They all laughed with excitement.

Andrea went for water, and Tina mounted his mouth. She wanted the same as Andrea, to feel what she had while she muttered the dirty words only his cock heard. Tina watched him as he made busy with her labia, when he tasted her for their first time. She leaned back to hold him as the street light caught the comely roundness of her breasts, which he cupped to knead. She ground her pudenda on his tongue, and his arousal once again filled her hand. Andrea returned to mount him – his torso best ridden beneath a hood of women. If this would be his deathbed, he could not have been happier than when he orgasmed, as Andrea convulsed her climax and Tina gripped his head while her juices gushed. Andrea climaxed again and when Tina turned they kissed on the lips for a while, oblivious to their prone partner.

Tom watched their silhouettes against the night light as they made love woman to woman. He needed them again. Andrea lay on her back, her head in the corner at the foot of the bed, Tina's rump above her face. He stood at the corner to penetrate Tina while Andrea licked at his balls and at his length going in and coming out of the shaved flesh of this well-built 'mujer' from Mar del Plata. If Andrea had difficulty reaching his testicles orally, stroking them, pulling them between his legs, when he withdrew to release his pressure, she took him in hand to draw it down to masturbate it herself and drink and swallow all he had. He gloved her hand to drain the fruits of their pleasure, consensual, as all things should be.

*

Sunlight bathed his room with warmth as he drifted in and out of sleep long after the lovers had left him. He could still taste the shapes of their motionless bodies lingering on the bedclothes. He took in the last of the sweaty sweet fragrance from the air as a warm breeze from the street found the open window. He thought of horses, of when Juan showed him a mare in the middle of a field not far from Pilar a few weeks earlier. Cormick had turned off the road and driven through high grass, stopping at a coral beside some stables. Juan and he spoke, and Juan asked Tom if he liked the horse standing close by. A roan mare with one white sock, she looked strong-boned, and her mane had not been hogged. This placid pony had maybe played a little polo but not much, or the long hair on her neck would have been clipped, and she might have been rounded up from the Pampas that day from the look of her. Juan held her tail to present her sideways. He dropped it, walked away ten yards and ran at her haunches. This overweight man then sprung from the earth, clear of the mare's rear to land, light as any feather, on her withers. She stood for him as he took her mane by his left hand and kicked her with his jute-soled espadrilles. They took off, free as the wind, totally tackless, out of the coral and through the three-foot grass. Juan cantered her in a wide circle, clockwise, then galloped, then cantered, then changed from right to left with a subtle weight move, and they rode anticlockwise. The figures of eight they moved in were, at first, large, yet decreasing, Juan rode her after a while in a

170

gathered canter in smaller figures. If his hand gripped her, his legs felt her, and something else, unseen, made them move as one. They rode into the coral and Juan stopped her in front of Tom, sideways as before, let go his hand, and rolled over her back to land on the earth behind. Taking her tail once more in his right hand he asked "now you like my mare?"

Tom swallowed, then exhaled. "She's great, Juan. But you, you're the greatest!"

"I love her, Tommy. She my novia. Sweet Mariposa, dulce de leche." He held his left hand close to his mouth, fingers and thumb pinched and gestured a kiss. "Unbelievabubble!"

Juan had not been at Pando's the previous day, Tom thought, as he emerged from his half-sleep. He took a shower and rinsed his lovers from his body. When he stepped into the street, his satisfaction had been more than physical, and looked forward to the weekend in Wallywhychoo.

11
Gualyguychui

Empanadas had been left for the boys to eat, and Eduardo laid out a plate of mixed olives with salami, and cut a French stick. Soft, ripe peaches and figs completed their comida. Then they drove the Peugeot out of the underground car park, onto Alvear, turned left and made for the outskirts. Passing the tall residences of Recoleta, talking about polo in Pilar and Wallywhychoo, they drove on through Palermo, to take the highway north to Entre Rios, located between the rivers Parana and Uruguay, part of the vast tract of land the Spanish had named Mesopotamia. The Yerba mate harvest, along with sheep, poultry, linseed, tobacco, and rice, had earned it the title it shared with Iraq, its own verdant landscape bordered by two rivers, the Tigris and Euphrates.

"Conzuela comes from Mexico next week. I want see her, a lot" Marcello said. Tom thought of Santa Barbara.

"We had a lot of fun then. How is Nadine? Did you hear?"

"I think she go back France now. She OK, Pablo say me."

"That's good. Will she go to California again, do you think?" Tom asked.

"Pablo play Bagatelle this season, so he probably bring her with him after. He like her muy mucho. He say me he play British Open in July, then Deauville, before come here for season," Marcello told him.

"What about all his other girlfriends?" Tom asked.

"They chase him, but he no care. He love only Nadine." They laughed. "The girls from Los Estados Unidos – they have money, but they too old for him."

"What, thirty! That's not old. I'm thirty-nine," Tom said.

"You a man. Is different."

"Eduardo, what do you think? Is he right?"

"No, he's a playboy, like Lalo," he grinned. "Like you."

"How about you?" Tom asked.

"I have my girlfriend. I am happy." Eduardo, older and wiser than his brother, had a steady girl, Carolina, his 'novia estable'. "She is a teacher. You will meet her soon. She is sailing from Venezuela on a training ship with her school. "

"Sounds great, Eduardo. Is she a good sailor?"

"This is her first time. She was very excited to go. I miss her." She must have missed him too, this tall, young, strong-jawed son of a playboy, who had listened and learned all the Colegio Cardenal Newman school in San Isidro could teach him. Marcello had no doubt spent more time at the Country Club honing his sporting skills. Eduardo did have a polo handicap; he played off two goals, Marcello three. Ricardo, their younger brother, aged twenty-one, had chosen to work after school, and moved to Brazil where his US employers were training him at the University of Rio de Janeiro faculty of Engineering. They paid him well, and he took little time away, but when he did, he would meet his family in Wallwhychoo, the place they would always call home. Ricardo would arrive at Paysandu Airport, outside Wally, at eight o'clock. Javier greeted them at the family home on the farm where he had also grown up. His father, a gaucho, died suddenly, and Javier became general factotum to support his mother and sister. They lived in their own house close by the Barolo ranch house beside the polo field. Javier had aired the house for their homecoming, lit an open fire and heated the wood range to prepare dinner. Javier was part of the family and so long as they had anything to do with it he would always live there. His duties were light, though this was no sinecure, as they were many, and he earned enough to support his own, run a car, keep his own stock, and ride rodeo when it suited. He planned to marry later that year and the reception would be held in the main house. When the time came, they all went to meet Ricardo. Javier and he were closer in age, and they had played as children and ridden many innocent acres together. Tom sensed a bond between them that had prompted Ricardo's career choice. He more than his brothers bore the gravitas of responsibility for the lives, the land, the livestock. He loved his brothers, mostly Marcello, and their banter and ribbing could not hide from Tom, Ricardo's underlying cynicism, his fears for all of them. They stopped at a bar in town to drink beers and coffee, and eat cheese and ham toasties.

Ricardo had a new girlfriend. His brothers were delighted for him. What did she look like? What did she do? How old was she?

"She is thirty, an only child, loves horses, and me," he told them.

"Bravo, felice" and other words expressed their joy for their baby brother.

"Her parents? Do they work?" Eduardo asked.

"Her father has a coffee plantation near São Paulo. Fifteen thousand hectares." Bloody hell, thought Tom, a life-changer, as he felt concern for him now. *Then again there's a lot of idle land here too.* Back home Javier lit candles and opened some Chilean Chardonnay, as their mood became even more relaxed, sitting out on the verandah. The ratchet of crickets and croaking calls of the bullfrogs accompanied their warming down. Their evanescence contrasted with the waking of the night sky, a trillion glistering diamonds set in an inky backdrop around the highlights of Orion's Belt. When Tom looked to the flagstones at his feet, a hairy spider the size of his hand moved slowly towards him.

"Christ, look at that!" the englishman exclaimed.

"It's OK Tom. It's safe. It won't bite," Eduardo said. Ricardo picked it up and took it to the far edge of the lawn where it could stargaze without fear. They retired to a dormitory which the brothers must have shared growing up. Being an only child his recollection of dormitory nights at school did not compare with the sense of brotherhood he now felt in his adopted family.

"Mañana a la mañana - chukkas. Buenos noches, Tom," Marcello bid him. Drifting into sleep the lid of an oubliette closed down on the Golfers bunk house.

*

Javier arrived at midday to wake them with tea and toast. The horses were ready to play and he had cut the grass. His espadrilles were black. He wore white, pressed riding breeches buttoned at his ankles. These riding trousers they called 'bombachos', meaning

174

knickers. If they resembled female undergarments, 'apple pickers' would have been more accurate due to their baggy appearance. He wanted some himself. They talked about it and Marcello would take him that afternoon to a local store where he could buy strong, cheap bombachos. Javier drove a large green Dodge with a goose-neck hitch which stood out from the open back of the pick-up, where he put their bags and sticks. Ricardo sat up front as the others stepped into the rear cabin of the truck. The military vehicle, stood high on the cross-country tread of its tyres, cleared the earth by two feet. Tom remembered the impassable mud roads at Las Heras. Javier took no chances. He drove the tree-lined farm lane embedding its leafy coverage into his tracks. When he turned into his yard, Lalo's '59 Chevy, gleaming in sunshine, greeted them with its twin headlights. Lalo did take chances, as Tom knew. Julia bought groceries on the road, and she prepared dressings and marinades in the kitchen with Martina, Javier's fiancé. They chatted with affection, and laughed a lot. Tom had not seen Julia as animated before, and it pleased him that his Argentine mother had a friend.

The chukkas were easy and relaxed, half the time Lalo, Javier, Ricardo, Marcello, Eduardo, and Tommy, forgot who was playing with who. They played farm rules, without an umpire or team shirts, no numbers on their backs. It turned into a free-for-all with a lot of loud laughing. The water table was high in the region and the remnants of the last rainfall gravitated to the centre of the field, in line with its length. When Tommy rode into the wet leaves, his horse slipped and fell to the right. His leg came out of the stirrup, so he landed on his foot, then quickly took his other out from its' stirrup.

"Es boluda, Tommy" Marcello shouted. "You OK?"

"Si, si. Ta bien." When he looked up, the sun dazzled his view of the horse being led away through the still woods, and yet an impression would remain with him of the detail within and beyond the copse on the edge of their enclave, in a way Corot or Pissarro might have. Gentle trails of smoke from the asado brushed the final strokes over a scene of shadows from thin trunks on a floor of leaf fall, wild flowers in the meadow where cattle grazed. When Lalo said "Basta" – enough, they dismounted the horses that Javier had shod, and walked them now across the crispy rustle of the earth's counterpane. Before they played, Javier had divided the carcass of a lamb, and staked each half to the side of a fire, lighting on the shaded side of the trees. The hot fat in its young flesh ran to the fire's edge and fuelled it from beneath. Flames leaped and lapped as it turned from red to brown. For a moment Tom thought of Andrea and how she became 'hot' to his licking.

They drew chairs around a stone table, and Lalo carved the succulent cuttings Eduardo had brought from the cooking lamb. The salads were fresh with oil from the region, and sunlight filtered onto the leaves and warmed them. Javier pulled a facón (small sharp knife) from a sheath within his wide cloth belt, to cut chorizo, and he passed the plate around the table. When he wiped the small blade he used it to lift slices of lamb to his mouth and ate some salad with his hand and some with the point of his knife.

Ricardo asked Tommy if he had seen the sword hanging over the fire inside the house. He had not. Ricardo explained that when Javier's father was growing up, he and Lalo would fence. Lalo had learned at school in BA, and he liked to practice with Javier's father. They wrestled and boxed as well, often, when they were not riding and shooting rodents or, later, chasing girls. They pursued these pastimes into manhood. One day, when Javier was six, the two men laid down their weapons on the floor. Javier stepped on his father's sharp blade, and his foot bled and they took him to hospital in great pain. When the doctors had treated him for any infection, his father then carried his young son, stitched and bandaged, to Lalo's car and they drove home, and he carried him again into their house. He hung the sword high on the wall, out of reach and harm, and he never fenced again. Ricardo asked Javier to show him the scar, and he removed his espadrille. A cicatrice from his toes to his heel remained where the wound had taken weeks to mend, and it had taken months for him to stand or walk normally. Before the double-edged facón became the utility tool of choice by the gauchos, its use as a concealed weapon had replaced the swords of the Caballeros. Javier's facon had never been used in anger, though he had found as many uses for it in his capacity as manager of an estancia that maybe had prospects. Marcello asked if he could use the pick-up, then left for town with Tom.

They turned left from the dirt road towards Wallwhychoo. "Any news from Conzuela?"

"Two days. Just two more days," he said. "My father take you the casino tonight."

"Where? Here?"

"Yes."

"Why? I don't gamble."

"He say me you meet with his friend, Alberto, at the casino."

"Oh. I didn't know," Tom said.

"Alberto know everyone. He a good guy." They stopped in the centre of town, outside a shop that sold equestrian equipment, including bombachos. He bought three pairs that he tried on. They fitted well and would button at his ankle. It must have been all the riding he had done, nearly every day since he arrived, but it shocked him that he could fit into clothing with a twenty-six inch waist. He had lost seven inches since he left Dublin in January. He must be down thirty pounds at least. He could wear his old wardrobe again. It was April and he felt flaco. Later Lalo drove him into town in his white Chevy with the hood down. The wind caught his hair and he felt like a movie star. *Let's go to the hop!*

Alberto stood at the steps to the casino. Like Lalo, he had broad shoulders and dressed well. They both wore cologne. Lalo lifted the hood and the three of them strolled the long street towards the main square. This Saturday evening seemed subdued, maybe with the end of Lent approaching, the good people of Wally were making a last effort to atone for their pasts, or their future, or maybe they were all in church. Anyway, as the men struggled to communicate with a mix of pidgin and semaphore, Lalo stopped them outside a café.

Alberto pointed out a young woman sitting at a table inside. She had long auburn hair, and when she saw him, she stood, tall in her high heels. A v-neck sweater hugged her to her narrow waist. Her make-up looked light. She did not need it. She was elegant, beautiful. When Alberto and Lalo had spoken with her she put her arm through Tom's and they started slowly down the street, a different street, with the same feelings, his pulse increasing. *Oh God, you smell so good.* She did not wear cologne. Soon they would be wearing each other. When they turned the corner she said, "Aqui," (here) and entered the doorway of a small hotel. Clean, cheap, their room was small with a marital bed, no TV, no videos, no distractions.

She pulled her sweater over her head, leaving a black satin bra covering her small breasts. Her long body, pinched at her flat stomach, widened at her hips which held her black satin panties and suspender belt. The clips pulled tight at the tanned nylons they supported. He held her legs, feeling the seems that ran their length from her black Cuban heels to the tops of her soft white thighs. He put his hands inside the stockings, his heart pounding, his cock hard inside his jeans. The belt over her panties, he could not remove them – he did not want to, as he manoeuvred his tongue between her lips when his thumb pulled the satin aside. If less is more, he wanted for nothing, nothing more, nothing less. 'Mas o menos' - more or less. 'Todo' - everything.

Both hands on her perfect arse, he gripped her to his burrowing. He could breathe only the taste of her, his nose on her love bud. Her hands were upon his head now, and she sighed with each thrust of his tongue. He dropped his mouth to her nyloned thigh, where he licked and kissed the fabric, over the clips to the flesh and back and up and back. She yawed for him, lunging and bending from her knees and arse. He stood suddenly.

"You're swell, baby."

"Que?"

"Fuck me." She understood. They both tore his clothes off. On her knees now she swallowed his erection, then lifted it to his stomach, cupping his balls, licking, sucking, swallowing, rolling them on her tongue, holding them there, all the while her hand gripping his cock, wanking it. Now he bent his knees and held her head. The vulnerability of his manhood excited him. His virility again sheathed by her mouth, blood pumped through his swollen vein. She drew back and cried.

"Eres fuerte. Si fuerte. Cogerme."

He knew what that meant as she turned and stood for him. When they finished, his thoughts drifted to two nights earlier when he had lain with Andrea and Tina. He might not survive all three of them but *what a way to go.*

"Querido, su nombre es?"

"Me llamo Tommy. Y usted?"

"Catalina."

As she stood in the baño doorway, he used his erection as a sight to her slender figure, adorned in her lingerie of the night, and said "Mira, Catalina, mira, mira."

Dawn had broken when his eyes opened again. He sensed her, wanted her, but she had gone. She left a note.

> *Gracias, Tommy*
> *Muchas Gracias XXXXX*

On the street the Chevy sat, hood up, engine running, with Lalo at the wheel. Had he been there all night? *Probably had his own tryst.*

"Buenos dias, Tommy."

"Buenos dias Lalo."

They cruised the streets of Wally, the controlled growl of the five-litre V8 announcing their departure. At 7.30 a.m. they pulled into a truck stop. The diner was quiet, most of the night hauliers asleep in the cabs of their long-distance cattle wagons. They would be filled that day with beef from the herds of Entre Rios and Corrientes, then driven to the meat boats destined for Europe and North America. By the time they would be offloaded their excrement would be running out the sides of these two-tier pantechnicons. The lorries parked alongside the Chevy were dry and odourless at their slumber.

Tom's Spanish was improving by the night; he found Lalo easier to understand, and over a big breakfast of ham and eggs, strong percolated coffee which they dunked with croissants, Lalo opened up. Yes, he had been a playboy. It was easy in a city like

Buenos Aires, its flagrant sexuality inured within a liberal society. It ran in the family; his own father fêted from the boardrooms to the bordellos of South America. Lalo had wanted to write novels about the gaucho lifestyle, and had studied literature at the University of Buenos Aires, just managing a third in between chukkas, rugby, tennis, cricket, and a lot of girls. He liked erotic poetry and hoped to write an account of his adventures. His critics condemned his lurid style and he kept stopping. He would have to close the door and shut them all out to finish his manuscript, written his way, from memory, with as much passion as he felt became it. Sex is sex, don't dress it up or tone it down. It is the most powerful force of nature, Lalo said to him, gesturing in Spanglish. Tom felt the same way, and his empathy filled in the gaps. *A good meal.*

They drove to the farm, and found Javier hosing the Peugeot. Everybody still asleep, they warmed by the open fire and drank water from the well. Javier reminded Lalo that they were playing chukkas at 'The Regiment' that afternoon. The garrison was situated on the edge of town. Lalo had been stationed there as a captain in his mid-twenties. Conscription did not exist, but his father thought it might straighten him out. It improved his polo and he went to four goals, and he had kept contact since then with the former cavalry regiment. They used his land for tank manoeuvres sometimes and this afforded him and his sons some status. Tom would play with Marcello, Eduardo, and himself.

Javier parked the Dodge and trailer at the lines beside the polo ground, and unloaded ten well-turned-out ponies from the Estancia Barolo. He had tacked them up before leaving. All that he had to do now was tie them and tighten girths for the first chukka. It would be a friendly game, and an officer had a pony Tom could try. They mounted and Tom circled the bay pony Javier had brought for him. The ponies were for the family, not for sale, and Javier tended them like children. He schooled and groomed them with patience and care, and he took pleasure from their performance even if he did not play himself on the day. The bay responded to everything Tom asked of him, and he assumed the position in the line-out. He was introduced to the Captain of the garrison team, Luis Macon, who shook his hand and smiled saying that it was his horse that he would ride. The chukka, unlike the battleground of the Mona Depot, was a delight, Tom's pony stopping, turning, as he read the play. The ball sat up on the firm, well-kept lawn, and he stroked the ball to an open goal twice. He made tangential ride-offs to backhand the ball to Eduardo or Marcello or Lalo who spoke with paternal assertion. At the second bell the players left the field.

Javier took the bay and held a smaller pony for him to mount. The little chestnut with a white face was lively, less experienced, but seemed to learn as he played her. She had a turn of speed like his own Marucha, and nearly ejected him more than once.

"Muchas gracias," he said to Javier when he handed her back to him at half-time. Did he like her, Javier asked him.

"Si, si, bien, bien – muy mucho." Javier was happy. A young groom brought him the Captain's pony.

"Señor" the boy said. "Para vos."

"Gracias."

She was grey with the large markings of her youth. *How pretty she is.* A benign look from her large eye beckoned and he winked at her. He took her reins and held them with the tuft of unclipped mane at her withers. Her girth tight, he raised his left leg to the stirrup and lifted himself over her saddle. She stood still for him. *Tranquillo.* Her ears pointing forward they moved off together, walking , then in a canter, slow, gathered, controlled, they began circling. They moved to the right and to the left with the lightest of touches from the squeeze of his strong legs. He balanced her one way and then the other, and only when his final message conveyed his intention did she follow his weight to change direction. In a chukka he would have to poise before committing to a play or line change, and he needed to stand in his stirrups to look about him as he read a situation. If all his signals said left as he held her taut, he might need to change right, and just as quickly back to left. This little mare, she could do it all. She made him feel worthy. He knew she would be his before the start of the third chukka, when she confirmed her ability with a seven-and-a-half-minute performance that floated and flowed, and he wallowed in her as he continued to stick and ball her after the final bell. He could not get enough of her. The Captain said he could continue playing her, and they took a break. Tom jumped from her and loosened her girth, and she stood, still calm, and the young soldier gave her water to drink as he sponged her neck. Five minutes passed before her girth was tightened once more, and he remounted to take to the field. Her energy had not left her as she engaged with revived vigour, and his heart pumped faster with her courage.

"You like this mare?" Marcello asked him.

"Yes." He agreed to buy her, and Javier made space in the trailer. Tom would forward $1,000 to Captain Macon post-haste. Now his string numbered four. They were invited for dinner in the mess but the weather was closing in and they all had reasons to return to BA.

Javier would look after the mare with no name, and Tom knew he would. He would see her again soon when he would give her a name. He thanked Martina, kissing her cheek.

"Muchas gracias por todo Javier. Buena suerte. Ciao" she said, shaking his hand.

*

When the Peugeot crossed the San Martin cantilever toll bridge over the vast Uruguay river, a sharp sheet of lightning, fifty miles long, shot over the horizon, then another, then more. The crimsons and purples lit the skyline with the menace of a Caravaggio. Mighty thunderclaps ensued and they were silenced by their noise more than their threat. Rain cascaded over the car, their visibility reduced instantly to no more than a car's length. Their outlook opaque, the penetrating chiaroscuro continued, and with more than two hundred kilometers ahead of them, this would be a difficult journey. Would the soft hood of the Chevy withstand the downpour they wondered, and Ricardo must be stranded at the airport. Javier had driven him, and they hoped the storm hit before he took off. What a night! All they could do was keep moving. If they broke down they could only move the car off the road and stay inside until the rain stopped. Eduardo cut the lights when the flashes

182

came. If only for a moment the way seemed clearer, they could only pray that nothing had stopped ahead of them. The potholes on the Pan-Americano would be their next threat.

"Take it easy, Eduardo. This road can destroy a car" Tom warned. He had seen vehicles on their sumps, suspension cracked, and wheels buckled. Eduardo knew the road a lot longer and he negotiated the lanes from experience, less with manic apprehension. The rain eased and they made progress, a moist breeze through an open window cleansing the air. They exited the main artery to the city, through the trees that gave onto Libertador, its many lanes a skidpan, and slowed to the lights. No other cars as the lights turned green, they moved towards Alvear, deserted by the boulevardiers — no tables, no chairs, no gazes, no trysts or rendezvous. The clean atmosphere might have been welcome, yet to Tom it felt more as if the party had finished. He stepped from the car where they left him at the foot of the one-way Callao 'Mañana, buenos noches' and heard only the soft splash as the jute of his soles met the pavement. The concierge was not at her desk and he took the lift to his room. There would be no clubbing that night, he thought as he closed the window. He read in bed, *A Moveable Feast*, a favourite Hem, restoring his own sense of the perpetual substrate, until he slept.

12

Downtown

Monday, midday, and grey clouds contained the damp atmosphere in Recoleta. He showered, shaved, and dressed, and wore leather soles when he walked to the Barolos. His mood became more sanguine, cheered by the activity in the household. Lalo enthused about his investments, Julia had received an invitation to lunch with some good friends, Marcello had gone for the car to collect Conzuela from the airport, and Eduardo was just happy for all of them. He would see them in the evening, and returned to the apart, then decided to drive around town. Its proud sentinel architecture stood at the edges of vast squares and wide green avenues with their own priapic monuments, encasing a byzantine bustle of black and yellow taxis as they raced between the megaliths of public transport. Despite his lack of agenda it all excited him. He turned into a side street and parked. Carrying a waterproof over his shoulder he strolled the narrow pavement. He bought a paper, *The Buenos Aires Herald* and took it to a café to read. His espresso had turned cold when he drank the first sip. He was waiting for nobody, not even Cormick the day he brought him to another café, God knows where, and left him for four hours, not a word of Spanish for company, while Cormick went to the passport office. He drank six coffees that afternoon, all cold.

When he left the 'Me Gusta' café, his *Herald* on the table, and said "Gracias" to the waitress, he walked, sometimes stopping at bookshops, trying to read headlines at kiosks, something other than the benighted economy, he hoped. The tinkle of an overhead bell announced his entrance into a music store. They sold early albums, jazz classics from the thirties and forties, blues recordings by Robert Johnston, rock and roll, just about everything he had ever heard, or heard of. In the second hand section he found cassettes. He had many of them as vinyl albums. He read the description of a collection of hits by Sade. Some he knew well and liked, others he did not know. His car had a cassette player and he bought it. As it played "Your Love is King" he drove past a club named King, and sniggered. He had found the music store in twenty minutes. Over an hour later he was still looking for Callao, and loving it, carefree, as the tape looped on "Smooth Operator". He did not know "Never as Good as the First Time" as its syncopated baseline began to resonate through the cab. Grounded, he caught his breath with a primal intake as waves of rain hit his windscreen. He felt a weight in his gut when the Doce stopped on Callao. He sat and listened to the sultry delivery of the sexy English singer as each phrase pulled him deeper into an inert abyss. She drenched him in sorrow, his thoughts rinsed by her lyrics until he had just one ... *Oh God, Sophie, what's happened to Joe?* Outside, the storm raged, a bellowing gale thundered down on the level land of the province of the city he loved now, his home. Inside his room, he lay listening, desolate. If he woke, it was to answer a knock at his door. *Who?* Conzuela threw her arms round his neck and they kissed their cheeks. She smiled.

"Tommy. How are you?"

It was good to see her he told her. Did she have news about anybody. Yes. "Nadine is better now. Becky is with her new man... I want go back next year. Marcello, can we?"

"Si." He kissed her. "What you do, Tommy? You want come the house?"

"Sure. I'll come after my shower. OK." The water ran to his feet and drained as he stepped to the mat. Marcello had left him a radio cassette player, and it played again: "Never as good..." He turned it off. *Later.* He opened the window, then closed it. *Leave my room alone.* He threw the waterproof round him and took the lift. He walked through the rain to dine with the family. When he made to leave, Marcello went with him, and they walked to Quintana. Le Club was shut – the sign translated to:

Storm damage – closed for repairs – come back tomorrow

"What we do, Tommy?"

"I saw a club called King today. Do you know it?"

"I know where is. I never been. You want we go?"

"Yes," said Tom. He drove. Marcello directed and told him he would leave him there. He wanted to be with Conzeula. He would go in if it was free and stay a few minutes only. So they went in, to a large open-plan bar with a mezzanine, and a stage and dance floor on a lower level. The intimate discretion of Le Club would not have passed muster in the lurid reds, golds and greens of this downtown discotheque. And when it seemed the only feature that might keep them there for one drink was its dim lighting, this gin palace was redeemed by the curvaceous figure of a solitary goddess. Not just the only goddess there, she was the only person in the whole place, apart from Marcello and Tom. They both stared, their jaws dropped. Her fitted dress hugged her from her ample bosom, around the curve of her rump, pronounced by her leaning to the bar, tracing her thighs to end at her knees. She wore black leather boots with high heels. Tom rose from his seat, when Marcello stopped him.

"She for me," he said.

"No, no, Marcello. I want her. You stay here. No, go home. Conzuela - remember."

"Maybe you and me together, yeah?" Marcello said.

"What?" *Might be fun*, he thought. Marcello went to the girl. When she turned to him, she revealed the face of a beauty queen. Marcello returned and Tom said, "I want her, Marcello."

"Is OK, Tommy. She no want both us. You go with her. Take me home, yeah?"

"No problema, Marcello."

Tom went to the girl. She was tall and *Gorgeous*.

"Por favor," he beckoned and waited for her while she collected her coat which she carried on her arm where a shoulder bag hung. At the car he opened the passenger door. She sat, then swung her legs to the footwell. He caught her perfume, French, maybe Rive Gauche. She gave him a look that smoldered with the first flame of a spill as she lifted her azul eyes to his, the hunger of his hormones voracious as she closed over the lids. He began to blow when he said "Rapido, Marcello." As the trio drove towards Recoleta, her essence carried them quickly. Marcello left them at the apart to walk home. Tom and Carla went up to the room. When she returned from the bathroom, she wore only a thong which hung from her hips. Her breasts were large, fecund, as was the roundness of her rump. She had strong legs and held them tight together. Her catwalk hips moved from side to side on high stilettos now. He lay naked beneath the sheet, and she joined him, kissing his neck, touching his thigh, then his arousal, and began to stroke.

As his explosion approached, she licked inside his ear, and whispered.

"I tell you something." *What could she want to say - something amatory?* "I say you. Es correct." *What, what?* "Estoy hombre – travesti."

When he understood what she/he meant he shouted "Jesus wept!" and pulled away from her, jumping from the bed. With a towel around him he told her to get up, and when she did he could only see a woman in a thong. He was incredulous to her claim as she stood before him, on the other side of the bed, still aroused by her voluptuous figure. She wanted him to want her the same way she had wanted him, but not by deception. She would have told him in the car but it had been uncomfortable with Marcello seated behind her. *If she's aroused, where is it?* Her deceit and honesty were revealed at the moment of his epiphany, when she removed her thong to reveal – his penis. He had used the thong to hold it back between his legs, and now it stood proud. After all that was said and done, it was an impressive piece. Tom released his frustration with laughter. Loud and hysterical, he might have lost his mind in what might have been a damascene moment when it occurred to him that Marcello knew all along. *Bastard, I'll get him for this.* He asked his name. "Carla". Whatever his name (Andy Rogers perhaps!) – had Marcello known? Carla left him her number and he wandered why. *Phew, that was close.* After passing beneath the bridges of the Pan-Americano, without stopping, he had walked right into the ladyboys den. *Boluda!*

*

Before morning the rain had stopped and the sun shone over Callao. Marcello dropped by for coffee and they went down to the breakfast room. Tom had not known it was there, nestled in the rear of his discrete denizen of desire. Marcello, anxious to know how the night had gone, asked him. Carla had been great, a marathon fuck. They had gone around the world at least three times. He had never had so much fun, he told his friend. All the time Tom looked for any giveaway signs that Marcello had been in on the 'joke'. He gave no indication, but gave him the phone number all the same. *He's a big boy, he can handle himself.* A little English schadenfreude.

"Tommy, you want move your horses to Wallwhy when you go back Ireland? Javier look them for you."

"Yeah. That's a great idea." Marcello was taking Conzuela for a long holiday to the Andes and they would stay there until the slopes opened at Bariloche. She loved to ski, and so did he. They would leave soon. Eduardo would be there for him, for whatever he might need, and Lalo still wanted to go to Montevideo.

"How about coming to Ireland when you get back," Tom asked him.

"Come with Eduardo. We can play some tournaments."

Marcello wanted to come and told him to make the arrangements with Eduardo. They discussed these things at dinner, and everything would be set in place. Javier could collect the horses any time.

13
Zorro's

Leaving the Alvear building, the rain fell again, and he went to Le Club, alone. It had reopened and when he entered he spoke to Sol. The damage had been minor, just some water through to the floor above the club. It was fixed, back to business. As soon as Jorge had poured his coffee, Tina appeared and they kissed on the cheeks. She had a friend with her, Veronica, tanned, well-built, a redhead with a broad smile. She was a big girl, intent on him. She kissed his lips and he stood back "Sheeert!" he said. *Steady girl, all in good time.*

She said "Sheeert!" back at him. He was definitely going to have some fun with Veronica. He took them with him into the rain and they ran down the street to his shelter. If Andrea turned up she would know where to find them. Veronica's lusty lips went to work, leaving nothing untouched. Tina picked up where she left off, and his choice of two genitalia kept him busy in a triangular tandem of lips to lips, flowing with the kisses of life. All three reached epiphytal ecstasy. When Tina rolled away, it was Veronica's thighs that engulfed his face as she held his cock in her mouth, drawing in its deep colours between her thick moist lips, teasing his meatus. Tina knelt at the end of the bed to fondle his thighs and clasp his scrotum in a tighter sac, all the better to run her tongue over his round plums, driving her prurience with such passion that she took his meat from the other mouth and sucked down hard on it with her own. Veronica turned about and used her mouth on his lips, and he tasted himself in her saliva. She cast a leg over Tina's head, her womanhood aching to be filled. Tina mouthed between her thighs, all the time squeezing his balls, gripping and wanking his shank. Tom had gathered Vonny's volumous chest to his lips now, teasing and tickling her sensitive nipples, sucking one intensely, then the other. Her response began in waves, and when Tina guided the pulsing shaft inside her friend, she groaned and gripped his coital substrate there, where they fucked. As his frenzied drive reached to its hilt, Tina's clasp enhanced his vigour further, then further still when he felt her tongue and lips upon his stiff organ. Vonny blew a longing moan as her arse quivered from the spurts of fluid that issued down his thirsty erection. Tina pulled it out to slake her own desire, as it volleyed its own chaser. She gagged and gurgled on its length, masturbating with her hand and mouth, and wasted nothing of the precious juice when she drank it down. She needed servicing and pushed Vonny off him to take him inside her. His hands on her firm breasts he kissed and licked, as he felt her vagina tighten about him. Vonny kissed Tina's breasts with him, and then applied her own sexual alchemy to his genitals, as she withdrew him for her own use. She fingered 'dulce de leche' from her 'cajeta' to apply to his glans, where she smeared and smoothed it sensually circling the shaft to its base. She took more of her spurted fluid and did the same again, then again, and once more to treat his testicles with the love unction. Then with her emulsified index finger she penetrated his sphincter, where she thrust deep inside, massaging his prostate. Two fingers now within, she gripped the base of his cock and hungered on its head. The vigour of her cocksucking increased the turgidity of his meaty tower, filling it to bursting with surged blood, and then his power shot ejaculated and she held his virile tool to see his cum hit Tina where she had wanted him. When he came, he cried out.

"Sheeert baby!"

She cried back "Sheert, Tommy baby!"

She was an animal, they all were, steam rising from their warm wet bodies lying on the wet bedding, the slaps of flesh on flesh, hearing their breaths, heavy with pleasure, inhaling their post-coital aromas, and body odours that nizzled in the perfume of the night. They slept until daybreak, when the girls left. As he showered he heard his phone. He took the call on the bed. Cormick wanted to know if he was coming to chukkas, at four o'clock. Then Marcello called. Joe had been seen, in San Telmo, Tango and slums, where the villas miserias skirted the bohemia of the sensual dance and Gitanos. Could they go there to find him, Tom asked. Marcello drove the Doce from Alvear to Avenida 9 de Julio, around San

Martin square, crossing Avenida Rivadavia. Tom recognized the route. He had driven there the day before, in the rain. Today sunshine filled the sky and he felt sure they would find his friend.

"My friend Fernando, he come here last night and see him in bar. He say he very different to last time he met, in Alvear."

"Was he OK? Alone?"

"He say me yes."

"Did he tell him where he was staying?"

"No." They parked and walked the narrow cobbled streets to check the bars. They went into every one they saw, and Marcello spoke to all the barmen, and nobody knew him. At midday, Tom thought, he would be sleeping it off, if he was drinking. When Marcello told one barman that Joe played the piano, he told him that a music festival would begin the following day and that might be a good time to come back. A lot of the bars had pianos, and Joe could be at home in any one of them.

"Marcello, let's come back tomorrow. We'll have a better chance of finding him then."

"Ok. What you do now?" Marcello asked. It was 1.30 pm.

"I just remembered. Cormick rang – chukkas – four o'clock. You want to come."

"I can't. I go cinema with Conzuela."

"Maybe I'll see you tonight then." Tom drove to the underground car park at Alvenida, where he transferred his sticks, boots and helmet from the Peugeot. Back at the apart he changed into a pair of gray bombachos and pulled on his espadrilles. He hit the Pan-Americano twenty-five minutes later. It was 2.30 pm. *Should make it.* There was enough fuel to get him there, but he would need to stop on the way back. He drove hard, missing the ruts and lorries, and on the slippy dirt track to the field much of the accretion of poultry waste had run into the hedges as the downpour had tamped and diluted its fetid stench. Mosquitoes swarmed with relish about the banquet at their low table. He arrived five minutes early. Cocine greeted him, Cormick had been held up. He mounted Blanca Flora to stick and ball across the field towards Zorro's when he saw him walking his way, and they stopped to chat.

"You like BA?" He asked.

"Mucho."

"Chicas?" They grinned. Tom asked about Blanca.

"El mismo" - the same - Zorro said.

"Where you go? Athos?"

"No. Le Club," Tom told him. "You know it?"

"No. It's good?" Tom raised his hand, fingertips on thumb, to his mouth and said: "Fantastico!" They laughed. When Cormick arrived he asked Tom if he would play six chukkas, possibly seven. Not everyone would make it, because of the rain. "OK." He stayed on Blanca Flora to play her first. She was fine. Then La Luce. She too was fine. And Marucha – fine. After a water break he played them again in the same order. The evening humidity became clammy and they drank more water. Cormick asked if he could play one more. "OK," he said.

When he finished Blanca Flora had sweat rolling from her neck, and when she threw her tail she flung sweat from there also. Cormick asked if they could play one more. "OK." The inside of his arms began to ache at his elbows as he took to the field once again, and his helmet was unable to absorb any more of his own sweat as it poured down his face. He wiped as he rode, with his stick hand, and still it fell across his eyes, blinding him when the ball was his to take. *Bugger.* He missed three shots completely, and his arms ached on. When 'chukka' was called, he dropped from his pony, barely able to hold the reins and leaned against her as she walked back to Cocine. Cormick pleaded with him once more. "I'll be the last one out there at this rate." Cormick begged. *What the fuck's his game?* Tom agreed. "Give me five minutes. He went to his car and found a dry shirt and toweled inside his helmet, then held a two-litre bottle of water down to his mouth, and drank half before pouring the rest over his head. He dried his face with the shirt. His arms were beginning to seize, as Cocine gave him a leg up to mount Marucha. Seven minutes of exhausting pain dragged him until he slumped in his saddle.

"Basta," he shouted. It was chukka, and he had had enough.

Marucha walked him back to Cocine, and when he saw Cormick, he said "That's it. I'm done here."

Cormick gave him water, and when he had cooled off he said to Tom "I have good news for you. Juan's brother likes Marucha and he will buy her from you." *Just what is his game?*

Tom checked that his keys were in his pocket and asked, "How much?"

"Ten thousand dollars."

With that sort of money he could buy ten more, and it did cross his mind. But he did not trust this Cormick and nine chukkas had not sweetened his mood. He sensed he was being set up for some sort of 'donkey deal' and he declined the offer. He would move his ponies to Wally as soon as he could get word to Javier. He did not tell Cormick of his intentions. He remembered he had a camera in his car, and asked Cocine to remove all their tack, including leg bandages. He returned with the camera, and when he had taken enough photographs for identification, he walked back to the car. Sitting at the wheel he could barely wind down the window. A cooling breeze was reducing the humidity and it would help him with the drive to BA. As he turned the ignition, the passenger door opened and a familiar figure sat beside him. It was the ogrish Serge. *What the hell does he want?* He began.

"Tommy. How you are?"

How am I what, sitting here with an equicidal fascisto like you? Is that what you mean, you bastard? "What do you want?"

"Habla Español, Tommy?"

"No."

"Association has torneado. You want I play you." *The hell I do.*

"No, you son of a bitch. If you were the last player in the world I would not want to be on the field with you or against you. Now get out of my car." Whether Serge understood or not, Tom did not give a damn, as he put his foot on the accelerator. *I'd rather have mosquitoes for company.* He took the old road from Pilar. It ran parallel with the motorway, where he knew he could get gas. What he did not know was that a new price hike, twenty per cent, had been announced that evening. Three miles out of town he sat in a half-mile tailback to a national filling station, where he remained for two hours. He played Sade, anything by her. Why had he not known her work better? Between fills there was time to switch off, and everyone did. Two hours was a lot of fuel, even at idle. About twenty car-lengths ahead, on the opposite side of the road a girl stood alone. She wore a tight mini skirt and sling-backed low heels. Her raven hair hung straight to her shoulders. She was not tall. He guessed she was professional, and wondered if she was really he, an Andy Rogers. As he moved closer, as she waited for her next trick, she turned her angelic face in his direction, and his curiosity rose. Female or male? She was too pretty and anyway the travestis stood beneath the bridges, didn't they? He moved closer, a double shunt this time, not quite close enough to be sure. Then the next car broke down, out of gas and the driver waved them on. Tom offered to push, but a fight would have followed so the cars drove around him, and he walked to the station with a can. Another car gave up the wait, all the while the little Doce getting closer to the mystery in the mini skirt. He could see that her swarthy olive features suggested indigenous blood, and her figure was as natural as a schoolgirl. When he came within twenty yards he gestured come hither. Her perfect proportions moved modestly over the road to his open window. Only when she bent to speak did the shock of just how young she really might have been ground him. He had read that sex was legal from age thirteen, but solicitation for money eighteen. What age was she?

He asked "cuántos años tienes?"

"Dieciocho" she replied. She showed him formal identification. He put his hand on the passenger seat, and she walked around to take a place in his life, if only for the briefest sojourn. It would be twenty dollars for the hour, plus the room, and she would take him to a motel close to the Pan-Americano. He filled his tank while his pretty little squaw waited in the comfort of his pretty little car. As they drove the short distance to their 'maison de passe', Sade sang "Cherish the Day". His empathy with this demure girl on the margins was so much more cerebral than physical, and yes he was excited by the life in her young eyes, but to treat her like a city girl would have saddened him. When he touched her he would be tender, as he hoped she would. And they were.

194

*

With much on his mind, it was a comfort that he had protected her briefly from the abuse of a Serge or some other roughhouse, while he cruised towards the epicenter of his own primal needs. He had found the underbelly to a savagery that belied the indigence forced upon it by an economy crippled with corruption and byzantine administration. More than that though, he had learnt something about himself, and when he had followed the cabs on Libertador, he pulled a sheet of notepaper from the drawer in the desk beneath his window, and started scribbling:

At a roadside I did not know where, I stood...

He put down his pen when a knock came at his door.
"Quien es?"
"Es VerOnica!" came her emphatic reply. When he opened the door, Andrea, Tina, and Vonny came in, kissed him, and made themselves at home.
"Hambre, Tommy?" She put some fingers to her mouth. He had not eaten since breakfast.
"Si si Vonny," he said. They brought bread sticks, strong hard cheese, peaches, and wine. And dulce de leche.
"Hacerte fuerte," she said. As he cleared his small desk and placed the provisions for dinner he knew he would need to be strong. He brought glasses, small tumblers and offered them the wine, red and white. Tina took a glass of red, the others drank Sprite from cans, and they sat on the bed in a row opposite him, as he pulled the corks. *Pure joy. The perfect picnic.* He drank the white, and they broke bread and cut the cheese. The peaches were ripe, their soft flesh sweet and fresh to their tongues, and tasted good when he drank the red wine from Cordoba. The succulence of the sounds of their feast began to stimulate more than taste buds, distilling fresh desire for more. He was 'excitado' and 'desperto', aroused before Vonny stood to sit astride his leg. She held open the confection with her fingers deep inside. She lifted her hand above her head,

following it with her brown eyes wide, her mouth agape and tongue out, to receive the slow viscous fall of the sweet brown caramel. She placed finger after finger on his tongue before consummating their mutual esurience with her lusty kisses.

When the tasting of tongues slowed, she removed his shirt and moistened his chest, where the dried sweat since Pilar lingered, and relished his maleness. The fragrant perfume of the sweet sweat gratified the growth of their arousal. She sucked his nipple, her caramelised fingers filling his mouth, and moved her free hand down. Tina and Andrea had removed their tight dresses and knelt now in their burlesque best to remove his bombachos. Vonny straightened her legs when they loosed his belt to pull the covering from his saddle-sore thighs. Nine chukkas on suede had left its mark, where they smoothed the caramel unction to soothe and arouse. On his needy erection their delicious devouring could only arouse. Vonny sat again, across both his thighs. The others stood to taste her breasts, his breasts, and kiss them both in a fourway embrace, lips to lips and back to breasts, savouring the sweet milk dessert, and his ejaculation jetted deep between the hips of this fine young woman. She stood once more, to release her own fluid, which she let fall, with his, above his chest, and the girls drank from her 'cajeta' and from his thumping breast. Vonny raised an athletic thigh clear of the girls and left them before the next course. Tom, recovering where he sat, felt heavy shoes fitted to his feet. They laced the commando-soled brogues tight to anchor him for what they next had in mind. In his repose he watched them as they sheered their panties down the length of their nylons where their high heels stepped out. They both smeared the caramel delight where the nylon met their intimate folds. *Knicker trouble.* The thought excited his passion while Tina wound hers about his face, and he could taste her sweet warmth with the smell of her sex. Andrea lifted his shoe to pull her small black panties onto his ankle, then the other. She sensually moved the damp nylon up and over his knees. The tight texture, at first uncomfortable, felt good as one girl bore down to kiss him deeply on the mouth, the other stimulated by his virile stretching from within the restraint of these bombachos, stroked the polymer moulded to his

196

penis, and frottaged his plums with vigorous tonguing. Tina's tongue forced between the folds of her silk to share the sweetness of his gag, then stood high in her heels to share her own folds with that place, and in their febrile fervor he found her sweet spot, and she burst into orgasm, and her own juice soaked the silk about his mouth. She gripped his hair as he continued to touch her, and when she tensed she came again, then, before she was done, he gushed his pleasure, arching into the nylon with his fuck muscles and Andrea gorged on the membrane that had so excited them.

Vonny took him by the hand and lead him to a corner of the bed. Andrea lay diagonally with her face up on the corner's edge. Stood above her, his legs astride the mattress, bestride her hungry eyes and pouting mouth, Vonny placed a pillow beneath the back of her head. Tina stood with her back to him, then dropped to her knees where her ass stood up for him. Andrea's hand on his hard cock, she opened Tina's passage for him to enter, the grip of his soles on the carpet supported his thrusting rhythm. With the ache now gone from his arms he lifted them to his head, and he drove into the swarthy rump of the woman with afro hair, from hoof to hip. He rode her as he had ridden Mariette in Del Coronado, with loin lust, hands free. He wanted to take her by her mane as he had his raven French mare that day, and reached forward. Vonny took his hand, this time between her thighs. She had mounted the bed to face him, barefoot and upright. As she closed in he felt her belly, firm and warm, and wet. She had showered, she was hot she said. He drank from her flesh and held her waist. Her strong back supported her large breasts, his face between them now, breathless. He sank into her smothering and craved her muscular body. He drove his cock hard between the cheeks she bestrode beneath him, while Andrea masturbated its length and sucked at his balls. The stimulation innervated his whole body now. They all felt it.

Just as he thought he might snap, Andrea felt the pulse from his surge and drew his throbbing cock down deep into her mouth to take him, all of him, and when she was finished, he was empty. From his apogee of intense sensation, his mind now blanked, he could feel nothing. Beads of perspiration appeared at his brow, while his torso, drenched from its work and from the shower-soaked Vonny, began to emit a profusion of fluid. He wiped his face, and it continued, then again, and again, and it would not stop. Vonny took towels from the bathroom and dried both him and her. Tina filled a jug with water and they all drank. She filled it again and Tom drank it all. But he needed more and went himself this time.

Looking back in front of him was a face he did not know. It was ashen, harrowed, and could not smile. He drank from the tap and still he sweated and he could see the moisture emit, as soon as he wiped it. His first sign of recovery was his headache, and he swallowed codeine with his water. He wrapped himself in towels and wore a bathrobe to keep them in place. When he returned the girls had opened the window wider and the air conditioning spluttered. They could see that he was distressed, yet improving. Tina and Vonny kissed him on his lips when they left. Andrea stayed to watch over him. The bed was soaked and they threw off the sheets and turned the mattress. There were no dry sheets. They closed the window and turned off the air conditioner, and she dressed and lay beside him while he remained toweled. After an hour he had stopped sweating, and she removed the wet towels and dressed him in a T-shirt and sweat shirt. They embraced and she offered him her breast which he took to taste the milk that her child would have tasted for the four months since she had given him birth, and he slept there, content, cooling. She stayed until he woke, and he was grateful and she murmured: "De nada." When they were clean from the shower and were dried by the warm air that came in from the street, they left to get breakfast, and he walked her to Florida where she took the bus, home to her baby son. *Love is not a measure, no matter where you find it.*

14

San Telmo

He walked to Alvear and called on Marcello. All was well in the Barolo household.

"Tomorrow I rent car and drive Mar del Plata, with Conzuela. You want come?"

"Let's see what happens tonight, first. OK?"

"Today I go Hurlingham . You want come with me Tommy?" Tom sat in the passenger seat of the Peugeot and told him about the day before. "Nine chukkas! Is a lot, and las chicas. How many? You must take care. Too many chukkas, too many girls – they kill you Tommy."

He drifted into a dream as the sun warmed his arm on the side of the car, and his face absorbed its colour, and he felt well, and would take Marcello's advice. At Hurlingham they parked on a side street and walked into a stable yard. He recognised Ernesto Manzanares when they shook hands. He knew him from Dublin, last season. Ernesto, in espadrilles, they all were, stood skinny, and had a thin dark moustache which dropped to stiletto points down the sides of his mouth. His black hair, thinning, he wore to his shoulders. His shifty regard reminded Tom of playing against him when he saw the four goaler use his mallet to tease the belly of his opponent's horse, rather than ride him in a legitimate ride-off. And then later when Tom followed another pair on the line, Ernesto leaned down to lift Tom's foot from the stirrup. "Get off, you bastard!" Tom yelled, before losing his balance.

"Sorry," Ernesto said.

Ernesto's groom lived in the yard at Hurlingham. Not just in the yard, in a stable, with a horse when the yard was full, which it was most of the time. Gordo was short, very skinny, and in his dirty hands he held a stick of bread and sausage. He placed them on a crude cutting board and pulled a knife from his belt. On the ground stood an open bottle of wine. Ernesto fetched glasses, and Gordo cut the sausage. He held a piece to Tom with a tear of bread in his other hand. Tom's hunger could not stretch to that, and he declined.

"You hurt his feelings, Tommy" Ernesto said, grinning.

"Lo siento, Gordo" he apologised. He drank from his glass the acidic wine, if it was wine, and spat it out.

"What's this, piss?" and it probably was.

"It's Gordo's. He is poor. He does not have money for good wine."

"Don't you pay him?" Tom asked.

"He gamble. He never win." Tom did not believe him. Gordo's penury was almost certainly due to Ernesto's exploitation of this nescient nobody. His disdain for his fellow man was universal, as his sardonic visage demonstrated.

"Come on Marcello. Let's go." They drove South on the main street out of Hurlingam.

"This Ernesto, he's your friend?"

"I know him long time. His father is friend Lalo."

"I don't like him. I definitely don't trust him."

"He not so bad. But he is politico."

"I don't know what that means but to me he's a shower of shit!"

"What mean this? Shower..." Marcello asked.

"Ducha de mierda. Entiendes?"

"Like Pilar."

"Exactamiento!" Tom said.

"Your Spanish, it is good now."

"Mas o menos," Tom said.

Marcello drove them to a ranch closer to BA, and stopped outside a large cottage. He had some business there and suggested that Tom walk to the polo field beyond the trees. He trod a track of twigs and crispy leaves beneath the susurrus of branches brushing in the gentle breeze. Sun flickered the shade of his passage which gave onto the level of the playing ground, full size, three hundred yards by one hundred and fifty, boarded on both sides. These twelve inch high boards, painted red, were made from ten foot sections joined, outside the arena, by white painted stumps. He sat on one looking over the cropped lawn reflecting on the revelations of the past few

200

weeks. If he had ever questioned his reasons for taking up his sport, he had found answers where he had not sought them, excoriated the layers to discover an honesty where he found its raw soul, Argentina. Juan, Zorro, little Bruno, Lalo, Marcello, Javier, the horses, the girls, his Doce, the credits to his liberation. To others he might have been 'gringo' but he was no tourist and they had confirmed that.

The slow movement of an approaching horse came from the path through the trees now. When it stepped over the board, one hind clipping its edge, he looked up to see a young man clearly in dialogue with the pony, a bay mare, around 15 hands. The slim figure turned his horse to the right, parallel with the board, away from Tom, to drop a ball directly beneath his own foot. He tapped the ball forward a few inches, then lifted his mallet to tap it back, and repeated the exercise a few times, in a controlled rhythm. Tom had seen many young boys and girls who would do this on foot with short mallets, hitting the ball to each other, play little games as they learned the rudiments of team play, all the while improving their stick and ball deftness and hand/eye coordination. The better ones might then roll the ball back quickly with the back of the mallet to then catch its roll onto the front of the mallet, then lift the ball up to continue tapping in the air. Tom had tried, and managed to tap the ball three times in the air before slicing it away. It needed practice, and youth. Maybe little Bruno would get to like a shorter mallet and hone his skills, he thought.

The mounted teen, from where they now stood, close to the board on the halfway line, tapped the ball forward and immediately had it on the back of his mallet, and it was airborne. He tapped it up higher, with the back of his hand and then again to lift it some feet above his mallet, now vertical. With the head of the mallet he tapped again, then again, and once more, harder this time to lift it higher still. He gathered his mallet then with both hands, and as the ball descended, his swing met its sweet spot. It soared towards goal, and bounced once to sail through the middle of the posts. "Wow!" Tom stood to clap the teenager who had played the best tennis shot he had ever seen. He turned to acknowledge. They did not know each other, and it was not until, on the road back to BA, that Marcello told him the young man was Adolfito Cambiaso. He was fifteen and already playing with a five-goal handicap.

"He's amazing," Marcello said. "He'll be the best in the world. Ten goals soon."

*

Eduardo joined Marcello and Tom in the search. Tom drove his Doce across town to the edge of San Telmo, where they parked. The streets were full of gaiety, people singing, dancing, laughing - fiesta. The bright, garish costumes worn by many dazzled beneath mobile lanterns on top of banners which trailed streamers of every colour. Some revelers wore gorilla outfits, many more clowns, their faces heavy with grease paint, their eyes disguised with mascara or concealed behind the holes of hand held diamante masques, harlequin domino, leopard print with feathers, black and white. Tights that complemented clung to hips and rumps and fit legs as the parade moved from street to street. Horns and drums in conflict did not sound discordant in a convoy so bizarre that every bar they entered was empty. Nobody needed to drink when the street offered this many mind-altering options. So the three walked one behind the other against the flow, enthralled by its hypnotic atmosphere. For a while they forgot their purpose as they imbibed the spectacle. The throng heated the night air with smoke from wood torches, steamy bodies, and pungent perfumes.

When suddenly the horizon candesced with lightning streaks it seemed their manic dance had been heard, and the street was invigorated, the sonorous claps of thunder its plaudits. The breaks closed around the masquerade, and when the rain fell it struggled on until it dissipated into every direction, lights extinguishing, smoke dispersing, banners abandoned. The boys took shelter in a bar, half full with drenched maskers. Stood in front of them a line of figures leaning at the bar, in lurid, tight tights and high heels. Some held the sticks of their domino, not to their faces now, others had removed their headdress. When they turned to gaze at Tom and the brothers, their visages ran with trails of mascara down to painted cheeks, their deep colours smearing with its black into a grotesque rearrangement of who they were, truly were, or who they wanted to be, and it was in their faces that cried for them Tom now saw the pathos of the putas, the pederast putas. Every dropped mask revealed a young male, a 'demoisel' of the district. Some resembled the concupiscent coquettes of Le Club, whereas others seemed more furtive in their curiosity.

"We need to go" Eduardo said.

"Yes, Tommy. We go" added Marcello.

"No, no. I'm gonna stay a while. You go on, take the car if you like." He had come this far and if Joe was close by then he would find him.

"Are you sure? These are all gay. They might hurt you." Comfortable with his sexuality, he had never felt threatened by homosexuality, most especially the third sex, the androgynous, the 'Andy Rogers'.

"I'll be fine. You go. I'll see you later."

"We take taxi. You take care," Marcello told him. When the brothers had pushed through the crowded doorway they pulled their jackets over their heads and ran through the emptying street. Tom bought a beer and looked for a table. He aroused a lot of curiosity, but whenever anyone approached he asked if they had seen his friend. Nobody knew Joe, although there were many musicians, pianists in the bars all over San Telmo that night. They all reassured him that Joe would turn up."Es Fiesta".

When he could see nothing of the bar but the pretty boys stood around his table a sense of tragedy descending on him, he heard some notes from a piano breaking through the puling falsetto of their voices. A short, slim flat-chested transvestite sat at his table and pushed a bottle of beer to him, unopened. He would not be deceived here. With the freedom of honesty he accepted the drink, and told the boy that he was not gay, just looking for his friend. The boy said he might know him. Take me to him, he asked the boy, and when he took him by the hand he trusted him. Moving through the bar though was like the time when he had been in Florida, in a pick-up bar, and roaming hands touched his modesty, as he now felt hands and thighs against his own and shemale breasts rub his arms. *Some gauntlet.*

Again he heard more piano notes, louder now. When they stood behind the piano stool where a pianist sat beneath a black Fedora with a red rose bandana, the boy looked up at Tom and gestured: "Tu amigo?" Tom's eyes intensified, the room silenced about him, as he looked down to the figure crouched over the keys. If Tom did not know who he was looking at, he did recognise the piece he was playing, and only one musician on the planet knew it. The rapid run of riffs continued after the lights went out, candles and tea lights sat on every safe surface and from the lid of the piano, light reflected on the pasty complexion of the musician engrossed in 'Sophie's Song'.

"Joe. It's you. It's me, Tom." Joe heard nothing when he played. Tom put his hand on his friend's shoulder. "Joe, it's me Tom."

"I heard you the first time." He turned. "How did you find me?" He spoke through the high red gloss of his lips, his eyes distant.

"That's not important. I've found you. That's what's important."

"Get me a drink then."

"What do you want?"

"Whatever you're having." Tom left him to push his way through the revelers, then looked back to see Joe passing the window, outside. Tom followed as soon as he freed himself, and ran into the road. Soaked by the rain, splashing into puddles sitting on the cobbled surface he could see the large hat disappear into an alley to his left. As he turned the corner, the hat vanished through an entrance. Tom ran fast to reach the doorway before it closed. Wind and water rushed in behind him as he was swept to the foot of the stairs. He could see Joe on the landing where he was closing another door. "Stop, Joe. Please. Talk to me."

Joe let him in. The small red room, lit only by a candle, red, contained little apart from its wide bed, and on it lay the voluptuous undulations of a young woman wearing only a black bikini bottom. As she turned to face him she said, "Hola, Tommy". He knew the voice and stepped closer.

"You?"

"Si, Tommy. Es mi, Carla." She rolled over in the half light for him to see her arousal.

204

"What the?... How?...Joe, what's happening?...Wha, wha, what the hell are you playing at?" The storm over BA had funneled into a whirlwind in San Telmo. Tom was head-down in the manic entropy of its vortex. "Jesus fucking Christ, Joe. Help me. For God's sake, help me understand, Joe."

Joe calmly poured his friend a large whiskey, and made him drink it as he held back his head. He poured him another when Tom sat on the edge of the bed.

"You OK, Tommy?" the glamorous bedfellow asked him.

"No! No, no, no. Don't ask me that." He lay across the foot of the bed and started to hit the mattress. "Fuck you, Joe. All the people you've fucked up, and you turn up here, in this shithole. What the hell's the matter with you, you selfish bastard?" He swallowed more whiskey. Joe poured him another.

"Please, Tom. Please don't make this worse than it looks. There are things you don't know. I hope you never have to."

"Me voy," Carla said.

"Don't go because of me," Tom said.

"Is better I go. I see you tomorrow, Joe." She kissed his cheek and left him with his friend. Joe made up a bed on the floor, where Tom fell into an alcoholic sleep; Joe lay with his demons, listening to the gusting rain.

*

When Tom came round, he was alone. His thick head made unclear his dawning recall, as he inspected the sparse contents of the room. Looking at scanty lingerie discarded about the floor, two-day-old newspapers, countless burnt-down candles and an English translation of Jean Genet's "Our Lady of the Flowers", Tom got the picture. Joe had jumped horses from mares to stallions, and he had taken a crash course. And it looked like he had cleared out. It was not a whiskey hangover he felt as he cruised back to his room in Recoleta that morning. He had found his friend, and Joe's demons were becoming his own. He feared for Sophie now. She, like him, would at first feel relief that he was found. But how would he tell her about Joe's startling shift in sexuality? Then if he did not tell her, what she would not know might not hurt her.

As he drove he recalled how Joe had appeared in the dim light of the casa de puta. He wore purple leggings stretched tight from his thighs to his ankles, and stood tall in red stilettos. A transparent sarong, tied at his waist, hung to his knees. Beneath an Afghan jacket he wore a white satin blouse open to the waist, and he had painted his own mask, grey-white, with eyeliner and mascara, and added a touch of tristesse with black teardrops down one cheek. When he removed his hat, a cascade of blond hair fell to his shoulders. *Joe has red hair.* Tom could not tell if Joe's transvestite clown was coming out or hiding. Either way, he could not believe that his friend, who had fornicated for the northern hemisphere with as many girls as his fifteen-second rule would allow, had slid the length of the gender spectrum. Tom felt the burden of responsibility to keep his friend's secret, but he needed to talk, to someone. Joe's indulgence compromised his friendship and his allegiances. He called on Marcello.

"Hi, Tommy. How are you?" Eduardo greeted him. "Marcello has gone with Conzuela now. They come back next month," he told him. "What happened last night? Did you find him?"

"Yes, he was in the same bar, at the piano."

"The gay bar? Why was he there?"

"Joe plays piano. He's a jazz musician." Tom did not want to reveal everything, and became guarded then about the encounter. He did want to go back though. Maybe he could work something out with Joe, if it was not too late. He remembered the number he had given to Marcello. "How can I contact Marcello?"

"He has his Movicom," Eduardo said.

"What's that?"

"His cell phone. Here, I have his number. Let's call him."

"Marcello, it's me Tom. How are you" He told him he had found Joe and he was fine, and living in San Telmo, near the bar where he left him. They made small talk for a while and Tom said he called just to say goodbye because he would be back in Europe when he and Conzuela returned. Marcello told him to make the arrangements for him to visit with Eduardo that Summer. " OK I'll do that. Have a good trip. Love to Conzuela." Before he put the phone down he said " By the way, do you still have that number I gave you? You know, the girl from King, I think she was called Carla."

"I lose it," Marcello said. "Why you want it?"

"Oh, you know. She was great. I'd like to see her again." Not only could Carla lead him to Joe, if he had gone AWOL again, he did not want Marcello to discover the truth about her.

"Ciao Marcello." He hung up.

"Fancy driving to San Telmo, Eduardo? I just want to be sure he's gone."

"Sure."

They talked on the way about Ireland. If they arrived in time, they could play the Derby Tournament in June, and the fifteen-goal Horse Show in August. They would play matches every weekend and practices during the week, and they would stay with him in Virginia. Eduardo said they would like to travel, to Scotland maybe, and Tom could lend them a car for that. They would pay for their tickets and they did not expect wages, only their board and lodgings, as friends. Conzuela might visit.

The street cleaners were still clearing the detritus from the gutters and doorways. They drove over the cobbles until they found the bar – 'Me Gusta Tambien'. Tom turned right, then left, and pulled up beside the door he had followed Joe through. Inside they climbed the stairs where the door to the red room was open. It had been cleaned. A large person of dubious gender wearing a black satin dress and fishnet stockings had followed them. Eduardo spoke and was told that Joe checked out, with his young friend. Without a forwarding address they no longer knew if he was even in the city. *Back to square one.* The trail had run cold again.

"This woman, she told me he has been here one month at least, with his girlfriend."

Tom wondered why she had been alone in King, and tricked him into taking her to his room. Had Joe known? Yes, there was much he had to learn.

"This is the wild side of town, Tommy. Let's go home." Tom thought Recoleta was pretty wild too.

*

In three years Joe had never spoken of his family, apart from his errant wife. Tom had met only Sophie, and Carla and some of his amourettes.

Dear Sophie,

I write to tell you that Joe was here in Buenos Aires yesterday. I write 'was' because when I returned to his apartment today, he had packed and gone. He has not left any forwarding details and again nobody knows where he is. I know you will read this with mixed feelings, but I want you to know that he was well, playing piano – I discovered him in a piano bar playing your song – and that when he re-surfaces I am confident he will be clearer about the future. There is nothing more to tell you, for now. When I return to Ireland, soon, I shall call. If I see him in the meantime I shall contact you immediately.

Love, Tom.

He did call that night but there was no reply. In some ways, not wanting to say anything hurtful, he was glad he had not spoken with her, and posted his letter the next day. Sitting up in bed, he turned on the TV. A Clint Eastwood spaghetti western in English with subtitles - "El Bueno, El Malo, y El Feo" – was showing, and in spite of its laconic protagonist he noted a few new words for his Spanish lexicon – 'feo' (ugly) resonated as his thoughts took him to the piano bar again. The word sounded like 'fear'. How ugly fear is when you're running from the rain to take shelter in a storm, the only time you can be who you want to be, come out from behind your mask. And then some clumsy do-gooder stumbles upon you to excoriate the pretence and take you back to where you fled from. *I did this to Joe last night.*

Tom felt gauche and loathed himself. *Forget Joe.* But he could not.

On the street a young woman walked towards Quintana. Her curly platinum hair sat on the shoulders where she carried a small bag. Only she knew that she had just arrived back in BA , on the bus from Asuncion. He dressed and walked to the corner. A distant thunder rumbled.

15

Flavia

When the black door opened he saw Sol, the manager, and she greeted him this time with kisses to his cheeks, drawing back the purple velvet curtains across the entrance to the club room. Inside was quiet, and at first sight empty, no eyes moving in its recesses. He turned to the bar. Jorge reached for the coffee jug. On a high stool at the far end of the bar the platinum blond perched, her legs crossed, looked over to him and said, "Buena noche," as she cleared her throat. He smiled and moved closer.

"Encantado." He had not used the word for charming before, it just came out as if he now was a passenger.

"Al final" she muttered.

"Que?" he said.

"Al fin nos encantramos" For weeks she had watched and waited on her stool, and every time he left with this one or that one, or those, he had done so without seeing her. From her lost look, she fixed on the delight in his eyes, and felt found. When she stepped down from her high chair onto her two inch heels, her nose came to his chin. *Just a little girl.*

"Su nombre es?"

"Flavia." It sounded like 'flabbier', and he smiled when he said it back to her. She could not know the reason for his amusement, but was happy that he liked her name.

"Y Tu?"

"Tommy." And she repeated it. He liked the way she said it. She squeezed his hand when they walked down the street, one to one, not rushing. With the overhead light on he could now see how very pretty his friend really was. Her flossy hair only a touch more pale than her complexion, her eyes benign, she was very small when she removed her shoes. Her make-up barely noticeable, her features radiated as a child at a festival. Sol would not have allowed a minor to enter the club, so she had to be at least eighteen, he reasoned. She

210

had an hourglass figure, round and well endowed, and wore a plain black close-fitting wool dress, and black tights. His hand in her hair, she flowed right to him, the lids closing over their eyes, sealing the bliss of their first kiss. He pulled the dress from her shoulders and lowered it to the floor, gently kissing her soft neck. She moved to the bed as he undressed, and they lay flesh to flesh, feeling their gaze, tender in the dark. The surrender of their second kiss, when their loving lingered longer than their longing, he slowly entered her. And when they had rested, they kissed again.

"Esta noche?" He said as she left. She smiled and squeezed his hand.

"Por la noche Flabbia." They laughed.

*

"What you want to do with your horses, Tommy?" Eduardo asked when he phoned in the morning. "Javier can pick them up today, if you like."

"Let's do it." They drove to Pilar and met Javier in the centre, where he followed them to Cormick's field. Cocine had brushed and bandaged them for chukkas that evening. He had no idea they were leaving. They loaded well and Javier set off for Wally. Although Tom did not owe Cocine or Cormick money, the deal had been $1,000 for each pony all told; he gave Cocine $100 and thanked him for all his trouble. He and his family would live well on it for a while. Maybe his wife could get better cuts of meat with less fat, and buy their little girl Pettina a toy or a new dress. They all waited for Cormick to arrive. Tom wanted to explain. They drank mate as the reality of Cocine's circumstances became clear. His house, little more than one room, was heated by a stove over which a stew pot hung. It could not have been heating for long – the stale, musty smells of poverty pervading the atmosphere. These people had nothing, and Tom, though humbled, felt warmth that they enjoyed the happiness of their child who knew no better, and probably never would. When Cormick did not come, they decided to leave and the little girl kissed them goodbye. The ponies would be halfway to their new home as they took the slip road onto the motorway after Pilar, when a familiar figure appeared at the roadside. It was the Indian girl he had taken to a motel the last time he played at Zorro's. This time he waved and drove on. She waved back, and he hoped Pettina would find a better way.

*

The girl at the apart desk gave him a note when he arrived. Flavia would be with him at nine o'clock, and left a number if it did not suit. They could get dinner, he thought, and put the note in his wallet. In his room he read a while, and ate some soft peaches. It was not that he was a slow reader, more that he liked to read slowly, maybe only one chapter a day, a few pages. He would ingest each word, sometimes out loud, double-check meanings with his pocket dictionary, and read a passage, if not an entire chapter, again.

"Cena?" He greeted her at his door.

"Si, por favor." He placed his cheek to hers. *Let's eat first.*

In the weeks that he had lived on Callao he had not walked beyond the corner of Quintana, day or night, and did not know where they might go, but he hoped she shared a sense of discovery in their steps. They linked arms towards Le Club, where she turned him right on Quintana, a dimly lit street with bare tree, small cafes, bars, all quiet in the early evening. Two blocks on, where it met Plaza Recoleta, a few couples strolled and chatted, against the hum of the traffic on Alvear. At tables on the terraces to the side of the square, men, women, awaited assignations or something to happen which might change their lives, if only for a few hours. Tom and Flavia crossed the solid terra between the old trees with long horizontal branches supported by municipal posts. Some trunks had circular seats, elsewhere single seats sat about heavy iron or wood tables. When they had finished their promenade, they embraced.

"Cena ahora?" He said.

"Si, Tommy darling." His smile became laughter as he thought of her looking for that word of affection which she would say and hoped he understood. "Mira," she said. The brasserie on the corner

212

of Quintana looked warm inside and the board hanging beside the entrance carried an extensive menu. They both had their appetites and they would eat there in the French Quarter, breaking bread and laughter, and he imagined boules being played outside where lovers made their trysts. The tall blond patronne of the Brasserie George showed them to a table which stood in a loose box, similar to the individual 'horse boxes' in his school study where he would sit in silence during 'prep'. Now he shared that place and could enjoy it in conversation, with alcohol, with a girl whose age was that of his in his last year of school. He drank Quilmes beer, she drank water.

"Flavia no bebo."

It did not surprise him that she did not drink alcohol. He had not met many women in South America who did. What did interest him was her habit of referring to herself in the third person, and when she said Flavia does not drink, she wagged her index finger at the same time as shaking her head. He asked her if she smoked.

"Flavia no fumo."

And when he began to ask if she… she interrupted him, and as honestly as he had ever heard anybody say anything she said "Flavia es una prostituta."

Sat on a bench behind a fixed table, there was nowhere for him to fall or hide as he put his hand to his mouth.

"Schhh!" He looked around the room. Nobody, it seemed, had heard his Paraguyan paramour, as they now heard his choking laughter. *Perhaps they all are.* She excited him as he also thought he would *need to watch her.* They both ate beef, and dipped their papas frittas with shared hands and passed pieces of salad, her hand to his mouth, his to hers, she drank from his glass and let the frothy head dribble from the corners of her mouth to gather it with the back of her hand and lick it back to her. He watched and sighed, and rolled his eyes behind their lids, and gave her his hand. Her tongue coiled his fingers with a sliding weave as she kissed them away from her. Forever began. In their room the love became as natural as children playing. Candlelight was more than they needed to freely caress all they were, and when they were fulfilled, the memory of their first kisses immersed them in timeless slumber.

"Que passé?" he murmured as in a half sleep, moving his arm. Awake now, it had been nothing – a flash of the incubus had stirred him from his dream. His movement had pulled the sheet and she felt its draw, sensual on her breast. She turned and embraced him with longing elation. When they had enjoyed their bodies they slipped into the night, to revive it with their lovemaking each time she felt his slightest touch. He opened the shutter and the fresh air of Sunday morning filled the room, and they loved more, bathed naked in the warmth of the sun rising over the Callao skyline. Their bliss was unequivocal when they laughed over language errors as it was when their deep gazes locked them in their tenderness. It was so when they realised some incompatibility, whichever of them was on top when they faced each other. In her involuntary throes she would cut back with her pelvis, nearly breaking his penis. *What's this, a bloody chastity belt? Or a contraceptive?* When this happened a few times, they decided he should enter from behind, and not only did things improve, they got better and the special moments were as tender as they dared to remember.

From behind he would hold her breasts and the flat of her stomach, lift her thigh to take her that way. She would turn her face to his to catch his silent breath, grown heavy from the perfume of her passion. So compelled were they in their world of two as one, distanced from any sense of ineffable ending, their immunity from reality became myopic. That day they stayed where they woke until sundown, and were their own provisions. They returned to Georges after dark to eat steak and breadsticks. Her jersey dress looked as good on her as the first time he removed it, and they paced themselves until it was time. Their routine continued throughout the week, although she did return to her own place in Palermo to fetch fresh clothes and a gift for him. This was a candle with two wicks, with a multilingual pamphlet that explained how it represented the first major milestone of a girl after reaching the age of fifteen. A girl's 'Quince Años' depicted the fifteen most significant people in her life until that age, and after that she could make her own choices.

214

Her rainbow candle was her gift to him. He felt the responsibility of love, and it was not a burden to him. Flavia would wake when he recorded a word or more in the middle of the night, and whisper.

"Te amo, Tommy darling."

He would love her right back as night people do. If she sold it when they met, they gave equally now.

16
La Boca

Three knocks at his door, and again as he pulled himself to his feet, taking his watch to see it was only six-thirty, he said "Quien es?" *They'd better have a bloody good reason.*

"La policia, señor."

Two police officers stood before him when he opened the door. The young woman spoke some English, and told him they wanted him to accompany them to the hospital. Somebody he knew, they believed, was seriously ill.

"Quien?" He asked.

"Señor Henderson."

"Momento." He dressed without delay. Flavia was sitting up.

"Cual es el problema?"

"Mi voy al hospital. Es mi amigo, Joe. El esta enfermo."

"Flavia voy contigo," she said, and jumped from the bed, threw on her dress and shoes. They both wore fleeces into the cold dawn. The police woman only knew what the hospital had told them, and Tom had been contacted as next of kin. *Christ, it's that serious.* He had been taken to the Hospital Britanico, in Recoleta, where they now walked through a small vestibule up to the emergency room on the first floor. The antiseptic aromas of morphine and disinfectant filled the quiet landing, as Tom had been with foreboding each time he visited his father the week he died. Death is never a preparation. A blind over the viewing window shielded the patient, and when the door opened, Mr. Stephan Velasquez spoke.

"You are Tom Standing?" Tom nodded. The consultant's manner was calm. "Mr. Henderson is dying. For three hours we have done everything possible for him. It seems he does not wish to fight and is resigned to his demise. I am very sorry."

The quivering surge of grief he then felt, as he sniffed back his tears and held onto the arm of the man who had fought for him, overflowed, as a priest, leaving the room, excused himself: "Mi permiso."

Resting on the upturned hand of his friend lay a crucifix. Both his wrists were thickly bandaged, so too was his neck, and his face had drained of all colour. His freckles had fled him, and his bald head made him infantile. Carla sat at his side. It was she who had told the hospital where they would find Tom and they sobbed now on each other's shoulders in a sorrowful embrace, and Flavia held them both. They let go when the Consultant spoke.

"He is going." They surrounded Joe as he faded, when the beat on his monitor flat-lined.

*

Velasquez, raised in London by his English mother, had lost his Argentine father when only ten years old. He offered his assistance to Tom in making the necessary arrangements concerning his friend's final resting place, and he would contact him later with a proposal. Tom asked Carla what she would do, and she told him she had family and friends in BA, and that she would be OK. He should not worry. "La vida sigue." And life would go on, if not quite as it always had. She would take him to Joe's room. There might be things he would want. The district only added to his inner misery, his anxious face, both grief-stricken and angry, utterly perplexed. Flavia could only comfort him by holding his hand. He could not feel her when he paid the driver, who would take them no further. Carla said it would not be far and she led them through a labyrinthine enclave of unmade alleys, with open sewers and vermin, small children wearing only vests, barefoot. Inside a shanty shack, she showed them an iron bed with a filthy mattress. A torn dress, moved by a rat dragging it over floor was the only covering. He pocketed the Genet novel and they left. It could have been a leper colony, it certainly earned its caveats, and he gripped Flavia and wished he had not brought her to such a place, where a friend could have only perished by his own hand if his own place matched its darkness. Carla had found him slumped in the doorway of his slum dwelling in the barrio of La Boca. How was Tom to find out now?

"Tu vives aqui?" No, Carla did not live there. Away from the shacks, she left them where they found a taxi, and disappeared along a winding street. They showered back in their room, then lay down to sleep. He could not, and sat at his desk. He closed the window to shut out the cold wind. Then he saw the novel where he had left it. He picked it up and a note fell out.

Tom,

If you have this then you know the worst. As my friend there have been many things I wanted to tell you. Please be patient a little longer and you will understand, I hope. Now you need to contact David Atkinson at:

Smythe, Durden and Atkinson,
59d, Old Brompton Road,
London SW5.

He will know what to do, to see me home safely. It's been a gas, old boy. Time to shuffle off.

Love, Joe.

From things Carla said, Joe had come to Argentina early in December and they met at King night club. She stayed with him at The Alvear Palace Hotel and they flew to Florida for a week, West Palm Beach. She was his first shemale, although he told her he had always been homosexual. Tom also knew that was not true, but the Florida visit made sense – it fitted in with what he heard when he was there in January. When they returned to BA he began to wear drag and shaved his head to wear a blond wig. He immersed himself in his alternative life, removing himself as far as he possibly could from his past. They moved into an apartment in San Telmo. It had all they wanted, apart from one thing – a piano. So they went to the many bars in the barrio and he would play to entertain. He refused

218

payment, but the proprietors insisted on plying him with wine, especially when they noticed how much better he played under its influence. He became popular as 'Nancy' from Nuevo Yorky. As natural as it seemed to Carla, Joe was often restless, like a man on the run, and he cruised many bars, without warning, stepping into this one or that one, lighting up the sleaziest gay bars in the wildest side of town on the most out-of-tune, broken-down uprights. Joe Henderson had played Carnegie Hall, the Hollywood Bowl, he had appeared on the *Ed Sullivan Show*, he had toured the world – yet in whatever desuetude he found an instrument, his inebriant Latin renditions of his own canon beguiled the transsexuals and sex tourists of the district, and he drowned in its depravity.

One night as he and Carla were returning to their apartment, they were followed and seriously assaulted in the street. Four young muggers beat them to the ground before taking all they carried. Carla nursed her man for nearly two weeks, and it became clear he had lost his nerve to return to the streets. She would shop, for basics and wine, and when he drank he listened to cassettes. His life imploding, his will slipping, the evening of the masquerade Carla coaxed him out so that he might play. In fact he had to, the robbery had cleaned him out, and he had not been to American Express in weeks.

The bar Tom found him in had agreed to pay twenty dollars for a three-hour set. What Joe had not needed was his old identity being revealed and he fled from the scene in the middle of a storm to find his lover where she waited in their new dwelling, the red room in a bordello. Totally broke, Joe left Tom there, where he had followed, to find a squat in La Boca, where he remained before Carla found him slumped that awful night. She tore clothing into strips to bandage his wounds and tied tourniquets around his arms. His neck continued to haemorrhage despite holding the cloth on its lacerated flesh. The blade had not severed an artery yet the blood-letting was profuse. She had pleaded down the mouthpiece of the only working phone booth she could find, and the hospital agreed to send an ambulance if she would meet it and show them the way. She ran back to find him the same, still bleeding, and tore more clothing to repeat her tending, leaving him once more to meet the ambulance before it turned back. At the hospital, when the curtain fell on Joe's final act in his own grand-guinol production pressed indelibly in Carla's desolation, Velasquez asked her if she knew of any next of kin. She only knew Tom. He notified the police and called to say he could meet Tom that evening. At eight-thirty Tom let him in to his apart room. They discussed the possibility of Tom travelling to London with the coffin. It would need to travel in a refrigerated atmosphere, in the hold. He advised an early departure. Tom would contact Joe's solicitor, David Atkinson, in the morning to make the arrangements. Velasquez' observation of Joe's choice of dress did not surprise him.

"I have seen everything in this city. My query is, if your friend had made his choice, then what terrible thing has brought him to this? Sex is the most powerful drive in us all. I believe the answer will be of that nature."

"You don't think there is any doubt?"

"In my opinion he took his own life. The official position might be homicide, given where it happened and that he was clearly vulnerable. The fact that he was English might be sensitive, political, so I cannot say where the authorities might stand on that. Perhaps homicide is better for his burial in the UK, though I hope this will not cause a delay if they have to wait for a forensic report."

"Joe would prefer cremation, I'm sure. Cleaner, final. When will you know from the police?" Tom asked.

"Tomorrow." They shook hands and Velasquez would call when he knew.

*

In the brasserie they had made their own, in the city she helped make his, the timer had stopped as they stood to leave.

"Vamanos."

Tom handed the patronne some notes as the waiter arrived with their meals.

"No hay necesidad, señor" she said.

"Por favor, señora."

"Gracias Senor." She touched his arm.

"Adios."

In as much as death is an end to life, the party was coming to an end. The lovers held on to each other all night. The passion of their love consumed them as their lovemaking subdued and they found time for their tears, as they kissed their warmth. She kissed his eyelids when they bent their heads to face each other, then blew her kisses right to his lips.

*

Velasquez rang to say that Joe's body could be released. He also told him that the official line would be murder to facilitate an enquiry. There were people they wanted in the barrio and they could make this stick. "You have not heard this from me," he added.

Before leaving Argentina, Tom Standing believed he would be contacting a shipping agent to transport a pallet of ponies to London, not the body of his closest friend. When he called David Atkinson, the solicitor said he would handle everything through his office, and he would contact an international funeral director immediately. When all was arranged there would be a ticket for him at the main airport in BA. All he had to do was accompany the coffin to Heathrow where he would be met. He should expect to leave within forty-eight hours.

"Alright Mr. Standing. That's it then. I will call you with the details."

"Did you contact Sophie – in California?"

"Not yet. She is on my list."

If Tom sensed closure, he knew also there was more to come. Velasquez had to be right. Joe had not perished in an irascible loss of control, certainly not at the hands of others who might be found guilty. Something else had sent him over the edge. But what? Who?

"Flavia voy a comprar." She left to get bread and fruit.

He called Eduardo to tell him the developments.

"We did not hear from you in two days. We have been very worried. This news is terrible for you. Please, Tommy, anything I can do to help just let me know. I'm here all week."

"Thank you, Eduardo. A lift to the airport would be good. I'll call OK?" He did not want to leave BA in a hearse. They could talk in the car about playing in Ireland. His other reason returned from the supermarket with warm rolls, cheese, and soft peaches. They drank, and ate, and loved, and life did go on. They did not leave their room until morning, and it would never be long enough in coming. Atkinson rang before they got up, and said that his ticket would be at the Iberia check-in desk. He understood that the flight would touchdown in Madrid before going on to London. He should be there at eleven for a one o'clock takeoff, the next day, Friday. He held Flavia tighter now, and she knew.

They walked to the plaza. It was different to that first Sunday. This day was sunny and cold. Everything seemed different, changing from how it had been for them. When they went back he shut the windows and blinds and they loved as naturally as they had from the start. The world could change all it wanted. Later they dressed for dinner and walked to Alvear. Eduardo greeted them. His girlfriend Carolina – short dark hair, tanned, athletic, generous smile – welcomed them, talking to Flavia about Paraguay, where she had taken some schoolchildren to Acunción to play soccer a year earlier, and how they had loved it. Lalo and Julia hugged and kissed Tom. They were all very sad. The paradox of an evening of endings he had hoped to avoid came when Julia brought in their young maid Carmelita. She held a baby, Christian, just three weeks old, and they all looked at his wide eyes and felt his hope. It uplifted them all, something new. They all said good-bye. Eduardo would call for him at nine, and they would return the Doce on the way.

"Mañana a la mañana," he said. They breathed the air of Libertador as it choked into Alvear through the slipstream of Recoleta. It was cool and good to feel on his face as his hand about her neck felt the cheek where her tears fell. He had cried his tears he thought.

"No llores querida." – don't cry, darling, he said. " No mas, nunca no mas." He tried to console her.

222

"Se que me esta dejando" – I know you are leaving me. "Flavia a esta solo" – I will be all alone. As would he. They forgot their fate for a few hours in the natural sweetness of their surrender to the night, and when it delivered them to their last dawn, they loved some more.

When Eduardo knocked, Flavia murmured "Momento."

"Tommy, Eduardo esta aqui. Rapido, rapido. Debemos dejar ahora. Es la hora." Time to go. They packed, everything from messages to mementoes, not touching. He cleared the bathroom but did not shower. He would skip that bit this time. He took the top off the mouthwash and emptied it down the sink. He would bring something of her to London. He followed Eduardo to the hire office, checked the car in, and settled his account. As they drove away he saw a boy sponging the little Doce, so much a part of his time there. On the twenty kilometre drive to Ezeiza, the international airport, Eduardo said he had spoken with Marcello, and they had agreed to travel to Ireland with Tommy's horses, if he was happy for them to do that. One of them could fly free as a groom in attendance and would have access to the ponies in their holding area. They could bring all his tack free of charge, part of the package, the shipping agent Bullrich had told him.

"Sounds fine, Eduardo. Let's do it."

"OK. Javier will keep them fit, and I will organise passports for them, and for me too. You remember Navarro?"

"The guy who makes the saddles? I'd completely forgotten about him. Are they ready?" Tom asked.

"I think so. I will collect them. They are $100 each." Tom had seen his work. His saddles were the best, and he had ordered three, all suede-topped with smooth sides, cut back at the pommel. He used a composite foam to fill the seat, and it would last as long as the leather.

"$100! No es nada." Nothing was right, saddles like these might cost over five hundred sterling readymade, more if made to order. And the shipping cost of the ponies would include them, as well as the bridles, rugs, and mallets. Should he buy more, he asked Eduardo.

"I can ask him to make another for the new pony, if you want?" Yes, he did want.

"Do you have a name for her ?"

"Yes, I do. Flavia."

"Felicitationes, Flavia. Tommy, te ama muy mucho." They all laughed and she kissed him.

"We need to come in the middle of June if we play the eight-goal tournament, and the horses will need rest and time to adjust," Eduardo said.

"If they are fit, a few days should be fine. It'll be summer so I'd say they'll acclimatise quickly," Tom said. He relaxed as he talked about the new season and the visit from his 'hermanos latinos'. He whispered:"Va a venir tambien?" – would she come too?

"Tratar de detenerme." No, he would not try to stop her. They smiled.

"I need to give you money for Navarro" he said to Eduardo.

"That's OK. Give it to me when we arrive. I don't know the exact amount."

"I'm going to give you some anyway when we get to the airport. If you think she needs any, give her some please. I am nervous about giving her money. It might insult her." He gave Eduardo five hundred dollars when she went to the bathroom.

"That should cover everything." They shook hands and wished each other good luck. Eduardo moved to the exit when he saw Flavia. They said farewell.

17
London

Aware of nothing other than leaving somewhere to go elsewhere, and knew he had to, he sat, a passenger. When he pulled his notebook from a pocket it was merely to gaze at empty pages. Desolate, he lay back, inert when not drowsing. Half empty, the liner took him into another night, to leave behind a continent that had touched everything about him. It had inflamed his passion, expanded his self-knowledge, stretched him beyond boundaries he had not even known existed. It had sucked the life out of him and kissed it back deeper than before. Undisturbed during the three-hour stopover at Madrid, he remained in his seat immune from his European reality. A sign held up in Arrivals at Heathrow alerted him to that reality now as he read his name. He met David Atkinson, a tall cavalry type in grey suit and black brogues. He folded the sign to place it in a bin as they made their way to the morgue. Joe was waiting, the lid of his coffin open to confirm his arrival.

"What happened to his hair?" Atkinson asked.

"It's a long story. Not now, please." Attendants removed the coffin to the awaiting hearse. Tom Standing and David Atkinson sat in the back of a chauffeur car where they discussed the funeral arrangements. A service would be held at the St. Marylebone Crematorium in North London the next day. The cortege would leave from Atkinson's office at 2.00 p.m. for a 3.30 p.m. service.

"Who made these decisions?" Tom asked.

"Joe."

"When? How? I've known Joe a long time."

"A few years ago, he had some kind of breakdown, and we talked about it then. He wanted to be cremated, in London."

"He must have foreseen what was coming."

"Look, Tom. Joe knew his demons, and he feared they would defeat him in the end. His life was a time bomb."

"I know, I know. Nearly every day was helter-skelter with him. What a pianist, though."

"I hope we can get together later. I don't want to say too much just yet, but he gave me this for you." Tom took the letter and Atkinson added, "Joe instructed that you should not open it before the funeral." It did not seem a lot to ask. He put it inside his jacket.

"What about Sophie?" he asked. Atkinson spoke with her and she would be in London later that day. He told him the Will would be read on Saturday morning at 11.00 a.m. in his office. When the chauffeur dropped him off in the Brompton Road, Atkinson told him to take Tom on to where he needed to go. He had not thought even that far ahead so chose a boutique hotel on Queensgate. Travelling light meant he would need a suit, and rang Moss Bros. They sent round a grey suit, black brogues, white shirt, and a black tie. He slept for five hours. After he showered and dressed, he strolled up Queensgate in loafers, chinos, and a blue shirt then walked up some steps into a bar he remembered from his city days. He sat on a stool and waited. For what? This was not the corner of Callao and Quintana. He drank a glass of wine as the bar became busier. A girl nudged his arm.

"Sorry." She had big eyes and smiled like she meant it. When a stool became available she sat beside him. He heard her ask "did you hear what I said?"

"I'm sorry. Not tonight." He left. He missed Flavia, he missed their apart as he turned on the light of his new room, and he knew the feast was where he left it, in the city where he had found his own impulsions.

*

He crossed the Cromwell Road at 1.30 p.m., suited with a black tie in his jacket pocket. His left shoe squeaked on the pavement of Onslow Gardens, the suit a better fit for a rental. Atkinson offered him a sherry before leaving with Sophie, who had arrived early and was waiting in one of the two cars. They held each other as she broke down sobbing into his shoulder. He had felt as she looked to him with her glazed black eyes, and he gripped her harder. The steady progress through heavy traffic befitted the convoy of three cars in its procession through Hyde Park. If he had been going to a Test Match he might have been talking sport with the driver, exchanging banal banter and vapid platitudes, confirming their position in a scheme of things. A few words from Joe at that moment and all would have been right with the world. His scheme had not played out well as his benighted votaries followed him now into the cemetery parkland. Tom saw Sophie to her place on the front pew, and walked back to offer his shoulder as a pallbearer. As Joe was carried, Magda Olivero sang "Vissi d'arte" from Puccini's *Tosca*, and the outpouring by all found Tom's own tears falling down his shirt. When they set him down, Joe's bald head visible, Britten's carol "That Yonge Child" grounded the congregation. Tom sat beside Sophie and held her shaking hand. A swelling of latecomers needed to be hushed as the Minister stood up to the dais to deliver his eulogy. Beside Sophie another woman, also wearing a black veil, held her head in her hands as she whimpered at the account of a life she had clearly known well. *I think I know her.* When the curtain came down on Joe for the last time, a medley from Oscar Peterson played them out into the warm weekend sunshine. Tom looked for the forlorn woman but she had gone. When David Atkinson shook his hand Tom asked if he knew who she was.

"You mean Celeste. Joe's sister." For the first time he heard her name. Atkinson told him she would be at the reading the next day.

"They were twins you know." He had not known. Joe never talked about her, only his wife sometimes.

"And the music? Were they his choices?" Tom said.

"Joe always had a sense of the dramatic. He loved opera, and the Puccini was his choice."

"When? When did he tell you?"

"Years ago. He just never knew when it would come. Like I said, he fought a losing battle constantly." *My God, all the time I knew him.*

"And the Peterson? I know he loved him, even played with him one time," Tom said.

"I didn't know that. He left that selection up to me. We both liked him." Atkinson went on to say that on Joe's instruction, anyone Atkinson wanted to join him would be welcome to the best dinner in town, and then maybe they might take in some jazz. They were in the mood for therapy.

"What'll it be? Indian or Chinese? Chelsea or Soho?" Chinese in Soho, they agreed, then they could walk to Ronnie Scott's. First they needed to change. Tom dropped Sophie at her hotel on Park Lane. He would collect her at 8.00 p.m., in three hours. He left her in better spirits as they kissed each other's cheeks. He went back to Queensgate. He soaked in the bath with a minibar for company. Vodka, whisky or wine? They all felt good by the time he stepped from the bathroom to dry on the bed in his robe. Then he remembered the letter Atkinson had given him, to be read after the funeral.

Dear Tom,

Well, my curious friend, if you have not opened this already, I am dust and ash now, and not before time. Apart from the booze and the incest, my greatest crime has been not to spare the world of one of its most inchoate bastards sooner. The accuracies to which I refer are:

1. The Booze - you know all about that one.

2. The Bastard - I never did tell you that I was born the wrong side of the sheets. As for the other bastard – fuck him. As for this one, well I'm fucked now, so what the hell?

3. The Incest - That will take a little more explaining.

Celeste and I were born November 10th 1951, in London. Our mother abandoned us at birth, in a doorway, we later found out. We went to a home for destitute children, where Emer adopted us and took us to the west coast of Ireland, and cared for us as her own. We loved her, and when she died from the 'flu in 1962, she had taught us how to rear chickens, milk goats, and fish in the streams and in the sea from a coracle. We would get wood from the nearby forest, and sold milk and cheese in the village to buy what we needed to live. Emer had plenty of books, and we could read and write. She had a piano and taught me the rudiments before she left us. We loved her. As our dependence on each other grew I loved Celeste,

228

and she loved me, in that way that is taboo – the forbidden kind. We lived happily, in our ignorance, until the fire destroyed our home when we were sixteen.

We packed our bags and came to London. Bloody hard, old boy – no blacks, no dogs, no Irish. Anyway, it seemed I was a better pianist than I realised, and took work playing in pubs. One day a man from a music school talked to me about getting some formal training. He was Rupert Marshall, and he arranged a scholarship. That was it, I never looked back. Celeste and I thought we could be 'happy ever after'. No sodding luck – some rival grassed us up when he found out about the incest. It's been turmoil ever since, both of us torn between guilt, shame, we would be interlopers, outsiders, pariahs wherever we went together. We just had to split, to survive. I was heartbroken – I know she was. I sent her money, and after a few years there would be plenty of it. But success could not bring me what I longed for - my Celeste. I love her now as I always have. These last three years, since we met, my descent has been fuelled by jealousy, loneliness, making compromises with substitutes. But there is no substitute for the real thing. Now you have discovered me with Carla I am shit out of options. If becoming a transvestite could have saved me and given Celeste the freedom she needs, from me, from us, our past, then maybe she could find some happiness. I have left her well provided for. She will need support. Can I ask you to be her friend? Can I ask you to be Sophie's friend? Can I ask you to be my friend? Can I ask you anything anymore? If I can, please look after Celeste. She is wonderful. I trust her to you.

Good luck my friend,
Love,
Joe

At 7.00 p.m. he walked up Queensgate towards Hyde Park. He had to meet Sophie. If the warm Friday evening, calming from the weekend exodus, did not reflect his anxiety, it did allow him time to think how he might console her when he told her of the letter. That

229

is, if she had not received one herself. Walking along Rotten Row, Knightsbridge to his right, the evening sun cast his shadow over the sandy soil. He had ridden horses along that tree-lined avenue some years before. On July 20th 1982, at 6.40 p.m. Pacific time, he had called a friend in London, from Portland, Oregon. As they were speaking he heard a thud, and she said, "Oh my God, what's that?" She looked out her office window at a scene of carnage. The IRA had detonated a nail bomb, killing eleven soldiers and seven horses. On Sunday May 18th 1980, he had been woken by a similar thud in Portland when Mount St. Helens erupted ninety miles north in Washington State. Somehow tenuous links between the West Coast and London, Sophie and Joe, were reminding him of how fragile nature is, no matter how distal, as broken twigs crunched beneath his feet. Stepping down the Park Lane subway the nature of Joe's conclusion might have made some sense to Tom as the sequelae of his friend's sexuality began to unfold.

In his pocket he had Joe's letter and on it a note of Sophie's room number. He crossed the lobby and took the lift to the third floor. She let him in, and they hugged. "Why?" she murmured. *Oh God she doesn't know.* He poured them both whiskey, and they stepped onto the terrace looking out towards the Park.

"Come inside, Sophie. I have something to show you." She sat on the bed and he handed her the letter. He poured more whiskey and moved a chair in front of the terrace door to sit. She turned the page and let it slip, her head down, shoulders slouched. Tom sat to hold her gently. When she lay to sleep he covered her, and drank whiskey until he slept at the terrace door.

The next morning he entered the boardroom of Smythe, Durden & Atkinson. At the far end of the polished surface of the long table sat David Atkinson, a woman to his left, in mourning.

"Hello Tom. I don't believe you've met Celeste Henderson, Joe's sister."

When Tom approached, the woman reached an arm towards him as she raised her head, removing her veiled hat. When her red hair fell down her pallid cheeks to cover a blue birthmark, Tom drew his breath:

"You!"

About the Author

Malcolm Kidd, born in Ireland and raised in England, is an active author, former polo player and coach living in the Northern Irish countryside with his wife, two children, two retired polo ponies, two dogs and numerous chickens.

His first novel is a fictionalized account of an extended polo season beginning in 1989 and details the Irish polo team's exploits in Pakistan and one player's search for a lost and vulnerable friend – his own lifelong passion for the sport having intensified following death, divorce and moving house/country all within six weeks. Polo had helped kindle many dynamic relationships and served as a keel at a time of uncertain swell. Free to travel, with polo his passport, he discovers sexual liberalism and duplicity where he least expects it and tragedy once more.

#0460 - 030417 - C0 - 229/152/15 - PB - DID1803193